THE PALACE OF THE SNOW QUEEN

The

PALACE

of the

SNOW QUEEN

Winter Travels in Lapland

BARBARA SJOHOLM

COUNTERPOINT

BERKELEY

Some of the material in this book originally appeared in different form in the following publications: the *New York Times, Smithsonian Magazine, Slate, Brick, Antioch Review,* and *American Scholar.* Additionally, Chapter 4, "How the Wild Reindeer Was Tamed," appeared in the *Antioch Review,* Spring 2007.

Stanzas from two poems by Paulus Utsi, "Shoreless Shore" (coauthored with his wife Inger Huuva Utsi) and "As Long as We Have Waters," first appeared in an English translation by Roland Thorstensson in *In the Shadow of the Midnight Sun: Contemporary Sami Prose and Poetry,* edited by Harald Gaski (Karasjok, Norway: Davvi Girji, 1996). Permission granted by Nils-Gustav and Stina Huuva.

Library of Congress Cataloging-in-Publication Data

Sjoholm, Barbara
The palace of the snow queen : winter travels in Lapland /
Barbara Sjoholm. — 1st ed.
        p. cm.
ISBN-13: 978-1-59376-159-2
ISBN-10: 1-59376-159-7
1. Lapland—Description and travel. I. Title.

DL971.L2S746 2007
914.89770434—dc22

2007011762

Cover design by Kimberly Glyder Design
Interior design by Megan Cooney
Map by Kat Bennett
Printed in the United States of America

COUNTERPOINT
2117 Fourth Street
Suite D
Berkeley, CA 94710
www.counterpointpress.com

Distributed by Publishers Group West

9 8 7 6 5 4 3 2

To Betsy

Warmer Climates having all the comforts and necessaries of life plentifully bestowed upon them, are but a more distant home; where we have little else talk'd of, than what we daily see among our selves: but here it is indeed, where, rather than in America, we have a new World discovered: and those extravagant falsehoods, which have commonly past in the narratives of these Northern Countries, are not so inexcusable for their being lies, as that they were told without tem[p]tation; the real truth being equally entertaining, and incredible.

Johannes Schefferus, Lapponia, *1673*

CONTENTS

I
Early WINTER

II
Mid WINTER

III
Late WINTER

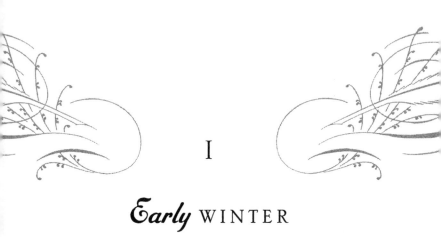

I

Early WINTER

1. THE BLUE HOUR

I ARRIVED IN SWEDISH LAPLAND at two fifteen in the afternoon on the overnight train from Stockholm. Mid-November and already it was dusk, the *blue hour,* when the slate-colored snow looks colder than white. The five others who stepped off in Kiruna, from the almost-empty train grinding on to the Norwegian border, vanished into cars or the one taxi. The station was deserted; not a single traveler remained to ask for directions to my hotel. A fluster of snow filled the air—strange, hectic snow, blowing in the refrigerator-cold light of a solitary streetlamp.

On the train approaching Kiruna, I'd put on all the outdoor clothing I'd brought with me, but still I was freezing. My lungs gasped, my boots slipped on ice. I began dragging my heavy wheeled suitcase uphill, hoping to see the name of the hotel. There it was—Vinterpalatset, the Winter Palace—log-built, dark and substantial in the whirling snow. I pushed open the door to warmth and light, Swedish pop on the radio, a nod of welcome from a pale-blond receptionist with black-rimmed glasses.

"Just one night?"

"Yes," I said. "Tomorrow I go out to Jukkasjärvi."

"You know the Icehotel isn't open for three weeks?" she asked, pitying, hoping I hadn't come all this way to be disappointed. But then the rhythm of Swedish often sinks to a commiserating note at the end of a sentence.

"I'm going there to see it being built."

Upstairs in my room I unpacked—long underwear, thick socks, blank journals, dictionaries, travelogues, calcium pills with extra vitamin D. The fairy tales of Hans Christian Andersen. I took a shower to wash off the grime of three flights and a seventeen-hour train trip. I looked out the window of the Winter Palace, back down at the brick railway station and over at a mountainous shape in the near distance. It glittered feverishly with work lights, like some modern-day Mordor, and must be the enormous iron ore mine I'd read about last summer when the idea of this winter journey to the far North first took hold of me.

My partner of many years and I had broken up in March, and by July I felt the need to do something of greater consequence than just sit in our newly remodeled kitchen and weep. With the future I'd depended on suddenly gone, it seemed important to take a step—any step, but preferably something grand and challenging—out of my misery and back toward life. At least I could get away for the Christmas holidays. Perhaps I'd take up my Norwegian friend Ragnhild's long-standing invitation to visit her in Tromsø, high above the Arctic Circle, in deepest winter. As a Norwegian translator and traveler, I'd been to Scandinavia many times but had never spent a Christmas there. I wrote to Ragnhild and began reading works of history and early travel tales about the Nordic lands. Then came 9/11 and the pervasive sense of fear and dread that followed. My notion of a short holiday grew into a three-month trip to the far North. I wanted to get away from everything familiar, even my country. I wanted extremity and silence, a winter world to mirror my sense of loss, an absence of sunshine while I found my bearings again.

For weeks I'd longed for the moment of arrival, and yet now—staring out the hotel window at the winking white lights of the mine—I felt frightened by the early evening, unprepared for this frozen new world. Friends in Seattle shivered when I told them where I was traveling. "But won't it be cold? Won't it be *dark*?" It *was* dark, and it also was, given the inevitability of our planet's tilted swing around the sun, bound to get darker and darker until the solstice, a month away. Suddenly I was uncertain. Was walking into a longer and longer night such a brilliant idea for me, who had been teetering on the verge of depression most of the year?

I turned from the window and my eye fell upon Andersen's fairy tales. Long ago, a child in California, I'd read "The Snow Queen" and marveled at the story of a boy captured by an icy empress who brought him back with her to her palace in the far North. As soon as I'd heard about a modern-day ice hotel in northern Sweden that was rebuilt at the beginning of every winter and that melted back into the river every spring, I'd longed to see it.

Tomorrow I'd head ten miles outside Kiruna to the construction site of the Icehotel in the village of Jukkasjärvi, where every year a team of builders and artists come together to make something out of nothing, a living space of mounded snow.* I wanted to understand the process, how imagination and hard work could turn frozen water into architecture. But I also wanted to see the

---

* Back when the Icehotel was the only hotel built of ice in the world, the decision was made to give it an English name (without an article preceding). In more recent years, Icehotel has gone to all capitals and a trademark, as in ICEHOTEL®.

Snow Queen's palace of my childhood dreams, to walk through the corridors and feel myself inside a world of ice and snow. "The castle walls were of the driven snow," Andersen wrote, describing the palace where the queen held court, "and the windows and doors of the biting winds. There were more than a hundred halls, according to the way the snow drifted; the biggest stretched for so many miles, all lit up by the intense Northern Lights; and they were so big, so bare, so icy cold, and so sparkling. . . . In the middle of that bare, unending snow hall there was a frozen sea."

That frozen sea inside a fortress of snow sometimes felt like my heart, and I had a determined curiosity to walk to its center and see if it was really "cracked into a thousand fragments," or if it could be made to melt again.

I went downstairs and asked the receptionist where the town's center was and she, on the phone, pointed vaguely upward.

I set out along a path that wound up a snowy hill to streets of shops and offices. I craved the semblance of daylight, and yet electricity's brightness seemed strange to me that first day in Kiruna. Inside the hotly lit stores, banks, and post office, I saw ordinary people going about their business—buying groceries, depositing money, sending packages—normal tasks performed as if in the middle of the night. But it's not the middle of the night, I kept reminding myself in wonder. It's the middle of the afternoon. Children let out of school rode their bikes on the snow-packed streets or pulled each other in sleds; elderly women in fur coats and hats pushed *sparks*—a kick sled on runners with a box for groceries. I bought some cheese and crackers for later and scanned *Svenska Dagbladet*, whose headlines screamed of a nursing home scandal, not the bombing of Afghanistan. I felt the concerns of my country and its real and rhetorical wars moving off the front page. Then, oppressed by the darkness, I went into Café Safari, where the interior—painted ivory wainscoting and patterned apple-green and rose wallpaper, deep sills for flowering begonias—was cozily Swedish with no hint of Africa. I opened my journal, made some notes on Kiruna, and again tried to remember why I was here during *mørketid,* the dark time, when life was buried and sleeping under snow.

"Everyone raves about the light of the North in summer," Ragnhild had told me on a sunny day in Tromsø a year and a half ago. "I can find it a bit boring." I was visiting her while doing some research for a project about women and the sea, and had arrived on one of the coastal steamers. Ragnhild, a novelist in her sixties, with a brush of white hair and an infectious laugh, met me at the dock. We strolled over to an outdoor café to drink iced tea, and everyone was in summer clothing under a blue sky. It was May but very warm; the sun beat down deliciously on our faces.

"Yes, the famous midnight sun!" said Ragnhild, gesturing to the tanned people all around. "But, really, is it the least bit *interesting?* Light is something you can get everywhere. You can go to Bermuda and get light—and be warm too. What's *more* fascinating about the North is not the light, but the dark. Come back in six months, you'll see something quite unique. I know you imagine our winter as pitch black, day and night. But during the day, when it's dark, it's not really like night. It's blue, polar blue, and the snow is blue too. And we have our lights on, all the time. It's . . . festive."

Café Safari was certainly festive, and so were the lighted shops across the street. But when, after a long time of writing, I came out of the café, the icy wind grabbed me by the throat and bitter darkness fell over me. Evening seemed to sit on the white snow like a massive flock of ravens.

I walked down to the library to check my e-mail. Surely there would be messages from friends, wishing me well at the beginning of my pilgrimage. There were. Even my ex-partner wrote hoping I'd arrived safely. My heart still stirred in anger and love to see the familiar name. How hard it was not to want, even after all that had happened, to warm myself at that old fire. I erased the message reluctantly and brought up the online version of the *New York Times.* Everything was as violent and terrible as it had been yesterday. I decided to unsubscribe, and felt as if a heavy blanket of despair slipped from my shoulders.

Three AM, bolt awake. My body insisted it was time to get up, even though it wouldn't be light until—when? Nine thirty? Ten?—and only a pale blue light then. I was nine time zones away from Seattle, and I lay in my twin bed wondering what to do for the next few hours until breakfast was served. I looked over at the window. Snow was falling heavily, illuminated by the outside floodlamp under the hotel eaves. I switched on the bedside lamp and saw the contents of my suitcase spread out carelessly over the second bed. Scandinavian hotels rarely have queen beds, and this can be good when you're on your own. You don't automatically glance over at the other, empty pillow. It made me feel like a child again, happy and safe, to snuggle in a narrow bed, and suddenly I remembered I hadn't come all the way here, past the Arctic Circle, just to feel sorry for myself. I'd done far too much of that already.

I pulled a sweater over my nightgown and sat up, unable to take my eyes from the torrent of snowflakes outside. In *A Description of the Northern Peoples,* from 1555, Olaus Magnus, an encyclopedic ecclesiastic whose multivolume treatise on the North is a compendium of wonder and warning, wrote:

Cold burns the eyes of animals and stiffens their hairs.

Cold allows fish to be kept fresh for five or six months without salt.

Cold causes copper, glass and earthenware vessels to break.

Cold allows games and most delightful shows to be held on the ice.

Cold opens up all pathless territories to travellers and hunters.

Cold makes the skin peel off one's lips, fingers, and nostrils, if they touch iron.

Olaus Magnus was perhaps the earliest travel writer to describe the icy far North. He wasn't the first writer to lay claim to some understanding of Scandinavian history and geography—he was preceded by the Roman historian Tacitus and the medieval Danish scholar Saxo Grammaticus, among others—but he was the most awestruck and exhaustive, the first to really give a sense of what winter up in the North was like. A Catholic bishop, Magnus left Sweden when Lutheranism became the new state religion. Magnus spent the rest of his life in exile in Rome, trying to conjure up for himself what had been so strange and marvelous about where he came from and to explain the Nordic landscape and customs to the Vatican in hopes they might take steps to keep Scandinavia Catholic. Magnus's first task was to complete and have printed an elaborate map, the *Carta Marina,* which superseded all previous attempts to chart the Northern seas and lands. Its illustrations are famous: Sea-monsters munch schooners, hunters harpoon seals, Lapp skiers glide by with bows and arrows, horses draw sleighs across the frozen sea, dragons fly, and reindeer prance. The exuberant detail of this Northern map delights any close scrutiny. The

Northern provinces are called Biarmia, Scricfinia, Finmarchia, Lappia. It was Lappia, Lapponia, Lappmark, and eventually Lapland that seemed to stick, and to eventually become short-hand for the entire far North.

A Description of the Northern Peoples was a classic Renaissance treatise of lore and learning, begun in order to explicate the *Carta Marina* but eventually growing to many volumes with charming woodcut illustrations. Although Olaus Magnus claimed he grew up at the latitude of 86° (not far from the North Pole), in reality he was born in the south of Sweden and never traveled much above the Arctic Circle during the years 1519–21, when he made his way through the wilderness to Norway and back again to Sweden, collecting tithes for the Pope. He never visited the northwestern coasts of Norway, much less the North Cape and the coastline bordering the Barents Sea. Nevertheless, Magnus glimpsed enough to ignite his imagination and to form impressions of everything that later travelers would also note about the North in winter: the refrigerating cold, the starry dark, reindeer, winter markets, and the possibility of snow also being a great deal of fun. Snow and ice clearly enthralled him, and he spends many chapters explaining the harshness and the beauty of cold climates. Magnus was the first in history to really consider the snowflake.

Lapland, as the haunt of reindeer, wizards, and a marvelous people who skied and hunted, entered world literature through Magnus. Tacitus had written of the "Fenni" in AD 98 and the Byzantine historian Prokopios of the "Skrid Finns" in 550, while other travelers and historians had made note of nomad hunters dressed in skins who slept out in the open. But it was Magnus who memorably described the "Scricfinns" by their "wonderful speed," which they achieved "by means of certain flat planks, curved like bows at the front and attached to their feet." These were, of course, the indigenous Sami on their skis.*

More than a hundred years later Johannes Schefferus, a Swedish scholar in Uppsala, took on the task of explaining Lapland in more detail. Now the Scricfinns are called Laplanders (in the English translation), and they are discussed in much more detail, often critically. Along with giving accounts of how the people of the North lived, traveled, ate, and prayed, Schefferus hoped to show that Lappish black magic had *not* influenced Swedish victories in the Thirty Years' War, as was widely rumored on the continent. His descriptions of Lapp Shamans and idols had the opposite effect, and were some of the most popular parts of the book, creating and reinforcing stereotypes of the Lapps as primitive devil worshippers.

Although, like Olaus Magnus, Schefferus never actually trekked into the far North, he collected and recounted information from fur merchants, tax collectors, and priests who'd ventured into what was now the increasingly disputed land above the Arctic Circle. By the time Schefferus was writing, the various Nordic and Russian kingdoms all had an interest in the thousands of square miles of tundra, mountains, and coastlines above the Arctic Circle. The borders kept changing, and the Sami were often the subjects of two or three different countries, sometimes all at the same time.

Johannes Schefferus's *Lapponia,* published in Latin in 1673, with illustrations of reindeer, sleds, tents, and drums, was translated into French, German, Dutch, and Restoration English (as *The History of Lapland,* in 1674), and helped create a taste in some

---

* Sami, also spelled Sámi or Saami, is both adjective and noun and doesn't change in the English plural. The Sami have called themselves Sami for as long as they have described themselves. However, the world has often known this people as Lapps, Laplanders, or the Lappish people. At times, even Sami referred to themselves as Lapps. The preference now is always for Sami. When writing about past depictions of the Sami, I use the older forms where appropriate; when writing about the contemporary Sami, I keep to current usage.

for journeys north. Most tourists, of course, tended to travel in the warmer months. As the nineteenth century drew on, it became popular to sail up the Norwegian coastline in summer and to cross into Sweden or the Finnmark Plateau to observe the Lapp nomads with their tents and reindeer. Still, there were those for whom winter in the far North would always be an attraction.

Frank Hedges Butler, Olive Murray Chapman, and Norah Gourlie were three British travelers who came to Lapland in the first decades of the twentieth century. With reindeer and sledge, they crossed the snowfields and frozen rivers of the Finnmark Plateau in Norway and Finland. They were curious about the Lapps, curious about the cold, curious about reindeer. All experienced difficulties getting information on how to travel in the North and what to expect (Chapman was told by a tourist official in Stockholm that "the cold was so great that even *breathing* was sometimes difficult"), but all pressed on, undeterred, to explore winter in Lapland and to eventually write books about their experiences.

Frank Hedges Butler was a wealthy wine merchant and world traveler who cofounded the Royal Automobile Club and the Royal Aero Club. In his younger years he was fond of ballooning; he also shot game in Africa and rode elephants in India. In 1914 he took on reindeer. With an entourage that included a Lapp guide and a Kiruna photographer, with provisions from Fortnum & Mason and a goodly supply of cognac, he made his way around a vast swath of the North, from Sweden to Norway and over to Finland, and then wrote about it in *Through Lapland with Skis and Reindeer*.

In the late winter and spring of 1931 Olive Murray Chapman followed in Butler's tracks, somewhat more modestly. Like him, she came up the Norwegian coast by sea, set off for the interior in one of the boat-shaped Lapp sleds pulled by a reindeer. A fellow of the Royal Geographical Society, she'd previously visited Iceland,

Cyprus, and Madagascar. *Across Lapland with Sledge and Reindeer*
told of crossing the Finnmark Plateau along rivers and through
forests, braving blizzards and spills. In spite of the hardships, she
managed to take notes for her book, to paint watercolors, and to
make a film of the Lapps that was shown in London.

Norah Gourlie first fantasized about riding a horse through
Lapland in the summer, but was told that the marshes and many
wide, rushing rivers would make for a difficult journey, and that
perhaps traveling overland in winter, as the peoples of the North
did, might suit her better. At first she was resistant ("But," I said,
aghast, "it's impossible; I should die of cold! I am only half alive
in London in winter. I adore tropical heat"), but by December of
1937 she was on her way north from Helsinki to spend several
months roaming, often by reindeer sledge, around the eastern side
of the Finnmark Plateau, and to write about the people she met in
A Winter with Finnish Lapps.

Butler, Chapman, and Gourlie all noted, when they gave their
reasons for going north in winter, how few other travelers they encountered above the Arctic Circle. Chapman wrote that although
most people visiting northern Scandinavia "take advantage during
the summer months of the numerous pleasure cruises around the
coast, they keep for the most part to the sea. . . . Finnmark is visited by very few, and in the wintertime, so I was told, by none."

The interwar years were a relative heyday for winter travel
in Lapland. With Germany's occupation and wholesale destruction of Northern Finland and Norway during the Second World
War, tourism dropped off precipitously and had a difficult time
recovering. Although eventually summer tourism rose again in
Scandinavia and passengers crowded the many ships sailing up
and down the Norwegian coast, relatively few individuals ever
seemed to think of spending their holidays in the dark and cold

of a subarctic winter. The Nordic countries had been on a mission for the last two decades to make winter tourism fashionable and profitable, and to this end, an embellished, tourist-friendly concept of Lapland—"Magical Lapland," "Untouched Lapland," "Lapland: Europe's Last Remaining Wilderness"—was key.

I made a cup of tea. It was still only four AM—hours to breakfast. I rummaged through my things, found a squashed Luna Bar, and ate it. I unfolded my map of northern Scandinavia, still uncreased and unspotted, fresh as the day I'd bought it. It was a big map that covered most of the bed, because all three of the countries where I was traveling were long, *long* countries. Their capitals were in the lower third, all at about the sixtieth parallel, all oriented southward. Oslo was for centuries the chief Norwegian outpost of the Danish kingdom, Stockholm was the imperial center of the Baltic, and Helsinki was alternately dominated by Sweden or Russia. The southern borders of these three Scandinavian countries are relatively vertical and conform to physical boundaries: A mountain chain separates Norway and Sweden, and Sweden and Finland are separated by the Gulf of Bothnia and by the Torne River. But once you're above the Arctic Circle into tundra and marsh, the natural boundaries grow less distinct and the lines between the countries become political, the borders less fixed.

If the far North seems far away, it's because it is. The distance from Oslo to Tromsø is about the same as from Oslo to Athens. Compared to some of the places I was heading this winter, Kiruna was not very northerly—perhaps a hundred miles up from the Arctic Circle, which marks the southernmost point where the midnight sun can be seen. Where I was going wasn't the Arctic, but the subarctic, and even *subarctic* can give a misleading picture when it comes to the weather and the landscape of northern Scandinavia. Because of the effects of the Gulf Stream along the Norwegian coast, the climate tends to be warmer in most places than it is at comparable latitudes in Siberia and Alaska. In Barrow, Alaska, human beings only manage to get through the winter in igloos or heavily reinforced concrete buildings. Yet at the same latitude, in Tromsø, there's a major university and plenty of nightlife. Its sixty-two thousand residents live in wooden houses with double-paned glass windows; during the early part of winter there's often no snow at all, though harsh storms blow in from the Norwegian Sea. Away from the coast, in the Swedish mountains and on the wide tundra plains of northern Norway and Finland, the snow comes early in October and stays as late as the end of May; even so, the land is inhabited by people who drive cars, work in office buildings, eat in restaurants, and shop in malls. By going north, I was hardly traveling to the end of the earth. I had, in fact, often crossed the line of the Arctic Circle from my earliest travels in Norway, when I had a summer job working on the coastal steamer and made the trip from Bergen around the North Cape and back.

I'd tried to tell worried friends that northern Scandinavia had every modern amenity you could wish for, but few believed me, and perhaps I didn't completely believe it myself. Certainly it wasn't to see Swedes and Norwegians driving their Volvos to covered shopping malls that I'd come north in winter. I'd arrived in the same spirit of fascination with the far North that southern people have always had, when they called these lands by other names: Hyperborea, Thule, Land of the People Under the Big Dipper, Scricfinia, Finnmark, Lapponia, and Lappmark.

Lapland no longer exactly corresponds, if it ever did, to any completely agreed-upon geographic area. Some dictionary definitions attempt to be precise, giving it an area of 150,000 square miles and boundaries of the Norwegian Sea, the Barents Sea, and the White Sea, and including not only northern Scandinavia, but Russia's Kola Peninsula. It's the name of Finland's northernmost province, Lappi, as well as the name of the Swedish province of Lappland. Swedish Lapland is a quarter of Sweden's surface area, divided between the counties of Norrbotten in the north and Västerbotten in the south.

I was in Swedish Lapland now, and would be in Lapland again when I traveled in northern Finland, but in between I'd be in the Norwegian provinces of Finnmark and Troms. Scandinavians tend to call their northern homeland Nordkalotten—the Northern Skullcap—a nickname for how the far North fits like a hat over the top of their several countries. To make things more confusing, Lapland was once synonymous with the Lapps who inhabited the far North, yet the Sami now increasingly refer to their ancestral homeland by its long-standing name, Sápmi.

Although Lapland, at least as a large overarching description, didn't correlate with an actual place on my map of Scandinavia, it still suited me to say I'd be spending the winter here. Why? Perhaps I liked the idea of traveling to a place that didn't quite exist. But it was also for practical reasons. To say I was traveling above the Arctic Circle made everyone shiver involuntarily. "Above the Arctic Circle in Winter" is short for *really far north, really dark,* and *really really cold.* "Lapland in Winter," on the other hand, conjures up a vision. Say Lapland and most people think of Santa Claus, reindeer, and fairy tales. I thought of all those things—especially fairy tales—myself.

Growing up in Southern California, I never saw a single flake of snow, nor had any of the neighbor kids. We used to sprawl during Christmas vacation on green lawns in our shorts and imagine what a real winter would be like. Was snow really cold, like

ice cream, or was it more like the spangled white felt that surrounded the base of our Christmas trees at home? Was it true all
snowflakes were distinct? The only snowflakes we knew were the
ones we cut, painstakingly, from folded white paper in school.
Every year at this time we heard familiar songs: "I'm Dreaming
of a White Christmas," "Frosty the Snowman," and "Jingle Bells."
As the warm sun beat down, some neighbors turned their yards
into Santa's workshop, or placed Santa and his reindeer on the
roofs and turned cans of white flocking on their trees. Illustrated
books showed cottages half buried in white, snowmen out front,
with children in caps and jackets throwing snowballs. We knew
the forts and figures were made of snow but what *was* snow?
Frozen rain? No, snow must be soft, we thought, a blanket over
the known world, a silent satin coverlet. What about ice? Ice cubes
we knew, snow cones and popsicles. But somewhere, up in Alaska
and the North Pole—far, far north, where snow never melted
at all—there were houses of ice: the igloos of the Eskimos, the
ice palace of the Snow Queen. Where it wasn't just a matter of a
white Christmas, but a perpetual one.

The hotel was utterly silent, and utterly black except for the pool
of light outside my window, which illuminated a hive of snowflakes—"white bees," Hans Christian Andersen calls them—
buzzing by. I folded up my map and opened his book to "The Snow
Queen." I slipped into the story of Kai and Gerda, of a friendship
frozen and redeemed, as if placing on an old turntable an LP I'd
heard a thousand times. I read about the troll who invents a mirror "which had the strange power of being able to make anything
good or beautiful that it reflected appear horrid; and all that was
evil and worthless seem attractive and worthwhile." When the

troll takes the mirror up to heaven to make fun of God and the angels, he loses his grip on it, and it falls and breaks into hundreds of millions of billions of pieces, some of which are turned into windowpanes or spectacles, and many of which become tiny glass splinters that get into people's eyes and make them see things askew and cruelly.

I read about the two children, Kai and Gerda, who pass many happy days in their roof garden above the city. I read about the splinters that lodge in Kai's eye and heart, about Kai's abduction by the powerful and seductive Snow Queen. She took him north with her and left him alone at the center of her ice castle, his skin blue-black with cold, his heart almost frozen, wracking his brain over broken pieces of ice, trying to spell out a word he has forgotten. What was that word? I always forgot until I read the story that it was "eternity."

That was how my sadness felt sometimes, as if it would last forever. But as I lay in my bed in the Winter Palace, having reached the North in winter at long last, I also felt the pleasure of knowing that I was warm and sleepy now, and that Gerda, Kai's brave and loyal friend, would come and save him in the end.

When I awakened, I'd almost missed breakfast. I threw on my clothes and went downstairs. I was no longer hungry; in fact, the sight of smoked salmon and three varieties of pickled herring made me slightly ill, and I contented myself with a boiled egg, a roll, and several strong cups of coffee.

By ten I was checked out and in a taxi heading to the building site of the Icehotel in Jukkasjärvi. It had stopped snowing and I was glad. The light was granite-blue, with a smear of pink. The sun hadn't quite departed for the winter, but it was hidden behind the mountains. The Kiruna streets were fresh white, the snowplows were out. We drove past the road to the iron ore mine, and then away from town, into a forest of evergreens.

"What did you think of Kiruna?" asked the driver.

I didn't want to hurt his feelings. "It's . . . well, it's hard to tell in the dark."

To be honest, I wasn't impressed. I didn't expect to spend much more time in what seemed to me only a way station, and not a very interesting one. Compared to many charming towns in Scandinavia, Kiruna seemed a utilitarian jumble of '60s-style buildings with only a few old wooden structures, like the Vinterpalatset, still standing. Kiruna and its giant iron ore mine were, not to put too fine a point on it, something of a blot on what the fairy tales and tourist literature promised me—Magical Lapland, Untouched Lapland, Lapland of the fairy tales.

Leaving town, the taxi drove into a forest of snow-laden firs and spruce. I was on my way to the palace of the Snow Queen, and the sun, not yet lost below the horizon, sent pink and gold rays into the sparkling branches of the Christmas trees.

2. THE ARCHITECTURE OF SNOW AND ICE

I WAS BURIED IN SNOW and yet I could move. The light was lunar blue, the silence immense. Had I just died? I seemed to be floating down a corridor of curved white walls to a radiant light source through an open doorway. Then I returned to myself. My boots crunched softly on the compacted snow beneath, and my breath made a cloud around my head. I was looking for the foreman, Åke Larsson, at the site and walking through a series of snow tunnels under construction. When finished, the tunnels would become a hotel, housing many hundreds of guests over the winter, most only for one night. Thousands more would walk the corridors and peer into the bedrooms, just to imagine themselves sleeping there.

I emerged into the central hall, a pool of granulated white light. At one end was a gaping hole that would become the hotel's entrance. At the other end of the hall was a frozen waterfall of riverine ice blocks through which slipped a diffused, cracked light. Cylindrical chunks of ice lay around, like broken columns at the Roman Forum. They would be levered, one on top of the next, to form the pillars in the hall. Here, under the vaulted ceiling, was action. Thickly padded figures strode back and forth with chainsaws, chisels, and scrapers. In spite of the flood lamps and power tools, there was something medieval about the scene. The woolen caps with earflaps looked as if they belonged to a centuries-earlier time. They warmed the heads of women and men with the cold flush of frostbite on their cheeks. *Chip, chip, chip* went the chisels. The blue ice in the columns was being shaped and smoothed by hand.

From outside, the Icehotel looked like a series of bulldozed hills; inside it was both reverently quiet and bustling as a cathedral under construction. Snow's insulating properties made it possible to stand in a room and hear nothing of what was happening a few feet away. It was unlike any space I'd ever found myself in. Even in its unfinished state, the interior aroused awe in me—not the claustrophobia I'd been expecting. The light suffused everything and gave definition to the packed snow crystals curving up to form an arch above my head. I was surrounded by a substance both gossamer and weighty. Inside the Icehotel it was hard to know up from down and where my body was in relation to the external world, which had been reshaped by light. Although it was only snow, it was far different than standing outside in snow.

That was landscape; this was architecture.

The winter of 1740 was bitter cold—one of the coldest in European history. Rivers froze to record depths, birds dropped like meteors from the sky. On the River Neva in St. Petersburg, not far from the Winter Palace where Empress Anna Ivanovna reigned, a three-room Palladian villa in ice went up, the marvel of all who saw it. Carved ice plates froze to an ice table in the formal dining room.

Two ice pillows and two ice nightcaps sat on the turned-down ice sheets of the ice bed. The dressing table was jumbled with carved boxes and bottles; over it hung a mirror of ice. From outside, the ice palace was just as remarkable, surrounded as it was by twenty-nine trees, with birds and a fountain, all of ice. From ice cannons shot ice balls fired with gunpowder. The ice came from the Neva and was transparent blue, an enchantment.

Anna Ivanovna was the despotic niece of Peter the Great. A horsewoman and hunter of enormous girth, she kept loaded muskets by the windows in order to shoot at passing wildlife. She maintained a court of fools and dwarves and made jesters of the scions of ruling families. The ice villa was designed as a honeymoon retreat, to sadistically mock the marriage she forced upon an aristocrat and one of his servants. But it was also meant as entertainment, the sort only an empress could provide, for her freezing subjects.

Anna's ice castle was perhaps the first grand frozen palace in history, but it was far from the first structure built of snow or ice. As far back as the 1500s, the Swedish bishop Olaus Magnus was describing how northerners used sheets of ice to make windows for storehouses and stables. He even had a short chapter in his book titled "On Snow Castles Built by Young Lads," in which he told of boys fetching "huge masses of snow" for construction. "A building of this sort," he wrote, "they sprinkle continually with water, so that the snow, being bound together by water, may become more effectively hardened as the cold comes on." On the other side of the world, in Yokote on the Japanese island of Honshū, children have traditionally built small domed houses of snow where they hold parties to celebrate the God of Water.

Winter carnivals and fêtes were the rage in North America in the last two decades of the nineteenth century, when ice castles went up in Montreal; Québec City; St. Paul, Minnesota; and Leadville, Colorado. The Montreal ice palace of 1883, designed by A. C. Hutchison, in the style of Canada's Parliament building, was the centerpiece of a gala festival and brought fifteen thousand tourists from the United States and abroad to join the city's inhabitants in torchlight processions, concerts, and costume balls. For several years, each winter carnival and ice castle, built of ice cut from lakes and rivers, was grander than the last, and writers vied to describe the sight of ghostly alabaster walls lit up at night by newfangled electric lights and of fireworks that turned the palace into "a great heap of jewels."

Of course, these palaces were subject to the weather, especially to the danger of sudden thaw. Walls melted almost overnight and symmetry failed. Everything from thunderstorms to blizzards could make the festivities uncertain, as well as epidemics of influenza and fickle public interest. The technology of cutting ice from lakes was forgotten, as refrigerators replaced iceboxes. Yet, over the years, these winter cities had spurts of building. During the Depression, St. Paul built a series of art deco ice pavilions. In Quebec, the '60s sparked a series of abstract palaces, more like Henry Moore sculptures in snow than fortresses. Manufactured ice replaced ice blocks from lakes, and then cast snow replaced them both.

Snow and ice castles are still built in Europe, Minnesota, Alaska, and eastern Canada, but it's in Asia that the art of ice construction has not only flourished but expanded beyond the wildest dreams of the architects who designed Anna Ivanovna's villa. Beginning in the 1950s, Japanese high school students built structures of snow and ice in Sapporo on the northern island of Hokkaidō. Now Sapporo hosts the world's largest displays of ice architecture, and two million people turn up each January and

February to view massive replicas of Versailles and Red Square. Harbin, China—another cold, cold place with plenty of cheap soldier labor—is home to the Ice Lantern Festival, where gargantuan frozen sculptures of buildings line the streets.

Most of the ice structures at these festivals, which include ziggurats, Hanging Gardens of Babylon, Bavarian castles, Egyptian pyramids, and Moorish palaces, are not meant to be entered. They're more properly called statues than buildings—polished, glittery, fantastically detailed exteriors. Even though St. Paul's celebrated ice castle of 1888 had a great hall where six thousand people attended a wedding, and though Leadville's castle interior was just as grand, with an ice skating rink, two ballrooms, and a merry-go-round, in general the concept of the ice palace has meant spectacle, not comfort. Ice castles have been constructed as glorious ice candy, to be looked at, not lived in. The Icehotel in Jukkasjärvi, in contrast, was not particularly spectacular on the outside, being more or less a series of white molehills on the land. It wasn't built by an empress, much less in a grand city. It existed on the periphery of Swedish Lapland, in the country's northernmost province, in a village of only a few hundred people. It was minimalist, vernacular, sacred in its shapes. It was meant to be experienced from within.

Ice architect and construction foreman Åke Larsson, when I found him, proved to be extremely tall, gauntly good-looking, with gray stubble and cool blue eyes. Impatient, not so much at being interviewed, but at losing the little light of midday, he marched me quickly around the site, hand-rolled cigarette at the corner of his mouth. He kept a watchful eye on the construction and occasionally interrupted our conversation to huddle with men bulldozing large piles of snow back and forth. Born in Kiruna, he grew up "down south" as they say here, then knocked around Uppsala and Stockholm as a self-taught woodworker. He's not a trained architect or engineer; he first made furniture for his family and then, when form grew more intriguing than utility, turned to wood sculpture. Åke headed up north again in 1993, after hearing some rumors of ice sculpting contests and igloos in his hometown of Kiruna. He persuaded his friend, Arne Bergh, also a sculptor, to come along. The two of them each took a chainsaw in hand and were instantly converted to ice. "Compared to wood, which is what we worked in before, ice was so forgiving," Åke told me. "So easy to cut and shape. And there's no problem afterwards with storing it, or trying to get exhibits. You create something. It lasts a while. It melts and is gone."

Now Arne is the artistic director of the hotel and Åke is the main architect and foreman; they're both part owners. During the summer Åke works on the design of the hotel. Beginning in late October, he waits anxiously for the weather to get colder, and as soon as the temperature drops sufficiently, the building begins. It takes about thirty-eight days to shape the Icehotel, a growing challenge, since the hotel gets larger, but the amount of time to create, a time frame dictated by temperature and the tourist season, remains the same. Some years it's simply too warm to begin before late November, and even then there's a danger of the roof collapsing.

The hotel had been under construction for three weeks and still had three weeks to go before the scheduled opening December 13, St. Lucia's Day, when a choir of angelic girls would sing and the double doors would be thrown open to visitors from around the world. Although this year construction was more or less on schedule, the weather always threatens with a pattern of freeze and thaw in November, before winter really settles in. It was getting colder now, fortunately, but the days were short, with only a few hours of light to work in.

The Icehotel is one of the largest snow structures in the world. When the hotel opened in December, it would have sixty bedrooms, forty of them basic, with just a bed of ice: ice blocks covered by a mattress and reindeer skins. Twenty larger suites would have been designed by artists working in snow and ice. There would be a chapel, a long central hall, another hall of sculptures, and the Absolut Ice Bar, where the tables, chairs, bar, and even the glasses are made of ice. During the coming winter season, around thirty thousand people were expected to visit the hotel; another four thousand would plunk down good money to sleep in a sleeping bag on one of those beds of ice.* Since its beginnings in the early '90s, the Icehotel has become big business, its statistics measured less in number of snowflakes piled up than in kronor, pounds, and euros taken in by Jukkas AB, the parent company of ICEHOTEL®. As a primary sponsor, Absolut Vodka played a role in shaping the venture commercially (and is the only brand of alcohol served in the bar). Fashion photographers figured out that it was an ideal backdrop for a fashion shoot. *Vogue* photographs of Kate Moss and Naomi Campbell were displayed prominently in the reception building, and the Icehotel got a boost when Campbell complained of almost dying of cold. Rock videos were shot here; television commercials and occasional TV specials were a regular part of the winter. Yet, a large part of the hotel's trade was corporate: Swedish and international businesses looking to mold team players sent them here for a snowy night or two to bond.

* In the winter season of 2006–7, approximately 13,000 people would spend a night in an ice chamber in the hotel.

In November there were few tourists to be seen, only a couple of spectators like me, staying in the warm wooden cabins near the growing mounds of snow, and a small cadre of workers, both paid and interning for room and board. In the Icehotel's offices off the warm reception area, complete with a central fireplace, the publicity director, Helena Sjöholm, and her assistant fielded calls from journalists, advertising directors, and television producers from around the world. Helena had been upbeat and encouraging since my first e-mail to her; she was blond, efficient, and welcoming, much given to exclamation marks when writing in English. Eventually she would confide that winter is a "stressy" time for her, however much she enjoyed her work. The bustle was beginning: Desk clerks took reservations by phone, fax, and computer; employees unpacked high-end Swedish souvenirs in the gift shop; and all the enterprises that had grown up around the Icehotel—from the restaurant across the road, to the kennels nearby where the owners of some of the dogsledding businesses kept their dogs— were gearing up for the tourist invasion in another few weeks.

Before Åke rushed away from me to attend to the dance of backhoes and tractors, I asked him what architecture inspired him. The great cathedrals of Europe, he said. His admiration went to "St. Peter's, for the size; Rheims, for the beauty; and the new Polish cathedrals. And of course, la Sagrada de Família in Barcelona. Gaudí's ideas of vaulting were based on the Romanesque and are structurally very sound."

Eventually I'd learn that Åke and Arne had studied up on arch theory and had designed wooden and steel forms for three different styles of interior rooms and corridors: the soaring Gothic of the main hall, supported by the tall, heavy columns of ice and buttressed from the outside; an arch for the corridors, rather like a simple drawing of a house, with straight sides and a somewhat

peaked ceiling; and the catenary arch, which was used in the sleeping rooms and suites. *Catenary* comes from the Latin for chain and
describes the shape that's made when you hang a chain between
two fixed points. The resulting open loop is flexible and, more
importantly, balanced. Turn it over and you have a catenary arch,
where the weight is distributed evenly, giving the shape simplicity
and strength.

From the outside, the Icehotel looked like just a lot of lumpy
tunnels. From the inside, it resembled a monastery, where the use
of the load-bearing catenary arch made for a low-slung spiritual
architecture. Antoni Gaudí, the Catalan architect who had created
a score of buildings in Barcelona and elsewhere in Spain, had often
worked with interior vaulting and arches in concrete; and concrete
as a medium had a lot in common with snow, being both malleable
and heavy. The amazing thing was how such simple material could,
merely through its shape, suggest sacredness and peace.

After over two hours of stomping through snow and standing in icy corridors, I was chilled to the bone. I returned to my
cabin for a cup of hot tea and to warm up my frozen fingers and
toes. Only the fact that the light was fading, and I wanted more
photographs and a better understanding of the building process,
sent me out again. It was only one o'clock, but the sky was pink
with sunset in the west, and blue shadows were creeping over the
snowfields down to the river. The din of machinery broke into
the cold air as everyone worked hard to make the most of the
shrinking light.

There are several ways of constructing a large frozen building.
One is the ice-block method, used first in Anna Ivanovna's palace
on the Neva and later in the Norman-style castles of St. Paul and
Montreal. Using teams of horses, men harvested large squares or
rectangles from rivers and lakes, just the way they did to provide

ice for refrigeration. It was this frozen masonry that gave the great ice castles their fortress look; block ice lent itself easily to making turrets, towers, battlements, and processional archways. Often the fortresses were surrounded by trees of ice, the great doors flanked by carved lions and horses. In the forecourts, sculpted cannons fired ice balls. In keeping with the fortress-style architecture, invented mythologies promoted mock battles between warring elements. St. Paul's winter festival always featured the storming of the castle, complete with fireworks.

Another model of snow construction is the igloo, the traditional winter home of the northern indigenous peoples of the North American continent. The nomad Inuit, working quickly, cut rectangular slabs of snow compressed by high winds, and place the slabs in a spiral whose diameter decreases as it rises higher. Once the dome is created, the builders light a fire that softens the interior walls so they glisten wet. At that point the fire is quenched, and a hole is opened up in the top of the dome. The melting surface of the igloo's interior refreezes, this time into a ceramic-hard finish, making the inside of the dome a cocoon, impervious to storm and cold. When new snow inevitably buries the dome, the Inuit move on.

The Icehotel's construction takes elements from both these methods: fortress and igloo. Pure, faintly blue ice from the nearby Torne River is harvested to create windows that bring light into the main hall and some of the rooms. Melting the interior walls of some rooms with a blowtorch to achieve a glass-like surface has its origin in the igloo model. But most of the snow-building technology here in Sweden, comparisons to the Romanesque and to Gaudí notwithstanding, could very well have come from the United States Army. In Greenland in 1959–60, the army created Camp Century out of cast snow. They experimented first with plowing snow over inflatable hemispheres to make snow domes that froze in shape, and then tried removable metal forms. Their research proved that compacted snow has a quality not unlike concrete, the molecules bonded together into a solid compound. This is something many children who squeeze fresh feathery snowflakes into balls already know.

Cast snow, that is, snow plowed over forms to create load-bearing, vaulted tunnels, is the method that the builders of the Icehotel employ, but these days the snow doesn't come from the sky. Every November a snowblower gets busy churning out a substance that is like snow, but slightly stronger, a mixture of snow and ice nicknamed "snice." Water pumped into the snowblower produces in all some fifty thousand tons of building material. Backhoes shove the snow up and over specially made crossbar-reinforced steel forms the size and shape of boat sheds on runners. Often people climb on top and spread the snice around with shovels to make the thickness uniform; the sides should be three feet thick, the top fifteen inches. The workers take walkie-talkies and measuring sticks. The snice is full of air bubbles and needs a good chill of at least 14°F (–4° is better) to condense and compact. As soon as the snow seems strong enough, sometimes within twelve hours, usually in about two days, the inner forms, on runners, are pulled out by tractors. As Åke explained, if the temperature's not cold enough, you know right away. The snow-ice mixture holds or it crumbles immediately, avalanche-like, once the forms are removed. The big steel forms are then tractored over to a new segment of the structure and the process begins again. Although snow structures are subject to something called "creep," which is the process of snow compacting, the shrinkage only makes the hotel's structure tougher, as fluffy snow particles change to ice and create a hard shell. The Icehotel, except to claustrophobes trying to sleep in the honeycombs of snow, is safe. No part of it has ever collapsed except during the first stages of construction and at the end, in April, when the sun begins to turn the roofs into transparent glass and open up the ceilings to the sky.

Once the big tunnels are created for the main hall and corridors, the time-consuming finish work of shaping the sleeping rooms and suites begins. Some of that had already started; workers were cutting doors at regular intervals and then shoveling excess snow from the individual bedrooms. After the room is hollowed out, blocks of ice are brought in for the bed, and a ten-watt halogen bulb or two are hidden in the crevices. On the blocks are laid a wooden platform, thin mattress, and reindeer skins. No lamps, no prints on the walls, no TV, no Gideon's Bible in the nightstand. Nothing mars the pristine whiteness of the cell. With a candle and a thermal sleeping bag, it's ready for occupancy—that is, for a quick dash out of the clothes and into the bag before sleep. The suites and public areas, on the other hand, take more initial work, as well as upkeep. The rough surfaces of their interior walls are smoothed by hand and hot water and sometimes blowtorch (a process jokingly called "sneezing" from the act of applying "snice"). The suites are made ready for the arrival of artists, who will then turn them into environments: conceptual, abstract, or realistic works of art.

When I was alone in the Icehotel, I often felt its spiritual aspect: the silence of its monastic cells, the sheer magic of its arcaded sacristy. There was something church-like too in its stated purpose of bringing people together. Yet from my first visit I felt the holiness of the building's architecture coexisting with frozen glitz and clever advertising, which often recalled another Andersen story,

"The Emperor's New Clothes." It is, after all, rather a brilliant strategy to convince visitors to fork over hard-earned money to sleep in discomfort by assuring them that an ice bed is the most refined of luxuries, and extraordinarily fashionable.

The success of the Icehotel at projecting an image of icy swank is largely due to the vision of one of its founders, Yngve Bergqvist, a self-described "cultural entrepreneur." I didn't meet Yngve on this first trip to the North, but I heard his name constantly. He'd originally come to Kiruna in the 1970s to do environmental assessment for LKAB, the mining company. From there he'd migrated the ten miles to Jukkasjärvi, where he bought a former Sami almshouse and turned it into an inn and restaurant. He was bullish on the beauties of the Torne River—one of the only undammed rivers in Sweden, and indeed in all of Europe—and soon was organizing whitewater-rafting trips in summer. Like others in the north of Sweden, he found himself pondering a way to attract more tourists, especially in the "off-season," which of course in subarctic Scandinavia is far longer than the "on-season" of summer. Not by chance was Kiruna's annual Snow Fest inaugurated in 1986 at a time when increased automation in the mine was eliminating well-paid union jobs, and families were leaving.

At the same time that concerned northern citizens were looking for a way to draw more visitors to the North in winter, artists had begun to explore the possibilities of snow and ice as sculptural mediums. In 1989, the relatively new Swedish Snow and Ice Sculpture Association decided to hold its annual November conference in Jukkasjärvi because of the village's proximity to the Torne River and its wide flat shores. Its chairman, Rune Sandmark, approached Yngve Bergqvist about hosting the event and brought over to Sweden two Japanese ice artists to help them learn how to harvest ice from the river as well as to lead carving classes.

Although the initial carvings melted in unexpected rain, the dozen or so Swedish ice sculptors who attended had a wonderful time.

Yngve had already seen the power of snow and ice to attract tourists. During the winters of 1987 and 1988, he had traveled with others from northern Sweden to Japan, Alaska, Utah, and Canada to see how other "winter cities" sold the cold. They arrived in Sapporo, the capital of the Japanese island in Hokkaidō, in the middle of its yearly snow festival. In addition to ice sculptures of animals, people, and objects, the Japanese artists had produced a copy of Jukkasjärvi's church tower in honor of their guests.

In 1990 the journalist Pär Granlund put the idea to Yngve of building an igloo on the Torne River and displaying paintings inside it. That igloo wasn't made of blocks of ice but was formed of snow shoveled onto a form and left to freeze. A local contractor created the forms of plywood, and a variety of people shifted snow onto the forms. Barbro Behm, an art teacher in Kiruna and an ice sculptor who was beginning to win prizes at international competitions, was one of the initial enthusiastic helpers.

The ART-ic event was a big success. Five hundred people made their way to the village to see it, and the next year, when several igloos featured the work of more artists, twice as many people came through the village. Just as important as the art was the environment and the fact that the builders had created 646 square feet of interior space. According to the Icehotel's official history, some visitors seemed intrigued by the notion of actually sleeping inside the igloo. Whether the idea came from a visitor or from the organizers is hard to say now, but certainly a light bulb pinged on above Yngve's fur hat, and a couple of years later the hotel was up and running. With Barbro Behm and other artists involved, the Icehotel was firmly about the architectural possibilities of snow and ice. Barbro herself wasn't much interested in the economics of running a successful hotel, but when Arne Bergh and Åke Larsson came on in the mid-'90s, the Icehotel began to enlarge its scope, particularly in regard to high-end tourism.

The tourist angle seemed to me the genius of the plan. In order to convince people to look at ice sculpture in a remote village above the Arctic Circle, you had to offer them a compelling reason to travel there and to stay. If the Icehotel had been merely a museum of ice sculptures, the ticket prices could never have covered the costs of its construction and administration, much less paid for artists to come and work there. But by charging visitors a hefty sum to stay overnight—along with airport transfers, restaurant meals, gift shop purchases, and activity packages—the Icehotel not only paid for itself, but made a profit for its owners.

The Absolut Ice Bar was the one part of the massive Icehotel structure that was reinforced under its blanket of snow. Its large dome, which from the outside looked like a whitewashed Greek church, was forty-six feet high and made of filigreed metal mesh. Snow had been backhoed on the outside, but in the inside, the snow had to be plastered on by hand. Three young workers stood on a platform up near the ceiling and stuffed balls of snow into the mesh and then smoothed them over. The workers were wearing dark snowsuits and boots, woolen hats with long earflaps, and woolen gloves. Again I was struck by how these bundled-up folk appeared to be laboring on a great cathedral of the Middle Ages. In spite of the backhoes and cherry pickers, much of the work here was agelessly labor-intensive. To see an indistinguishable laborer, head wrapped in wool, chipping away at a column or pushing a wooden wheelbarrow full of reindeer skins along a cloister-like corridor was to travel back into the past.

The simplicity of some of the tools, particularly the chisels, as well as the elementary roughness of the basic materials—stone (ice) and mortar (snow)—was in contrast to the sophistication of the technology that made this enterprise viable and successful, not only in the construction but in the marketing. The Icehotel is the delight of photographers, and countless dreamy and arresting photos, amateur and professional, have made their way digitally around the world. Indeed, the setting seemed made for the art and craft of light. The Absolut Ice Bar, in particular, always seemed to glow with unearthly light in the photographs, all luminous blue except for the bright tropical spots of color, which were juices in the glasses made of ice. I'd seen photos of the Ice Bar, its entrance through the cutout shape of a huge vodka bottle, the tables and chairs, the massive chandelier, its ice-bulbs in the shape of small Absolut Vodka bottles. Amidst this scene, well-wrapped human beings, strangely dark and substantial against the glowing bluish light of the room, stared at the camera in a daze, not quite realizing how inebriated they were.

On the other side of the Icehotel, an ice chapel would soon be added to an exterior wall, as godly a space as the bar was a sinful haven for human weakness. Of this chapel too I'd seen photographs, blue and white and uplifting, the room often illuminated by masses of candles. Its arched ceiling and frozen cross inlaid in the snow wall behind the altar was sacred architecture: backless pews of ice, covered by reindeer skins, with an altar of ice, candlesticks of ice, even a baptismal font of ice. Barbro Behm had had the idea for the chapel and had been its designer for the hotel's first seven years, but this year Åke had taken over the job. The chapel was part of the Jukkasjärvi parish and had a Lutheran pastor who presided over the increasingly popular weddings and christenings that would take place regularly over the season to come.

✳

After my tour, Åke turned me over to one of his associates, to my surprise, an American. And not just any American, but a Southern Californian. Like me, Anders Porter had grown up with his imagination turned to the sea, to swimming and surfing, rather than to the mountains. He'd thought of snow as something messy the few times he saw it: wet, drippy, uncomfortable. But as a theater major in college he'd grown interested in set design and construction. "Everything about theater is temporary, including the sets," he told me. "I like the idea of art being the creative process, not the product. So when I happened to read about the Icehotel, I knew I'd like to become involved. I sent them an e-mail, and they let me come last year and work for room and board to learn the skills. This year they invited me back as a paid worker."

There was something about the Icehotel under construction that stirred the imagination, that made you think of both grand gestures and impermanence, of fairy tales and Russian empresses, of Yeats and "All things fall and are built again, and those that build them again are gay." Many of those I encountered around the Icehotel—a puppeteer, a film scene designer, a theater director— saw in the Icehotel a backdrop on which to project their own visions. None minded that in the spring the whole structure would melt; it was that very prospect that seemed to enthrall them. The Ice Bar, the chapel, the vaulted, monastic cells all came from the specific requirements connected with building structures in which people could be separated from their money, yet few whom I met during the construction process had any interest in the hotel as a hotel. They shrugged when I asked if they'd slept in one of the rooms. "Once," they might say, neutrally. What interested everyone involved in the construction process was either the architectural possibilities or else the simple pleasure of making snow forts, using one's strength, working in concert with others to build something that would disappear in less than six months.

The high point every year, I began to understand, was *now*. After the Icehotel was finished, the structure belonged to the tourists, a necessary, but somehow sullying influence on the original purity of the material and the concept.

This year Anders would stay on throughout the entire season and do maintenance on the building.

"Maintenance?" I asked. "What maintenance? It's not like you have to paint the walls or replace the windows."

"Ah, but there you're wrong," he said. "Right from the moment it's built, the hotel begins a slow, progressive shrinking. The scientific word for it is *sublimation,* when a solid turns into a gas without ever turning into a liquid, as opposed to *evaporation,* when a liquid becomes a gas. The process of shrinking happens from the bottom up. That means the doors get shorter and narrower. We have to open them up regularly. And sometimes we have to reconstruct furniture, a table or chair in the bar. People, when they drink too much, can get a little silly."

Later that day I met a local girl, Karin, who was sneezing the walls in one of the suites. A few of the twenty artists who would design the suites had arrived, but more would be coming in a week or so. The workers were preparing the rooms for them. Karin would become a guide once the hotel opened; she confirmed that everything would change once the tourists appeared on the scene.

"I worked here last year and thought it was fantastic once the hotel opened, with so many people from around the world coming through. The art is like . . . it's like being in a museum all of ice. People walk around with me and their eyes get big to see it. They are amazed and happy. But"—she dropped her voice— "sometimes people drink too much in the bar. They don't know how drunk they are—because it's so cold. They think they are just happy. Then they get into their sleeping bag and—*uff da!*"

"*Uff da?* Why?"

"All over the bed, the floor. We have to throw out the reindeer skins—you can't get the smell out by washing. Or, people don't make it to the bathroom in the middle of the night. You've got to dig up all the snow with a shovel and replace it. The Icehotel," she ended, "is a work in progress. It's not like an ordinary hotel, finished when it's finished. You have to keep working on it all season."

"What's the strangest question you've ever been asked by a visitor?" I asked.

She paused diplomatically. "There are no wrong questions. People are curious about everything. But I remember once, someone said, 'Why is some of the Icehotel white and some parts clear?' And after a minute I realized what they meant—they didn't know the difference between ice and snow! Well, maybe they're from Florida. How would they know? So I have to explain—I say, 'The Icehotel could never be made of *ice*. It would be too cold.'"

3. THE PALACE OF THE SNOW QUEEN

THE BLUE THAT PRECEDED the early darkness began to wash over the icy construction site sometime before two o'clock. Or rather, the ever-present thin blue of sky and snow intensified as it darkened. The brief blue hour, softer, more subtle than twilight, resembled the artful tinting of a platinum photograph. The recognizable grew mysterious. The spruce forest thickened. A lone hooded crow flying overhead seemed to pull a smoke-blue shadow in its wake. Blue became a verb, as whiten is, as blacken: The snowy world blued. Blued into black.

It was suddenly night at three in the afternoon and, without the faint stain of light on the snow, insupportably cold. I went back to my warm cabin and lay down on one of the many bunks, exhausted and suddenly dispirited. How could I get over my jet lag if there wasn't enough daylight to shift my body's clock to Swedish time?

❈

I was awakened by the heart-jolt of a phone ringing. It was Arne Bergh inviting me to join him and a few others for an impromptu meal at a house nearby. It had somehow become seven o'clock.

When I knocked at the door, I found a Japanese film crew and a couple of the artists who were working on suites in the hotel. Arne was being filmed for a special program in Japan. All day I'd been around so many people in snowsuits and thick gloves, in woolen caps pulled low over the eyes and tight around the ears, or in fluffy fox-fur hats, that it seemed strange to see these small fragile heads, these bare necks and pale fingers so exposed and vulnerable. I took off my own heavy outerwear and scooted onto a bench at the long table next to Arne.

If Åke Larsson was a man to take your measure and perhaps find you a little wanting in some colder, cleaner vision of the world, Arne was open and welcoming. Lithe, balding, with the stubbled chin of all the men working here, he had warm, intelligent hazel eyes, the air of paying close attention. His cell phone rang perpetually; in between calls we talked. Although he must have been asked some of the same questions before, his enthusiasm was real.

There was about him a spontaneous, let's-think-it-up-as-we-go-along quality; he made the Icehotel sound like a grand adventure involving a cast of thousands, not a solitary spiritual quest. Åke was a foreman, supervising a dozen workers, but he had the air of a man pursuing a vision known only to him. Arne was openhanded, collaborative. If Åke conceived of the hotel as a cathedral in snow, Arne seemed to think of it as a Happening. They had been friends since their student days in Uppsala. Arne had also spent some time as a child in the military town of Boden when his father was stationed there. He'd gone to art school and had become a sculptor. The first time he came to Kiruna, in 1993, he'd been taken by the difference between making sculpture in metal and wood and making art in snow and ice, of making environments and ordinary objects as well as shapes. For Arne, function and form were hardly different, because the material was so inherently unusual. Like Åke, Arne was so enthralled by sculpting in this old-yet-new medium that he moved up north and cast in his lot with Yngve Bergqvist and the Icehotel enterprise.

In 1995 he and Åke were asked to create the ice cavern used in the film *Smilla's Sense of Snow*. Not only did they learn a great deal about ice technology, but the publicity helped their work at the Icehotel, which in Arne's case grew bolder and more theatrical. Although it was Åke who made a Medusa wig of icy snakes to fit over Naomi Campbell's head in the famous fashion shoot, Arne was the one who ventured to Nigeria to carve a huge block of ice, transported with great difficulty in refrigerated ships and trucks, so it could melt in the sub-Saharan sun.

In his role as artistic director, Arne had hired theater directors, Web designers, architects, interior decorators, even graffiti artists to design the suites. Personality, curiosity, confidence, a spirit of adventure—those mattered more than past experience working with ice. How many people in the world have worked with ice, anyway? But of course he also wanted a balance of styles. What I was to hear many times about Arne was that he was extraordinarily open to new ideas—the wilder the better.

Soon Arne had to leave for the airport to pick up another arriving artist, and I began talking to a woman down the table. Tjåsa Gusfors was a slightly built blond in her thirties who, like Arne, was also being followed around by the Japanese film crew. She whispered to me, with a laugh, that she was the sort of girl the film crews liked, because she looked so "typically Swedish," with her long flaxen braids and big blue eyes. The blond fragility was belied by her working history: She used to be a forklift operator and longshoreman at the Malmö Harbor. Tjåsa was now a puppeteer in southern Sweden who made her own puppets, costumes, and sets and gave one hundred fifty performances a year. She said she knew she had to come north after hearing about the Icehotel years ago. Although some artists come and do their work in a week or ten days, Tjåsa was here for three weeks. She wanted time to let her ideas develop.

After dinner I walked back with her and the Japanese crew to the suite she was designing. Tjåsa's room wasn't far along; she had spent a week just prepping it, smoothing the walls, ceiling, and floor. She'd connected up a Coleman stove, with a pot of melted snow steaming on its burner. She scooped out hot water with a ladle and used it to rub over the rough spots on the walls. "I want the walls to be like stone or plaster, that smooth." In the klieg lights, the bare walls appeared almost soft, without edges, and the vaulted ceiling made it seem as if we were in a whitewashed chapel somewhere in a southern land. On one wall, Tjåsa had created a radiating design of hexagonal ice blocks set into the snow. She'd carefully cracked the blocks so their fractures would capture more light. Behind this wall was a narrow crawl space, so that the design could be worked on from both sides. Later she would put in a revolving-wheel lamp, with filters of pale pink, green, and blue, behind the walls so that the ice blocks would seem to be illuminated from within and would cast faint stained-glass flickers on the walls.

"When we were figuring out the interior design of the hotel," Arne had told me earlier, "I said we should get rid of the paintings on the walls, the way they were in the ART-ic igloos. People can see paintings anywhere. I thought we should use only 'winter material.' The light should be cool, not warm. No candy-colored lights, like they use in China. That's not the effect we're after here." Tjåsa's use of filters was the exception here, not the rule.

When the first ice castles were built in Canada and the United States, electricity was new, and the lighting of the castles at night was part of what made them seem so splendid. Writers rhapsodized about the palaces as "glowing alabaster lanterns," even though the technology would have been very visible, compared with the possibility today of embedding lights in snow by using fiber optics and LED lights. The latter are 90 percent light and only 10 percent heat, important when melting is an issue. The basic electrical grid at the Icehotel consisted of ten underground "wells" connected to the village and inspected by a professional electrician. During construction, as I'd seen, outlets for power tools and floodlights were visible. Once the hotel opened, all that would be more or less covered over. In 1998, a Swedish light architect, Kai Piippo, had been hired to design the lighting for the hotel. He came with visions, most of which couldn't work, because of the reality of cold. Over the years the Icehotel had experimented with light in many forms, from filtered fluorescent tube lighting to halogen spotlights for the large ice sculptures. For Tjåsa, light was an essential part of the "mood" of her room, but many experiments lay ahead before she'd be satisfied with the effect.

The Japanese filmed her for a while as she worked, then they left and I left too. Tjåsa planned to work until midnight. She told me, as many people had today, that it was always the same temperature inside the Icehotel: 23°F, day or night, no matter how cold it was outside. They told me this as if it meant twenty-three degrees was actually a comfortable temperature for warm-blooded mammals like us to live and work in.

I went away for a week to the village of Överkalix, about three hours southeast of Kiruna, not far from the Finnish border. An old yellow parsonage had been turned into a writers' residency called the Barents Literary Center, though, to be strictly accurate, the Barents Sea was quite a distance to the north. I was lonely at the center, especially in the evenings after the staff went home. There was just one other writer, a quiet Norwegian man. The residency had come too early in my trip. I didn't have much to write about except the Icehotel, and I felt I'd rather be back at the vibrant construction site than sitting here trying to describe it. The days were short and snow fell every day. My jet lag still kept me up half the night. I made sketches with white chalk on black paper and took walks around the tiny town. The Kalix River, like the Torne River to the north, and like so many rivers in the north of Sweden, had once been an important waterway linking fur trappers and traders. Some of the first foreign travelers to Lapland had sailed up the gulf and then made their way up the rivers to the interior. The Kalix was still known for its salmon runs—but that was in warmer months. Its surface was frozen now.

I still didn't quite understand where I was in this vast northern world. Wet, heavy snow fell and then froze; the streets were icy, and there was really nowhere to go. Instead of wandering around and exploring, I sat in my room writing in my journal. Always it was the same question: Should I live or should I perish of grief? I'd been trying to answer that question since I was twelve and my mother died. Was there a point in learning to love and trust again? I sometimes thought not.

I reread "The Snow Queen" several times, surprised at how little of the story really took place in the frozen ice castle. Much of the tale was Gerda's long quest to find Kai. In order to discover his whereabouts, she had to go into, as she called it, *den vide verden*—"the wide world." She set off in summer, traveling by boat, and immediately lost her red shoes in the river. She was saved by a woman gardener who cast a kind of summertime spell on her; Gerda traveled barefoot, talked to animals, met a prince and princess who sent her off in a golden coach. She was captured by a robber family, reprieved from death by their daughter, the little robber girl, given a reindeer as a steed to take her north. Andersen, happier himself in Italy, was vague about the geography of the North. Gerda goes to Lapland and meets a Finn woman and then a Lapp woman; she says good-bye to her reindeer and continues on foot through snow and ice to the Palace of the Snow Queen, which seems to be located somewhere near either Spitzbergen or the North Pole. I felt cheered whenever I read about Gerda, but also cold. What about her shoes?

I cut short my residency and returned to Jukkasjärvi. Immediately I was happier, once again engaged in the international community of artists and workers. I was impressed at how much progress had been made on the hotel in my absence. Several of the tunnels had been closed off at the ends by walls of ice blocks; the columns in the main hallway were upright and smoothed; a double door had been set in the main entrance in what had been a gaping hole. The door was covered in reindeer skins, with handles of antlers, like something out of *Beowulf.*

The building of two more wings would go on from now through the official opening of the Icehotel in eight days, and the chapel had yet to be built, but the real focus now was on making the rooms fit for habitation and completing many of the suites. While the tractors and bulldozers continued to move snow masses around outside, more of the work was being done inside, as workers and interns trundled in ice blocks for the beds and put carved ice numbers outside the doorways. The doorways, I came to realize, would not have actual doors. Curtains would be hung, and that was all. At first I was taken aback by at the lack of privacy. And what about the noise? But one had only to step inside one of the rooms to hear all outside sound vanish. The snow was a terrific insulator, almost uncannily.

The tunnels had become a honeycomb of rooms now, and the only way you could observe what was happening inside them was to step over the threshold to see if anyone was working. This was how I met Maya Erdelyi, a Cooper Union grad who was here because she was interested in public art. Maya was smoothing and sneezing the walls of the so-called Cosmic Room. "It's going to have constellations of light embedded in the ceiling and a round bed in the shape of a planet." Her excitement filled the room as she spoke of the snow construction as a kind of Buddhist practice and the work that they were all doing as a symphony.

I thought both were true: Talk about nonattachment! The Icehotel was a fine example of art for art's sake, of pouring one's greatest efforts into something that was destined to disappear in a few months. Yes, a few figures and pieces of furniture could be rescued and eternally preserved in the Ice Gallery, and photographs could try to capture the essence of the project, but film or digital imagery could never truly grasp the sensory impact of being cold as you experienced this form of art. Creating the Icehotel was like rehearsing a symphony or putting on a ballet. It required careful coordination and the efforts of many to turn evanescence into solidity, just for a short while. It required cash and time and enormous labor, as well as the efforts of scene designers and stage managers, and the imagination and drive of conductors and impresarios. If the Icehotel were a theatrical production, Arne Bergh was its Diaghilev.

❄

As the exterior walls formed and the rooms took shape, the designer suites assumed distinct moods and styles. In one, two Swedes in their fifties were designing a room full of rock-and-roll paraphernalia. Peter Båvman was an art director in film; the other was his longtime friend and Web designer Ingmar Almeiros. They told me that their generation had been so influenced by music that it naturally came to mind when they had a chance to create a room. They'd carved a freestanding Fender guitar in ice and were now spending all their time chiseling the outlines of lyrics into the blank white walls. Dylan songs figured heavily. They'd also cut out individual letters of snow and inserted them between two clear slabs of ice. "We love the music, but we sometimes don't spell English all that well," Peter said. One of the plaques they'd just mounted on the wall bore this out: "Come in she said I give you shelter from the sterm."

Across the corridor were two Norwegians, Peder Istad and Espen Voll, who together were the leaders of a group called Minus°, which was formed to create conceptual art in ice and snow. Peder was a furniture designer, while Espen worked seasonally from January through April doing artistic installations for businesses and communities. They were against realistic art. "We try to generate feelings rather than words." What they liked, they told me, was the chance to work quickly and on a large scale, to make good design wherever they could. In their view, granite and wood were costly materials, time-consuming to work with, and ultimately such sculptures were seen and appreciated by relatively few people.

"Art is dangerous, usually," Espen said. "And many people are frightened of art. But here at the hotel, people are not frightened of looking at art in ice. Because they are fascinated by the material, by the ice, in a way they are not fascinated by wood. What we learn from working in this temporary but quick medium can be translated to other design work. Here you can make a big piece of public art in a week. Sponsors can see pictures; you can try a lot of different techniques."

Last year, they told me, they'd done a room with an interior shaped like an egg, and this year they also seemed to be fashioning ovoids from the piles of snow in the chamber, some of which had portholes lit from the inside and looked vaguely submarine, like something from Jules Verne. Unlike the good-natured Swedes playing Dylan tunes on the boom box across the hall, the Norwegians were earnest and a little severe. They weren't listening to music, but if they had, it would have been Estonian minimalist Arvo Pärt. I asked them if they'd come back to see their suite during the tourist season. "We prefer to keep the room in our head, as something pure and artistic," the Minus° men told me. "Although we like to *think* of people being interested in our design and responding to it."

There was room at the Icehotel for the avant-garde, for experimentation, but also for whimsy and for crowd-pleasing realism. I poked my cold nose into a shoveled-out room where Mats Indseth, so bundled-up that all I can really say of him was that he had blue eyes, was cutting into a big chunk of ice with a chainsaw altered so that about half its teeth were removed. Afterward he created the details of his figure with an "ice iron," a tool about two feet long, with a ruthlessly sharp, spade-shaped blade. His particular tool came from Sweden, but in general the best ice irons come from Japan, where ice sculpture is a fine art. "In Japan, hundreds of thousands of people come to see the ice sculpture competitions," he said. "Here in Europe, the interest is just beginning, really. If you do want to sculpt in ice, the Icehotel is the place to work and be seen. So many people have the chance to see your art here."

Mats's suite this year had an indigenous, circumpolar theme. In addition to what was going to be an Inuit hunter perched on a blocky mountain of ice, there was a large, Mount Rushmore–style face of a man cut into the snowy wall. He was supposed to be from Canada, one of the First Peoples. Mats also planned to create something on the opposite wall: a Sami drum frieze with runic figures, of Shamans, hunters, and reindeer. Another block of ice—a tall, rectangular slab—would be left essentially as it was, with a light fixture embedded somewhere inside.

The ice used in the hotel—for the weight-bearing columns in the grand hallway, for the bar, the tables and chairs, the beds, the sculptures—is cut from the Torne River in March, when it is at its thickest, and stored through the spring and summer in a huge, refrigerated building off to the side. The river freezes to a cloudy pale blue. Its color makes it seem mysteriously alive next to the granular heaviness of the snow walls.

I saw more examples of Mats's ice sculptures in an aluminum-clad structure the size of an airplane hangar by the construction site. This warehouse, production plant, and ice gallery was kept at a temperature of 23°F. At one end, slabs of ice cut from the river had been forklifted up onto shelving, layered with sawdust, and stored from March through the next winter. A small assembly-line machine produced glasses for the Absolut Ice Bar: uniform small blocks with a hollow core for vodka and juice. At the season's height, some two thousand glasses were produced each week.

The other half of the cavernous structure, separated from the ice factory, held four igloos of different sizes, created on the Inuit model, with a low door you had to crawl into. Three of the igloos were made from snow blocks, the fourth from ice, and could be rented by the night at any time of year. Helena Sjöholm had suggested that I might like to sleep in an igloo, so I'd have a sense of what a night in the Icehotel was like. I'd been open to the possibility until I saw the igloos sitting in the brightly lit hangar and tried to imagine a night passed in a sleeping bag in this cold building, surrounded by life-size sculptures. The ice figures were realistic, in the dramatic mold of heroic but conventional statuary: Inuit hunters and Viking berserkers with raised spears and axes, mothers and children, and huge renditions of bears, elk, and reindeer.

The igloos, I was told, were most popular in the summer months, with tourists who were thrilled at the piquant contrast between the midnight sun and green of summer and the chill of the Ice Gallery, at the mind-boggling notion of sleeping in an igloo in July. Now, the warehouse was mostly used to store ice bars and frozen furniture from last year's hotel. Objects of ice, some soiled or cracked, were piled haphazardly here and there, like so many discarded castoffs in a secondhand shop. In the dim corners were broken-off bear paws, candelabras, baptismal fonts, reindeer antlers, and child-size chairs and tables, all of worn-out ice, all unable to melt back into the river, held in the frozen captivity of form by refrigeration.

I went into Kiruna one day to do some shopping and to meet with ice artist Barbro Behm. Coincidentally it was our mutual saint's day—December 4. Barbro is the Swedish variant of Barbara. It also seemed fitting that St. Barbara was the patron saint of mines. Out the window of the café where we lunched I saw the looming white mass of the LKAB mine, which so dominated Kiruna's views.

Kiruna, in the mountains, was colder than Överkalix, but also often brighter, and this was one of the (relatively) brightest days so far. Barbro met me with a smile. "What a great day! You know, I feel so happy in October when the first snow arrives. Winter is my best time, the time when ideas come. It's so inspiring to live here, where the winter is so *long*."

Barbro was in her fifties, with a wide-open face, long gold-brown hair with a touch of gray, and a sturdy set of shoulders. She used her face and body to act out emotions, from absorption to indignation to surprise. Her English was excellent—she'd spent a great deal of time in the United States as a student—but the tone was always Swedish. After she finished one of her stories, she would laugh and say, "*Ja, ja,* that's how it is."

Barbro had grown up in northern Sweden and had been an art teacher in Kiruna most of her adult life. She'd been doing ice and snow sculpting for a good twenty years, ever since the resurgence of interest in working with frozen water. "This isn't new, the ice world," she said. "It's at least a hundred years old. But in the 1980s everything started up again, sculpture contests and ice festivals." Over the years she had traveled widely: within Europe, to Alaska several times, to Sapporo, Japan, and many times to Harbin, China, to take part in ice-sculpting contests. "Sculpture is a way to really allow people to see *ice*. For that reason I don't do representational sculptures. I prefer the abstract. I love angles and fractures over rounded shapes. I never use power tools, only my bag of chisels. I refuse to use colored lights. I refuse to compromise my sculpture. It's always about the integrity of the *ice*."

Every time she said *ice* her voice rose with enthusiasm.

Along with other artists and entrepreneurs in northern Sweden, Barbro had been interested in ice art as something that Norrbotten Province could use to attract visitors in the off-season. She, along with Yngve and others, had shoveled snow and experimented with different architectural shapes back in the early days when the Icehotel was more of a local scene, before Absolut Vodka had come on as sponsor, before the marketing had geared up to its current heights.

The idea for the chapel seems to have happened by chance. "I noticed that a block of ice had melted into a concavity on top and it reminded me of a font. I'm not religious, but I like the intense quiet of a church space that invites contemplation and worship." She'd suggested the chapel to Yngve and had then gone on to design its interior architecture and furnishings. Over the table she spread some photographs: Most of the crosses were inset in the wall behind the altar and illuminated either through natural light or invisible fiber optics. The pews were of ice, covered with reindeer skins. The pulpit and altar were of ice and had designs cut into their surfaces.

Barbro had designed and constructed seven chapels at the Icehotel and was now beginning to work with a hotel complex in Finland to create a chapel for them each winter. She was busy, judging competitions here and there and still traveling to do her own sculptures. She was trying to advocate for standards for ice artists, so that their work could be taken seriously. "Often," she told me, "you'll see a photograph of an object in ice, or a chapel or room or snow sculpture, and there you'll see the photographer's name credited, with no mention of the artist. But what we do is make art; we are artists."

Ice was a pure thing to her. "I don't compromise my art," she said firmly, shaking her head so her long hair swung. "When I was in Harbin the first years, I was the only artist working abstractly. I knew that if I did something different, something realistic, I had a better chance of winning. But no, I did my art, I didn't compromise. And they respected me. And now the Chinese are doing abstract art. *Ja,* that's how it is!"

She laughed. "I was in Japan—Japan is much more sexist than China; it's surprising. The Chinese are open, the Japanese, no. There were forty-eight teams in Sapporo one year, all men, all with chainsaws. I was the only woman; all I had were my chisels. You can imagine! *Ja!*" She made a face, then softened. "I never use a chainsaw. I'm interested in the *ice*. The ice decides. It's transparent. It has angles. It should be used *as is*."

She pulled out more photographs, including a series of four huge abstract pieces in a row. "This was Fairbanks, Alaska. I was working in a team that year, four women. We called ourselves Arctic Women. We were Kathleen, an Athabascan Indian; Nadia, from Siberia; Anita, Alaskan; and me, from Sweden. Kathleen had had the idea of using the theme of 'story knives.' These are knives that fathers give to their daughters. These were huge pieces, fifteen feet high. We had to be organized. We didn't have chainsaws, each just a bag of chisels." Barbro mimicked a sarcastic male voice: "'Oh, women don't like power tools, scared of them.' *Ja, ja*. But I believe that you should come to the competition with an idea that will work no matter what the temperature or the conditions." She smiled wickedly. "Some of the men, the men with their *power tools,* didn't finish. Some Italians came to us, 'Help us, Barbro, we aren't going to have enough time to finish, give us a suggestion what to do.' So I did, why not?"

Good-humoredly she added, "So many of these competitions, you see the men. Rubbing, rubbing, rubbing. *Polishing* their sculptures of naked women. The proportions are all wrong, huge rumps and thighs and breasts." She roared with laughter. "You see them polishing. No wonder they don't finish. Women don't do sculptures of men, generally. We do abstracts."

❄

Having lived here so long, Barbro was, unsurprisingly, a fan of Kiruna. But I still hadn't found it easy to get a grip on the town, which seemed modern and even ugly, dispersed over the lower slopes of Haukivaara mountain and stretching dismally out into the snowy plain. The Folkets Hus, a large community center, home of the tourist office, a cinema, meeting rooms, and the café where Barbro and I had met, loomed over a packed parking lot in the center of town. There were a few attractive buildings—the modern city hall with its tall clock tower and an enormous Jugendstil church on a hill, along with some neighborhoods of large wooden houses, but I was puzzled by the tourist literature that referred so cheerily to Kiruna as a "garden city."

I knew little of Kiruna's history and nothing of this part of Sweden. Although my great-grandparents Nils and Johanna emigrated from Sweden to Illinois early in the twentieth century, they came from the south of the country, a region rich with farms, lakes, and coastlines, and it was that summertime Sweden—of archipelagos and islands, sailboats and beaches—I was most familiar with. I didn't quite know what to make of this cold industrial town and its mine. I liked the fact I'd been given a borrower's card at the library and that I could wait my turn, among the Somali refugee youth, to use the computer there, but other than the library and Café Safari, the town held little interest for me, and Barbro's enthusiasm for it was touching but inexplicable. Such local boosterism wasn't shared by anyone I met around the Icehotel, which had created a world of its own, untethered to any locale but the banks of the Torne River.

It was a world I preferred too: a symphony, a Buddhist work-in-progress, a state of mind, a miracle of light and mystery. I knew that everything would change once the tourists came, and somehow I wished to preserve this moment. One afternoon when I was visiting Tjåsa in her room, still only very slowly taking shape, I asked her if she would be coming back.

"I'd love to. Arne is the one who decides."

"I mean, in a month or so, when people are staying in the hotel. Wouldn't you want to see all the suites complete, see people in your space?"

"I wouldn't come back to see this place full of people." She was adamant. "The best part is *now*, when we're making it, all of us together. Trying to realize some vision, or visions, out of piles of snow." She laughed. "I know it's commercial. It has to be. But Arne allows us to think of the dream behind the money. That's why I will only come back to make another room, another dream space. Next year."

For now, we agreed, the Icehotel belonged to the world of the imagination, fairy tale, and dream, as well as achieved art. Day after day the ice artists labored to realize a vision in a medium that many of them had never worked in before. They put on their woolen hats and gloves, turned on their boom boxes, shoveled and chipped and sawed and scraped, trying to create spaces that would approximate the designs they had dreamed up months before.

I walked around the site, well bundled up, breathing frostily, chatting, gradually more used to the cold, looking at the thickening walls of snow, the honeycombing of the rooms, the seemingly endless corridors of silence, and at the way the ice captured light from the departing sun's reflection near the horizon. "Snow has to do with shadows," Barbro had told me. "Ice has to do with light."

I would have liked to stay longer but the days were blueing darker now, and I had hundreds of miles to travel yet on my journey. One day soon I'd pack up my rolling suitcase with books and journals and put on my heavy socks and boots. Then, like Gerda, I'd set off into the wide world again.

4. HOW THE WILD REINDEER WAS TAMED

THE TORNE RIVER flows out of the high mountains between Sweden and Norway down into the Gulf of Bothnia. At Jukkasjärvi, it widens out to a lake. *Järvi* is Finnish for "lake," a reminder of the Finns who helped settle the area; *jukkas* has been variously translated as "meeting place" or "drinking spot." In late medieval times Jukkasjärvi was the site of a winter market where the Sami traded furs, skins, and dried fish for milled grain, fabric, iron kettles, and silver jewelry. It was where the tax collectors came to extract whatever the king needed in order to finance his continental wars. Merchants would arrive a few days before the tax collectors were due and would relieve the Sami of some of their goods in exchange for alcohol. There was once a great deal of drinking here, but in the nineteenth century Jukkasjärvi became a local hub of the revivalist Laestadian movement, a stricter form of Lutheranism still practiced by many Sami. If you walk a half mile from the Icehotel you'll come to the village, with its grocery, school, cluster of houses, and a red wooden church built in 1728 on the site of an earlier church from 1608.

One freezing blue-pink morning around ten o'clock, a man in full Sami dress appeared in the reception lobby. I'd signed up, along with a bachelor party of five Englishmen, to have an authentic Lapland experience, one that included a ride on a reindeer sledge and a meal in a traditional nomad tent. The brochure description made it sound as if all this took place deep in the Swedish wilderness, but in fact it turned out to be a site just down the road, next to the Jukkasjärvi church.

The Sami's hair was dull blond, floppy; his cheekbones wide. He was in his twenties, short, strongly built, with a shy glance and a bowlegged walk. I could see that the Brits, his age or slightly older, wanted to laugh at him and his clothes: at the Dr. Seuss–style cobalt blue, red-trimmed, four-cornered hat, at the blue cloth tunic over leggings of reindeer skin that came up over his knees, at the soft-soled reindeer-skin boots with the upturned toes. Later they would call him, unmaliciously, "funny little bugger," among themselves. I'd had a glimpse of the bachelors last night, when they had returned to the row of cabins after midnight, drunk as lords, jumped on their rented snowmobiles, and roared up and down some nearby mounds of bulldozed snow. Today most were dressed in outdoor gear supplied by the Icehotel: one-piece, front-zippered, black snowsuits with fleece-lined helmets of the same material, snow boots, and thick gloves. Although their accents varied (one was from India, another from the East End), they had a low-key air of entitlement. They were stockbrokers in the city and clearly had the money just to fly up to the north of Sweden for a weekend.

Ailo introduced himself and directed us outside to two snowmobiles with reindeer-skin-covered sledges attached. He drove one and a bachelor another, and the rest of us seated ourselves behind them on the sledges and held on tight. Out on the wide frozen Torne, the temperature was −13°F and the wind cut my face even though I'd slipped on a fleece balaclava. It was an exhilarating fifteen minutes though, for the blue sky was clear, a flush of sunrise pinking the bright snow.

We could have driven over to the site, but arriving by iced-up river made it more dramatic. A herd of half a dozen or so reindeer was waiting for us in a corral. They were pawing the snow for fodder and had the alert but resigned look of half-tamed beasts that were going to have to put up with whatever nonsense we thought fit. Some had no antlers; others had broken ones with brown, barky material sloughing off the white bone. Male reindeer lose their antlers in November or December and don't grow new ones until late spring. Females keep theirs over the winter and use them fiercely to gain access to feeding sites. "In the rut the bulls are male, but the cows are male in the winter," goes the saying. Memo to those who believe in Santa: Rudolf the Red-Nosed Reindeer could only have been female.

The reindeer wore colorful woven harness bands around their necks. Ailo told us he'd capture two of them for us to attach to the sledges so we could have a ride. Tearing after them through the corral, Ailo swung a rope with a slipknot circle. The intended reindeer, thicker than a deer, smaller than a horse, dashed off, wild-eyed, for another corner of the enclosure. Reindeer are speedy creatures, built to run from wolves and bears. But they are grazers too, and curious about people, a trait that's made it possible for the Sami to milk the females and harness them as beasts of burden and transport.

One of the bachelors, a tall, handsome Anglo-Indian, sporting a big Russian-style fur hat with earflaps, lit a cigarette. "Fucking cold here," he remarked. Two others were looking at their watches, calculating how much time it would take to get to the Kiruna Airport and then back to Stockholm and London. Another bachelor, shorter and plumper than the rest, who looked like Sleepy in *Snow White* with his small beard and dozy eyes, turned to the bridegroom and asked him how he was making out. "Bit of a pounding headache, I'm afraid," the almost-married man groaned. "I'll have to sleep it off in the plane. Tell me again what we're doing here in bloody Lapland. I don't remember a thing."

None of them addressed more than a polite remark or two to me. I sensed from some sotto voce ribald remarks made later ("Doesn't this reindeer pelt feel good, mate? You'll be getting a lot of this after next weekend") that my presence put a slight damper on the bachelor party atmosphere.

Ailo, meanwhile, had been successful in lassoing a big, active male reindeer. After a struggle, he managed to fasten a leather bridle around the animal's neck and two leather reins. Ailo then fixed a pair of long wooden poles to the bridle; they were attached from around the bull's haunches back to the sledge. The sledge was about four or five feet long and the runners curved up in front. He instructed one of the bachelors to hold the bridle and went off for a second reindeer. This one, a smaller, more docile female, put up less of a fight, and soon we were ready to each take a turn driving a reindeer around a small, go-cart-like track.

Ailo harnessed the reindeer cow to a second sledge and handed her reins to me to hold. He instructed Earflaps on how to step onto the sledge and kneel. "Slap the ropes on his back! He goes," said Ailo. The bull dashed forward, with surprising gusto. Earflaps whooped in alarm that quickly turned to glee. He slapped the reins again, yelping like a television cowboy.

The bachelors were now energized. The second one to try the big bull fell off his sledge and was dragged a little by the reins before he let go. This lent an air of danger to the enterprise, which made the bachelors all the more keen. Sleepy positively jumped on the sledge as the bull careened past us. He grabbed the reins and, standing, took on the air of a circus performer. Ailo caught them both as they came round again. The bull was winded, Sleepy triumphant.

Ailo gestured to me to get on the sledge behind the female reindeer. "She's not so fast as the other," he said. "Old reindeer. You must shout to her and hit with the ropes." I slapped at her rump a little and also shouted, "Gi'up," and off we went. I felt balanced on my knees, enjoying the pace. While we did run faster on the downhill than on the uphill, where she dragged, our pace was respectable. She sped up as we came to the cluster of bachelors, and Ailo caught her. Another bachelor jumped on, but was disappointed. "This one's too slow!" They preferred to be flung off the sledge. We all went around twice, then it was over. The second time I circled I was more aware of my surroundings: scrub birch and willow, black against the snow, and the almost shocking brightness of the hour or two of light, which seemed to scour the dusty film off my retinas.

Ailo said, "Now the reindeer are tired. We sit around the fire and have coffee and eat." He unharnessed the two animals and led them back to the corral.

When he returned, one of the bachelors asked him, half-mocking, "Is this how you get about? By reindeer?"

"We drive cars," Ailo said in his painstaking English. "This kind of racing, maybe once or twice a year, for festivals. My family has some reindeer, but not so many. You must have many reindeer to make money."

Ailo wasn't from around Jukkasjärvi. He lived about sixty miles north but had taken over the day's excursion from his cousin, who was ill today. His task was not only to provide a little adventure for us tourists, but to explain how the Sami had lived in the past and, in some respects, still live. Now he led us through the flap of a tent that was surprisingly roomy inside; it could have easily held twice our number. The tent was canvas, stretched over alder poles, like a tipi. In Sami it was called a *lávvu*. In the past the tent might have been covered in skins or woolen cloth, not canvas. Until sometime around the 1960s the Sami huts of bark and wood, permanently left in the landscape and snug against the snowdrifts and howling winds, were where the Sami would normally spend the winter. The tent was a structure for putting up and taking down, something to use during the long months of trekking. Now of course the tent was also used for tourist purposes.

Its snow floor had been covered with spruce branches, then padded with reindeer skins. Ailo built up the fire with birch twigs and a few logs. He said he'd make us a meal and tell us some Sami stories. Then he would show us the church next door.

One of the bachelors asked him how long all this would take, and reminded Ailo that they had to catch a plane at one PM. The brochure said this would be an all-day excursion, and I was paying the full price of nearly a hundred dollars, but there was nothing to be done. I was at the mercy of the bachelors, who were not in the mood to be instructed in the folklore and daily life of the Sami. They merely wanted to do one last vigorous snowy thing in Sweden before heading back to the financial world. They had admired Ailo's skills with reindeer, but now, again, they couldn't resist making fun of him.

"So, Ailo, where'd you get those reindeer trousers?"

"My mother made them for me. She makes all my clothes."

"Oh, I *see*."

Inside was dark and cozy, except where our backs met a slice of cold at the slight gap between tent and earth. He told us that the interior of the Sami dwelling is always arranged the same, and so are the people inside it. The mother is on the right side of the fire, the father on the left, the children alongside. The hearth goddess lives under a flat space where the cooking utensils are kept. The guests sit close to the door. In Sami life, guests come and go freely, hardly saying hello or good-bye, simply accepting coffee.

Water was boiling in the coffeepot. Ailo took out a leather pouch and dropped in ground beans. At the same time he'd gotten out a blackened iron skillet and was softening butter to fry up small pieces of reindeer meat. Here inside it was smoky and warm and one or two of the bachelors lolled back dozing, while the others checked their watches and hoped there would be no delays getting to Heathrow. They were hungry and quite uninterested in what Ailo had to say. But I was curious. I asked him about his language, his schooling, the politics of Sami culture. We spoke in English except when I threw in the occasional Norwegian. I gradually ignored the bachelors and their low-voiced comments about hangovers and travel plans and paid attention only to my host here in the tent. Ailo's earnestness, his steady and dignified determination that we understand something of his way of life, made it more than an experience I paid to have.

As I continued to travel in the north of Scandinavia throughout the winter and read more about the Sami way of life, these few hours with Ailo would serve me well. I'd recall the warm, smoky tent with the cold at my back, the woodsy snap of the birch twigs and branches on the fire, the white reindeer hair over all my dark clothes, the smell of coffee and the bitter-dark taste of it in wooden cups, the flavor of buttery reindeer and how good it tasted on the freezing cold day. Later I'd read that the arrangement of the tent or other shelter reflected ancient matriarchies. There was a goddess at the entrance, and a goddess of the bow watched over the weapons. The hearth goddess not only watched over the fire, but also gave souls to the babies in the mother's womb. I understood all that better, having been inside a tent, having had coffee when I was cold and food when I was hungry. In the future I wouldn't pay for an experience like this, and would even feel a little embarrassed I'd believed it would give me a sense of Sami life. But when I got back to my cabin at the Icehotel, the smoky smell of my clothes lingered for a long time and hinted that there was more to Lapland than the deliriously beautiful structure of ice and snow that was going up outside my window.

Before today, my only other close encounter with reindeer had been about thirty years ago, up in the Jotunheim mountains in Norway, where I was working for the summer in a hotel. There were a few Norwegians among us, but many of the staff were from England or America. Toward the end of August we heard that there was to be a roundup and culling of wild reindeer: Did we want to see them? Of course! All summer the cooks had served us reindeer in stews and as steaks, but none of us, foreign kids or city Norwegians alike, had ever seen one of the animals up close. We drove to a large corral where the reindeer had been herded in from the mountains. They were galloping round and round in a counterclockwise direction (reindeer always go that way). The sound they made, animals in fear for their lives, was a terrified croaking, almost frog-like. From time to time in the thundering frenzy, two or three men would wade into the herd, lasso and bind an animal, and drag it over a fence post. With its head pulled tight against the post, the reindeer's kicking legs took it nowhere. Then someone shot it in the head with what looked like a rifle, the bore right at the temple. I know now it was a special rifle that shoots stakes into the skull. Brains spattered, the reindeer died immediately. Nearby were a tractor and trailer where the reindeer were quickly skinned. Blood trailed in rivulets through the dry grass; the stench was stomach-churning. The butchers were covered in blood.

Although most of the men working with the reindeer seemed "Norwegian," a few were dressed in leggings and tunics, and we were told they were "Lapps."

I'd been in Norway over six months by then, working and traveling. I'd learned the language, had hiked in the glaciated mountains, and had seen the glorious fjords of the West Coast. I could dance a polka and make cream porridge. But I'd heard almost nothing about the Sami people, whose political and cultural renaissance was, in 1972, still in the early stages and almost invisible to the larger public.

Gradually, through the years I kept returning to Scandinavia, I learned a bit more about Sami culture and history. While researching a travel book on women and the sea, I spent some time with Lars Børge Mykevold, a Sami archeologist at the Árran Center on the Tysfjord in Norway. I was interested in the lives of the coastal Sami, in particular one Trouser-Berit, a hard-living, pipe-smoking mother of four who was renowned as the captain of a Lofoten fishing boat. I was hoping on my travels this winter to discover more about the Sami who live inland and who, even if they don't own reindeer themselves, are part of the culture of reindeer.

The reindeer (*Rangifer tarandus*) is a cousin of the wild caribou, which is found in the circumpolar north, both in Eurasia and

Europe. Unlike caribou, which migrate across the tundra in the thousands but often in loose, scattered groups, reindeer run in a tight herd, especially when pursued. The semi-domestic reindeer tend to be smaller and heavier than caribou, but the two share many characteristics and are equally well adapted to freezing temperatures, with large, splayed hoofs that make it easier to move on snow and swim in water. They have two very dense coats; the outer one has long, hollow hairs—five thousand hairs to a square inch. The inner coat is woolly and fine and almost three times as dense, with thirteen thousand hairs to a square inch. They can lie down on the snow without melting it, and cows can give birth in blizzard conditions and hardly feel the cold. The hair on their faces covers their muzzles, so they can forage and "drink" snow. Their nostrils are cunningly designed not to frost up; the large surface area inside warms the breath and prevents the moisture from turning to ice. Reindeer are so well adapted to the snow that they tend to suffer in warm weather. That's part of the reason they migrate—to either find more snow in the mountains or take to the rivers and sea. Of course they're also looking for food. Although reindeer eat willow leaves and the buds and flowers of sedges, they're particular specialists in moss and lichen, and in winter will dig below snow to find it.

All northern native peoples have hunted the caribou and reindeer and made use of the animal in a variety of ways for food and clothing. The Sami have had a relationship with reindeer, first as hunters, then as herders, for at least seven thousand years. It's quite probable that earlier in European history reindeer were to be found farther south. They are also found in Eurasia and were domesticated by such tribes as the Eveny in Siberia who managed to tame the beast in such a way as to be able to ride reindeer like horses. The Sami sometimes put children on their animals, and in olden times it was common to see cradles attached to the reindeer, but in general the Sami used the reindeer as pack animals and as locomotion for their boat-shaped sleds or *pulkas*.

The extensive reindeer herding practiced by the Sami is relatively recent in their long history. Keeping large herds only came into being around 1500 and was a result of economics: The wild reindeer stocks were declining, and maintaining a lifestyle based on hunting grew more and more difficult. Yet the Sami were able to use centuries of knowledge about reindeer behavior to tame individual reindeer and eventually control herds of hundreds and often thousands of animals. Accustomed to following the reindeer on their annual migrations, the Sami continued to live a largely nomadic existence even as more and more settlers came into the northern provinces and established farms and took over the forests and waterways.

The Sami's close association with reindeer is the subject of many folktales in Lapland. One legend from Sweden tells of a Sami man who was out working, in the old days before the Sami had reindeer. He met a girl from "Below," and bound her to him by cutting her little finger with a knife. They lived together in a hole in the earth. She told him to lie quietly for three days, no matter what he saw or heard. Then she left him. For three days he heard the most astonishing and frightening noises above his head, but he kept quiet all the same. On the third day the girl returned and took him to the surface. There was a herd of reindeer and a tent full of useful things, including lassos and skis.

Another story tells of two sisters who lived on a mountain. They each had their own hut, and they each had a reindeer they milked, and that was what they lived on. The reindeer didn't need tending. They came to the huts every morning and evening for milking.

One day the two reindeer began to talk. One of them said, "I'm leaving my old woman to be alone again." The other reindeer asked why, and the first reindeer said that the old woman was cruel, hitting and kicking her during the daily milking. The second reindeer said she would not leave, because her old woman was so good to her. "I have no heart to leave her alone and hungry." The two reindeer said good-bye, and the first reindeer became wild, while the second grew tame.

A hundred years ago a tame reindeer, called a *hark,* was a valuable commodity. Not only did tame reindeer draw the sleds that held food, gear, babies, and trading goods—but they were invaluable in leading the wilder herds on migration routes. For the Sami, reindeer made life in these northern latitudes possible. The animals provided food, skin for the tents, fur for sledge blankets, clothing, and bedding. They were milked, and cheese was made from the milk. Their meat was fried, smoked, and cured; the antlers and bone were worked into tools, utensils, and jewelry. Reindeer tendons were used as wicks for burning seal fat and for sewing together boats of sealskin and bark. The reindeer was a sacrificial animal in pagan times. It was also often a "helping" animal of the *noaidi,* the Sami Shaman. The drums of the Sami, used in ritual and divination, were made of stretched and dried skin and often featured small figures of reindeer painted on with inks from blood and plants. Once there were thousands of these drums in Scandinavia; now there are less than a hundred known examples, most in museums. Christian missionaries who called the drum the Devil's Bible destroyed the majority, often in bonfires.

The next day I borrowed a *spark* from the Icehotel and kick-sledded my way down the icy road to the cluster of houses that make up Jukkasjärvi, and went inside the church for a closer look. The Laestadian church is justly admired for the painted wooden tableau behind the altar, a lively, naive rendition of sin and salvation, everyone dressed in Sami costume. Founded by the Swedish Lutheran pastor Lars Levi Laestadius in the 1840s, the sect still holds a strong sway in northern Scandinavia (and in some communities in North America as well). Its followers hold strictly to the Bible, are conservative and teetotal, and have a tendency to speak in tongues when in a state of religious rapture. Laestadius himself was half Sami and spoke the language, which was one of the reasons the movement took off so quickly among the Sami; another reason was his fervent preaching against the evils of drink in a community that had lost many of its members to alcohol. But Laestadianism also had the effect of muting or negating the traditional Sami worldview, which knew all the world as sacred and which invoked a variety of gods and saw spirits in animals and trees.

The reindeer was long a totem animal among the Sami, inscribed on their knives and drums. To outsiders such animism was connected in ages past with the notion that the inhabitants of the far North were wizards, warlocks, and idol-worshippers who lived in a realm called Biarmia, where "the path of approach is beset by insurmountable perils," as Olaus Magnus wrote. "If any person should want to get beyond these, he must provide himself with reindeer yoked to a sledge (there is a copious supply of these creatures in that country, as of donkeys in Italy), by means of which he can cross the hard, thick-frozen ridges at an amazing speed."

The tent in which I'd sat yesterday drinking coffee and eating fried reindeer was just next to the church, on the other side of the graveyard. I kick-sledded over to the enclosure. No one seemed to be around. I looked at the tent from the outside and at the eight animals in the corral. I was embarrassed now about the sledge riding and about how the bachelors had treated Ailo. Already I couldn't tell which reindeer was the one who drove me around: Was it that small one with the long-suffering, big brown eyes?

"Are you my reindeer from yesterday?" I called to her, and softly apologized—for what, I wasn't sure. I remembered how the little robber girl kept the reindeer tethered up, but unloosed him to carry Gerda up to find Kai in the far North. First she asked him, though, if he knew where Lapland was.

"'Who should know better than I?' answered the poor animal. 'There I was born, there I have run across the great snow fields.' And his eyes gleamed, recollecting what he had lost."

My reindeer lifted her head, tame but with some wildness still in her, and looked at me. Then she went back to scraping the snow from the ground with her strong hooves, looking for the sustenance underneath.

5. TRAVELING IN THE DARK

THE COASTAL STEAMER MAKING its way up the Norwegian coast had few passengers and no other tourists. I rattled around in the communal spaces of the *Richard With,* and was the only break-faster in the vast dining hall, where an enormous smorgasbord of cheeses, meats, herring and boiled eggs, cereals, breads, pastries, juices, and hot drinks seemed to have been laid out, fairy tale–like, just for me.

I'd taken the train from Kiruna west over the high, cold mountain chain that divides Sweden and Norway. It's the north-ernmost railway in the world, an engineering marvel originally built to transport ore from Kiruna's mine to the ice-free port of Narvik. The train makes a dramatic descent through the moun-tains into fjord land: in summer, spectacular; on a winter after-noon, just dark. From Narvik I took a bus over to Harstad on the coast to catch the steamer that stops every morning on its way north. It's twenty-eight hours from Harstad to Honningsvåg, and I'd chosen to travel by sea in part for curiosity's sake—to see the coast in winter—and in part for nostalgia. One summer long ago I worked on the coastal steamer line as a dishwasher. I rarely missed a chance when in Norway to take the *Hurtigrute,* even for a short hop. For the most part, however, I'd been a passenger in summer, when polyglot tourists packed the ship's restaurants and lounges, and the panorama deck was thick with sedentary seniors writing postcards and reading. It wasn't the shortest day of the year today—that was still two weeks away— but this was the farthest north I'd come this winter, almost to the North Cape.

I'd had some weeks now to get used to the dark, but that was inland, in Sweden, where the countryside was blanketed in soft snow and radiated whatever day- or moonlight there was. Out here on the coast there was no snow, only raw lashings of sleet whenever I stepped out on deck, and eerie twilight before and after a day of a few hours. The moon sailed with us back and forth across the sky, a chill white disk, morning, noon, and night. "In the absence of the Sun, there are two twilights, one in the morning and the other in the evening, in which those poor remainders of days provide that the night should not be utterly destructive. And by how much the Sun is farther absent, the light of the Moon is clearer," wrote Johannes Schefferus in *Lapponia.*

Around ten in the morning, as we approached the end of the European mainland, the black coastal mountains turned to paler charcoal and showed themselves desert bare; suddenly the light was no longer bone gray, but—in the east—blush pink and tur-quoise, then hot rose, mango orange, the sunrise churning into sunset, all in two hours, with the sun below the horizon, invisible below the iron-hard water. Joseph Acerbi, an Italian traveler to these latitudes in the years 1798–99, wrote that the birds stopped singing as he and his companion approached the North Cape. That

74

was in summer; in winter, all life except the sea and the raging black wind seemed to have vanished.

In a version of Ptolemy's map of the world, printed in Ulm in 1482 (but originally created almost fourteen centuries before), giant women's heads are placed at the four corners of the known world. Their lips are pursed; they are blowing winds onto land. The wind-woman in the upper left—nearest to Ptolemy's idea of northern Scandinavia, an archipelago of large islands—looks to be blowing especially hard. Ptolemy, born in Alexandria in AD 90, drew some of his notions of the northern climes from what early Greek poets Hesiod and Pindar described fancifully as "Hyperborea," or "Beyond the North Wind" (*boreas*), and what Pytheas called "Thule."

None of them went as far as the North Cape, but it was Pytheas, a Greek geographer and astronomer born in Marseilles in 300 BC, who observed the sun traveling around the earth in a yearly cycle and who believed the moon influenced the tides. Pytheas first sailed out of the Mediterranean into the Atlantic to explore the North Atlantic coasts. After visiting tin mines in Cornwall and accurately estimating the circumference of Britain, he navigated his ship northward. He described a place he called Thule, six days north of the British Isles, where a congealed substance, neither air nor sea, bound everything together. Fog or pack ice, no one knows, or whether Thule was the Shetland Islands, Iceland, or Norway. He wrote a book called *On the Ocean,* but it has been lost, and his descriptions of the northern lands and seas exist only in excerpts.

No traveler seems to have followed up on Pytheas's interest in the far North for over a thousand years, though Tacitus's descriptions in *Germania* offer some of the first mentions of the "Fenni," or Sami. Eventually, it was a Norseman visiting the English court of Alfred the Great who described the coast where I was traveling now. King Alfred, born in 849, was the ruler of the kingdom of Wessex in southwest England at a time when a large chunk of the country was home to Danelaw. Alfred, probably the man most responsible for the fact that Danish is not spoken in London today, was also a scholar known for his curiosity about the world. In between battling new Viking incursions and reconquering land in England where the Danes had already settled, Alfred learned Latin. He translated and had translated many texts of history, geography, and religion. He also invited scholars to his court and welcomed travelers who could tell him more about the world. Alfred was especially curious regarding the North, about which so little was known.

In the early 890s, Ottar, a Norse chieftain, came to Alfred's court. Ottar's fiefdom lay far above the Arctic Circle, in the area of Tromsø. Alfred was so interested in what Ottar had to say about his travels that he or one of his scribes took the words down in Old English. A copy of this report is to be found in the British Library. It's the oldest eyewitness account of northern Norway and is particularly important because it was written down at the time, not transmitted orally for several generations before a cleric thought to inscribe it on parchment, like the Icelandic sagas.

In this narrative, called "Ottar's Report," Ottar describes where his kingdom lies—the farthest north that any Norseman lived. He spoke of the land as empty, except for some Sami here and there who fished on the coast and hunted inland. Ottar grew curious about what lay to the north of his kingdom and whether anyone lived in that wilderness. One day he set sail and traveled three days north, with land to starboard the whole way, and open sea to port. He came to the North Cape and sailed east another three days, and then another four to what must now be the Kola

Peninsula in Russia. On his return west, he came to a large "river" and sailed into it, surprised at how built up it was. There he found more Sami fishing and some "Biarmians" who had cows, pigs, and sheep. Everyone had reindeer.

Ottar was a brave man to go so far north, though I assume he sailed in summer. On this chill December morning, it seemed as if the *Richard With,* unpeopled and silent in this ghostly, luster-less light, was sailing off the edge of the world. Then suddenly the lights of Honningsvåg appeared, so pitifully brave around a little harbor.

We few disembarked to streets coated in gray ice, inches thick. I had no idea how to walk on this, especially carrying luggage. A local offered me a lift in his car the short distance to my hotel, but left me at the top of a hill that led down to the wharf on which the hotel was built. Slipping and sliding, I arrived at the reception desk to check in, then set off again, as if on an Arctic expedition, scrambling ungracefully into a town that seemed as though it had been constructed on a glacier, to the tiny museum.

The young woman working there, perhaps starved for com-pany, followed me around the exhibit cases, telling me that any college graduate who came to work in the provinces of Finnmark or Nord-Troms had part of her education paid, as well as hardship pay. Most of the bureaucracy turns over every two or three years; the people who live here year-round are fishermen and their fami-lies, or those who work in the tourist trade. Hard as it is to imag-ine, this little ice-encrusted town is the hub of the North in the summer months. Then, the coastal steamer and the cruise ships pour out thousands of visitors, and thousands more arrive in buses from all over Europe to see the North Cape.

Up until the second half of the 1800s, few tourists came north of Trondheim in Norway, and Norwegians and foreigners alike thought of northern Norway as horribly ugly, even frightening. But with the Romantic movement in art and literature, what had been hideous was now beautiful, what was desolate was now *sublime*. Increasingly lyrical descriptions of the midnight sun, of the grandeur of the lonely land and sea, of the opportunities for poets and painters culminated in the publication of some 250 books about the voyage north in the nineteenth century. In 1873 King Oscar II of Sweden and Norway (a union then) made a trip to the North Cape. The next year came the world's first midnight-sun cruise, chartered by an English company in London.

I left the museum in a storm of sleet and hail and perilously made my way back to the hotel, where I sat in my room the whole long evening, writing postcards and watching Norwegian TV. Violent gusts of sleet shook the windows, and the waves slapped onto the icy wharf. I thought of Ptolemy's map with wind-women blowing gales onto shore, and of Magnus's map, the *Carta Marina*, with its illustrations of sea monsters swallowing ships. I could not imagine being out at sea in this weather, when all that was north was pack ice and endless snow and roaring winds. North was the Pole, and the land where Frankenstein had chased his monster over ice floes.

It was dark and still snowing when Ole Kristiansen picked me up the next morning at nine in his battered Jeep. He was the friend of an acquaintance and had volunteered to show me around. "You'll know me by my hook," he'd said on the phone. A burly man in his sixties with a weathered face and shrewd blue eyes, he was on disability after losing his hand. He'd been around the world on merchant ships, had fished and hunted seals; now he lived on a tiny island off the coast with his wife, Anne, a German nurse.

Wet snow and sleet rocked the Jeep as he drove the hairpin-turn coastal roads and pointed out fishing factories and small harbors. (The hook had been replaced by an attachment that allowed him to shift gears.) The waves offshore were huge maws of black. Every year, Ole told me, friends and relatives never came back from fishing those rough seas. I'd had some unclear and adventurous notion of getting to the North Cape, perhaps by snowmobile, as a cheery brochure promoting winter tourism had advertised; instead I cowered in the passenger's seat as we drove higher up the mountain in the direction of the last promontory of Europe. But even following the snowplow we were hopelessly enveloped in whirling, lethal snow and couldn't continue. Ole assured me, "There's not much to see out at the North Cape anyway, this time of year. Just lots of weather."

Ole's island offshore was a speck of rock swirled round with stormy waves and connected to land by an icy causeway. It was noon when we arrived, too dark for a photograph. He showed me around as we waited for Anne to return from work. He and Anne had built the house themselves; they catch and salt their own fish, repair what's necessary, believe in making do.

He asked what I was writing about, why I'd come here.

"I wanted to know the North in winter . . . winter tourism." We both laughed.

"You should come back in real winter."

"This isn't winter?"

"No. No. This is just . . . the ugly time of year. Before Christmas. It's February to March that are the real winter months. There's lots more snow, and light. That's the time to go snowmobiling to the North Cape."

Anne arrived, attractive but stern and opinionated. "I'll tell you what you ought to do for your book—go out with the snowmobile crew—in the high mountain passes. Then you'll see weather!"

She started in on the Sami and soon we were arguing. Her opinion wasn't so different from that of some Norwegians, those who believe that the Sami refuse to be "normal," that they demand "special rights." I recalled a conversation during another visit here in the North one summer. I'd been on a bus, and my seatmate, an elderly farmer, had talked about these "special rights." I asked him what he meant.

"Soon you will have to ask permission before you pick a cloudberry while you're out on a simple walk," he said. "They think all the land really belongs to them. Them and their reindeer. Most of them don't even *have* reindeer now."

"But wasn't this land once theirs," I asked, "or at least in use for the reindeer migration?"

"It wasn't theirs," he said indignantly. "Norwegians have lived here for centuries. There was intermarriage. Most of the Sami who say they're Sami aren't really; they're just trying to get special rights. And then they go around speaking Sami, so you can't understand them. And they want Sami taught in the schools, that dead language, and signs in Sami, bilingual traffic signs! And what I really hate about them is how dirty they are. If you go out into the countryside, you'll see. If a snowmobile breaks down, they just leave it lying in their front yard. You can always tell a Sami house from a Norwegian house!"

Now Anne was going on in much the same way as the man on the bus. I'd heard this sort of convoluted reasoning before, in my own country, about all manner of people. These days it was directed at anyone in a turban or veil. People who managed somehow to be *worse than,* and yet with strange thoughts that they were *better than.* My skin crawled to hear this contemptuous spewing in a German accent. My own prejudice was at work: What right did a German have to an opinion about the inferiority of other races? No Scandinavian friend of mine would put the case quite so baldly. They were more likely to sigh and say, "*Ja, ja,* the Sami question. . . ." But there were certainly Norwegians who thought the same as Anne. I had met them.

Anne had lived in Norway for about eight years, ever since she met Ole while working farther south. I wondered what it was like to be German in the north of Norway, where every town and every village had been bombed and burned when the Germans pulled out in 1945. In the museum in Honningsvåg, there was a sign that read: WELCOME TO HONNINGSVÅG, ONE OF THE MANY VILLAGES WHICH WAS BURNT TO THE GROUND BY THE GERMANS DURING THE SECOND WORLD WAR.

Outside, the wind howled and snow beat against the windows, while Anne began serving up a dinner of potatoes and fish they'd caught themselves. I made one last try. "Don't you think that Sami culture is fascinating, though? That there's a lot to learn about it?"

"I don't really know any Sami," she said. "There aren't many here. You don't see them. I don't think they really have a culture, anyway. Not like ours."

I remembered Ottar's famous description of his voyage, ". . . the land goes on far to the north. But everything is completely empty except for a few places, where here and there the Sami live, hunting by winter and fishing in the sea by summer."

I would hear this again and again as I traveled through the North—that the land had been empty. That it was still a wilderness.

In Tromsø a week later I would meet a friend of Ragnhild's, the Sami journalist John Gustavsen. Adopted by Norwegians, John had grown up in Honningsvåg after the war, at a time when the Norwegian government was busily trying to assimilate all the Sami who'd somehow managed to escape assimilation before. It helped that the Germans had burned so much of northern Norway. When the government doled out money for rebuilding schools and housing, it promoted *Norwegianness* as the necessary and patriotic reconstruction of a ravaged country. By the time John arrived in Tromsø to attend high school, he had little sense of being Sami and didn't speak a word of the language.

John and I met in the cafeteria at the University of Tromsø. Short and slight, he had a thin, high-cheek-boned face. He had become over the years the sort of Sami I was fairly sure Anne would dislike: one who ceaselessly pointed out injustice and demanded what she called "special rights." Over coffee, he told me how he struggled as a teenager with a sense of identity.

"We were studying Knut Hamsun in class, reading his famous novel, *Growth of the Soil,* about the settling of North Norway. Hamsun wrote something like, 'No human being had lived on the land before then, only animals and Lapps.' I asked the teacher what this meant. Did it mean we were not human beings, we Sami? Had we not lived on this land for thousands of years? For answer, he threw me out of the class that day. That was my political awakening."

After Honningsvåg, I dropped south again to the town of Alta, which sits low and protected by rounded mountains on the Alta Fjord, at the mouth of the Alta River. Once, all this was covered by glaciers. When the ice receded, hunters moved in. In 1950 the first pictographs carved in sandstone were found. They date back six thousand years. In winter the ancient images are blanketed by snow; in summer, thousands flock to see the pictographs at this UNESCO World Heritage site.

Alta itself is new, mainly built up after the Germans destroyed everything. The older village is Bossekop, a few kilometers south of Alta and long a trading place, like Jukkasjärvi, for the Sami. Twice every winter for several centuries, on December 1 and March 1, a weeklong *Lappemarked,* or "Lapp Market," was held where the Sami came down the frozen Alta River from the Finnmark Plateau inland to trade with local merchants, who brought goods to Bossekop by sea. The Sami offered furs, skins, dried reindeer meat, and dried berries in exchange for iron kettles, coffee, woven cloth, and felt. They also acquired silver spoons and jewelry, for the Sami treasured worked silver and often had silversmiths make spoons according to designs they'd carved on their own birch spoons, cups, and boxes to hold butter.

The markets continued up until the Second World War, and Olive Murray Chapman described one of the last ones, in 1931, in *Across Lapland with Sledge and Reindeer.* Chapman began her trip across Finnmark in Bossekop with reindeer and a guide and ended up traveling by horse-drawn sleigh and then car to Kiruna. Although a Swedish tourist official had tried to dissuade her, she'd persevered in her desire to see the North in winter and to study that "picturesque race of nomads." An intrepid widow with a "cinemagraphic camera," she was perhaps the first foreigner to film the Sami. She took copious notes on everything about the people she encountered and their customs, and also illustrated her book with watercolors. Seventy years before me, she'd also traveled up the coast by ship, to Hammerfest, and then had taken a small boat to the Alta Fjord. This was her first impression of Bossekop:

> Then, to my surprise, I saw a number of what appeared to be gnomes running swiftly down the steep slope to the jetty. I was

beginning to wonder if I had indeed sailed into Fairyland; but, on closer inspection, these quaint little people proved to be Lapps on their way to the Bossekop market. They crowded on to the boat, almost tumbling over one another in their hurry, some carrying bundles almost as large as themselves. Many were under five feet in height, and with their quaint pointed blue and scarlet caps, and gaily embroidered tunics, might have stepped straight out of a Hans Andersen fairy-tale.

I'd come to the town of Alta to visit Laila Stien, a writer and translator of Sami literature. After a month of traveling on my own, Laila's snug wooden house was a welcome break from hotels and hostels. I'd met her when she came to Seattle for a reading, and I admired the spare, evocative prose of her short stories. Dark-haired, pretty, quick in her movements, Laila is one of northern Norway's best-regarded writers as well as one of the few non-Sami Norwegians fluent in Sami. Her Sami husband, Mikkel Gaup, is the editor of the cultural newspaper *Áššu,* published out of Kautokeino, a town on the Finnmark Plateau, about a two hour drive away. Their children are grown and gone, and Mikkel spends most of the week working in Kautokeino, so Laila and I were alone in the house surrounded by evergreens and lit by innumerable small lamps.

A week before the winter solstice, it was light enough to be called *daylight* only two hours a day. I had a hard time waking up in the morning and a hard time going to sleep. Sometimes I didn't stagger downstairs until eleven, when the window was a rectangle of pale blue light. I felt strange and not myself.

We tried to get outside each day, but there was more ice than snow, and walking was slippery on the frozen roads and fields. Laila showed me what there was of Alta—a shopping center, a college, a superb museum that explored the long history of habitation on the Alta Fjord. More than the landscape, what struck me most was the way the sunrise-sunset flared orange and pink across the southern horizon and turned the snow to pale tangerine silk. The sun was gone, but evidence of the sun was precious, proof that we hadn't been abandoned completely to darkness. Each day I turned my face to the direction of the light, craving reassurance and finding an austere beauty less comforting than magnificent and otherworldly. A burning band of vermilion behind a row of dark firs was nothing like the relentless sunshine of the summer, but it was, in a way, more heart-stopping in its reminder that the sun had not forgotten us. No wonder that the Sami worshipped the sun as father and the earth as mother, and had so many tales about the disappearance and reappearance of light and warmth.

One day Laila and I drove to Kautokeino to visit Mikkel at his newspaper office and satisfy a little of my curiosity about the vast tundra that lay on the other side of the mountains, through the Alta River gorge. We started out in the morning in the dark, but by the time we came through the gorge the sky was lighter, and I had a sense of breadth and space. The whiteness went in every direction under a pale blue sky streaked in the south with crimson and peach. This was a different world from the stormy dark coast. The Finnmark Plateau is the home of the reindeer Sami, who have a less fragmented history than the "sea Sami," of the coast. One of the reasons Anne could claim she knew no Sami and that there were few living around Honningsvåg was that most coastal Sami had chosen to assimilate rather than face continued discrimination. In 1930 a census taken by the Norwegian government showed that 70 percent of the community of one coastal Norwegian county identified as Sami; in 1950, it was 0 percent.

The two main towns on the plateau are Kautokeino and Karasjok. Sixty-five miles to the northwest, Karasjok is home to the Sami Museum, the Sami Parliament, Sami Radio, and an extensive library, while Kautokeino has the Sami Institute, the Sami Theater, and a college that specializes in Sami language, cultural studies, and traditional handicraft. Once these two towns were marketplaces for the nomad reindeer herders, who lived in *samebys,* or small Sami communities, all over the Finnmark Plateau. Not everyone who lives in Kautokeino or Karasjok is Sami, but most are. This is the heart of Sápmi, the land of the reindeer herders and Sami speakers, where the politics of being Sami play out.

I suppose I was expecting a colorful place, but the buildings were blocky and ordinary, and only a few people, mostly elderly, were wearing the *gákti:* a tunic for men and a dress for women, with hats and bonnets to match and reindeer-skin boots. We had a cup of coffee with Mikkel, who showed me around the newspaper office. Afterwards Laila and I visited a bookstore. Most of the stock was grammar workbooks, dictionaries, and children's picture books in Sami.

"Where's the literature section?" I asked Laila.

She picked up a copy of a book titled *Muitalas sámiid birra,* by Johan Turi. "This is the first book ever written in Sami," she said. "Johan Turi was a Kautokeino Sami who had to move south to Jukkasjärvi when the border to Finland closed, and the Sami on the Swedish side couldn't graze in their traditional places. Turi was a man who didn't fit in—he couldn't seem to hold on to his reindeer, he never married. He supported himself as a wolf hunter. Turi always wanted to write a book. By chance he met a Danish painter traveling in Sweden named Emilie Demant Hatt. They formed some kind of relationship and she helped him tell his story, then she translated it into Danish and got it published.

"After Turi's book, in 1910, there was a long gap. Sami wasn't really a written language; it wasn't taught in schools as a literary language. Sami writers had to reclaim it." She pointed to some collections and anthologies of poetry, to a couple of novels by the Finnish Sami writer Kirsti Paltto, and to several prose-poem works by Rauni Magga Lukkari, who lives in Norway. Best represented was the all-around artist-poet-singer Nils-Aslak Valkeapää, born on the Finnish side of Sápmi. Valkeapää had died just a few weeks before, at age fifty-eight. Several of Valkeapää's books of poetry had been translated into English and other languages, and he was one of the few Sami authors known outside Scandinavia. Most of Valkeapää's texts combined poetry in interesting typographical designs over the page with his drawings or with photographs. This was partly an expression of the man himself, but it also implicitly recognized the fact that few Sami could read their own language. Samis could take away much from Valkeapää's books just from turning their pages, seeing how the poems looked like reindeer herds in a corral or strung out over the mountains.

"A generation of Sami lost their language," Laila said. "It's only in the last twenty years that Sami has been taught on an equal footing with Norwegian in the schools here in Finnmark. The children who were put in boarding schools, including one here in Kautokeino, didn't learn to read or write Sami. These would be the writers of today. Most Sami authors who live in Norway write in Norwegian. Of course they must write in the language of the majority to be seen, but it's also that they have no readership in Sami. People *speak* Sami—most people speak it here—but they find it hard to read. That's something that Mikkel struggles with in the newspaper too."

Later we drove up from Kautokeino to some hills overlooking the tundra plain, to an extraordinary collection of six or seven interconnected buildings, Juhls's Silver Gallery, where Laila and the director of Beaivváš Sámi Teáhter, Norway's national Sami theater, planned to discuss turning her novel, *Vekselsang (Antiphony)*, into a play. It was one o'clock, perhaps, and already twilight was stealing over the sky and the snow. Against the blue shadows, the buildings with their swooping roofs and glass-paneled exteriors were bright with interior light.

Over the last forty years, Regine and Frank Juhls had built up a series of gold- and silversmithing workshops and display rooms in a manner idiosyncratic, luxurious, and also quite out of proportion to anything down below in Kautokeino's few streets with their utilitarian shops and offices. Inside, the architecture was, if anything, even more sweeping: curved ceilings of tongue and groove that ballooned inward like full canvas sails on a clipper ship; rooms on different levels; and a sense of spaciousness. Paintings hung everywhere, and small tables displayed ceramics. Long shelves of jewelry lined the white-painted brick walls, the pendants and pins often mounted on dried reindeer moss or birch bark.

German Regine and Danish Frank had migrated to Lapland separately in the '50s, drawn by the romantic notion of the nomadic lifestyle. They'd stayed to build this art emporium, which was a sort of dream architecture of billowing wood, more like the celebration tents of desert nomads than the Sami's utilitarian tents. But the Juhlses were inspired by Afghanistan, where they'd traveled in the hippie '70s. There was even a large and lavish Afghan room, with a convex ceiling of carved wood and tile, and low lamps and little tables covered in patterned rugs with copper teapots and cups set on them. In these rooms fabrics and rugs and pillows with mirrors and hammered brass plates and picture frames were for sale. They were made by Afghani craftspeople and the Juhlses sold them to raise money for the Afghanis.

While Laila and the theater director settled down over coffee at a table in one of the main galleries, I wandered about the place, looking at jewelry. Much of it was designed by Regine, according to the booklet I was given, and her inspiration was the plant life of the tundra and the migratory birds flying overhead. Silver and gold bracelets and necklaces had a nubbly texture, reminiscent of lichen and moss, sometimes of tiny berries and small cupped mushrooms. The earrings were airy and winged. But the Juhlses also designed traditional silver jewelry for the Sami, and that was a significant part of their business. For the Sami had once carried their wealth with them, in the form of silver spoons, cups, earrings, rings, and elaborate brooches. The nomadic life didn't lend itself to metalwork, but the Sami had long bartered furs and fish with Russian merchants, who brought goods up from Italy and the Bosporus, and with peddlers from southern Norway where silver mines flourished.

The Juhlses' daughter Synnøve—tall, blond, calm—came over to me, and we sat down to talk for a while. She had recently graduated from a German goldsmithing school and had brought her new husband, also a newly minted goldsmith, up to Kautokeino to join the family business. She told me that the gallery saw three thousand visitors in summer. Busloads full of foreign tourists on their way to the North Cape stopped and marveled for an hour or two, bought, and moved on.

"They don't stay in Kautokeino," Synnøve said. "No nice hotel here. They go on to Karasjok, where Rica has a hotel and now a sort of building called Sápmi, where they have a multimedia presentation about the Sami, that's connected with a big gift shop. That's where tourists get their so-called 'Sami experience.' Short and digestible. They could get a Sami experience walking through Kautokeino, but they probably wouldn't understand the least thing about it. The Rica Hotel chain is very powerful in the north of Norway. They more or less own the North Cape now."

"What do the local Sami think about your silver gallery?"

"They come to buy their silver, but otherwise it's a bit of a foreign place to them. We've always been outsiders. And in the '70s and '80s, when Sami nationalism was running high, our gallery was sometimes boycotted. The Sami are something of a closed society. They're suspicious of people using their culture, trying to make money off them."

I told her I'd been in the north of Norway before, but never in the interior, and never in winter. We both looked out the tall windows at the huge dark blue sky with the first stars beginning to come out. It was not quite two o'clock.

"I keep hearing about winter tourism," I said. "But I don't see any winter tourists."

"If people only knew how much more interesting Arctic places are in winter," she said. "In summer it's green and sunny, but the light here in winter is so special, so strange." Synnøve paused. "You know, because of films and photographs, people think they have seen everything in the world. But they haven't *experienced* everything. Ice. Cold. Darkness. Those are things you can't see. You need to feel them in your body to know them."

On the way back to Alta, driving across the icy white tundra, the northern constellations flung clear and diamond-sharp against the black velvet sky, Laila said that there was a time when neither she nor the director of the Sami Theater would have met at Juhls's.

"People have calmed down now. There used to be so much more anger from the Sami at others. It was a reaction to everything that had happened between the Sami and Norwegians for two centuries, and especially in the twentieth. The Sami children were taken from their parents and put in boarding schools, the language was almost lost, the culture nearly destroyed. The resources of the North are always in dispute. The farmers who paid taxes on their land *owned* their land. The Sami paid taxes for centuries, but they never owned anything—just the right to graze the reindeer on the plateau and in the mountains. The Norwegian state owns this land. The Sami had tried to organize earlier in the century, but in the '60s there was a resurgence of political activism that got stronger and stronger for the next twenty years."

I knew Laila hadn't grown up here but on the Nordland coast in the industrial town of Mo i Rana. She'd gone to the University of Oslo in the mid-'60s and majored in Sami Studies, the first year that Sami was offered. There were twelve others in her classes; only two of them were non-Sami. Even now, she said, "I don't know why I chose Sami, except that it was different from what everybody else did.

"Now there's no Sami department in Oslo," she added. "It moved to Tromsø. Very few non-Sami Norwegians study the language, even though Norway has the largest population of Sami in the three Nordic countries. If people want to study Sami they come here to the community college at Kautokeino. It's mostly Finns who come, not Norwegians. Sami is more like Finnish. That's perhaps the reason, it's easier to learn."

She herself had come up to Kautokeino after obtaining her university degree to teach for a summer. Here she met Mikkel, who'd grown up in the Sami village of Masi, on the Alta River. Mikkel was a teacher for twenty years before becoming the editor of *Áššu*. They married and settled down to raise a family, and Laila began to write.

What was her relationship to the Sami? I asked. I meant: as subject matter. I knew she rarely wrote about them.

"Until *Antiphony*, I didn't dare create Sami characters. It felt too politicized," she said, hands on the wheel, concentrating on driving. The studded tires crunched over the ice. "I've mostly written stories and taken my themes from the everyday—marriage, domestic life, problems, and all the usual sadness of life. I've got the sensibility of North Norway in my writing. Melancholy! But of course I have a very different experience than many Norwegians. Mikkel and I spoke Sami at home much of the time, so the children would grow up bilingual. We lived in Masi, a village of four hundred people, all related in some way, many working in Sami traditions of craft and art. My husband was a member of the new Sami Parliament for four years and a teacher for twenty years before becoming an editor. So you can't say my experience is completely typical. Yet when I finally wrote my novel, *Antiphony,* which is about three Sami women, three generations, I was very nervous about the reaction. Fortunately it was positive. Still, I wouldn't do it again probably. I feel my work with Sami culture should be as a translator."

The narrator of *Antiphony* is a Norwegian researcher-writer from Oslo who comes up to Finnmark to interview three women and write about them. The youngest of the three, the most politicized, tells the narrator sharply once, "Just admit it—you don't understand anything . . . of course you're not the first who hasn't understood very much. Over the years there's been a damned bunch of idiots up here."

We were passing Masi now, not that anything was visible, but I saw the sign. I knew that Laila didn't care for driving on ice, and I was a little unsettled too, by the vast dark around us. To distract us both, I asked about the demonstrations that had taken place here in the 1970s and '80s. The Norwegian government had planned to dam the vast river system of the Alta-Kautokeino for hydroelectric power. Norwegian environmentalists and the local Sami began a quiet protest, not only because the village of Masi would be inundated and lost, but because the Alta-Kautokeino river system had symbolic value. Like all the rivers in northern Scandinavia, it had traditionally been a pathway and a food supply. The Kautokeino River flowed through the plateau to the gorge, where it became the Alta. Frozen in winter, it was a smooth road down from the plateau to Bossekop for people to travel on foot and with reindeer and sledge. In late summer and fall it was rich with salmon coming upstream. Not only did the river provide fish for the Sami, but wealthy English anglers had been coming to the Alta for decades; in fact, in 1862 a section of the river was leased to the Duke of Roxburgh for a hundred years.

"The protests started slowly," said Laila. "Nobody thought we could win against the government, or that anybody but the Sami who were going to lose Masi would care. But something about the combination of awareness of indigenous rights and the environment had changed. 'Alta' became a big political cause during the '80s, and people came from all over: Sami, hippies from Christiania in Denmark, German environmentalists, Norwegian leftists. Here they all were in the summers, camping out near Masi."

In the end, the dam was built, but with conditions: Masi wasn't flooded. And something had changed. The enormous coercive state presence in Alta (10 percent of Norway's police force took part in controlling the demonstrations) brought national and international attention to this remote part of the world. In 1982, Nils Somby, a Sami photographer, tried to set off a bomb on a bridge and it went off too quickly; he lost an eye and his hand and was jailed when he got out of the hospital. Several Sami went on a hunger strike outside the Norwegian Parliament in Oslo, a terrible public black eye for a country that prided itself on its image as peaceful and socially progressive. More importantly, the Sami began to join with other indigenous peoples around the world and to cast their concerns about land use and culture in terms of the rights of indigenous people.

"We are only seventy thousand," the Sami said, "but around the world are three hundred million indigenous peoples." The protests in Alta were the beginning of modern Sami politics; from that time came a host of cultural and educational institutions, parliaments, and a new sense of pride in identifying as Sami. Of course, that also increased tensions between Sami and non-Sami and led to people like Anne believing that the Sami had "special rights" that diminished or restricted their own.

We passed through the gorge, and the lights of Alta welcomed us back to Laila's house among the firs. We were both relieved to be getting off the icy road. In Seattle, when telling friends about my trip, a few had asked how I could possibly travel around the North in winter.

"They have cars up there," I'd said, impatiently. "They have buses and planes."

But getting around never felt easy. The Sami have two hundred words for snow, nuanced and precise: soft, packed, new, old, fine, coarse, wet, dry, untouched by wild animals, or with a trace of them. Often, the words are connected with reindeer feeding and movement. The snow cover tells which way the wind is blowing and whether the reindeer can get to the lichen underneath. But snow is read in countless other ways, as a story of season and weather, and all those readings have a vocabulary.

I wondered what word was there for ice on the road and dirty snow spitting back up at the windshields? What word was there for traveling in the snowy dark, far from home?

The snow was swirling in a wind of icy white beads when I boarded the Nord-Norge-Expressen and left Alta at two o'clock one dark afternoon on a seven-hour bus ride south to Tromsø. We traveled along a snow-packed highway with only our headlights to guide us and, occasionally, where a village sprang up, a few streetlamps. Uphill and down—from the curves the bus took I could tell at times that we were probably traveling along the coastal fjords. Sometimes the bus was almost empty; sometimes jammed with schoolchildren, shoppers, and workers coming home. For a long while we traveled with a group of deaf children and two mothers or teachers. One five-year-old deaf girl sat beside me and made noises at me and touched my hand and smiled. She smelled of dirt and peppermint.

I looked out into the desolate black sky, where snow blew sideways and the huge wipers could barely keep it away from the driver's big windows, and thought how often in the last month I had traveled at nighttime, no matter what time of day it was. I left in the dark and arrived in the dark, and I saw nothing of the landscape but night and snow. The few settlements looked lonely, illuminated by gas station signs or streetlights. We went through them quickly, stopping only to pick up or let off a single passenger with a suitcase or shopping bag. Most of the time, like today, I had no sense of where I was, no sense at all, only that it was dark and cold out there, and I was afraid to get off and only wanted to burrow into my seat with my book and trust the driver.

Surrounded by the deaf children, their hands flying, I thought about going off the road into a fjord below, about dying far from home in a wreck in the snow and icy water. Surely it could not be right for humans to tempt fate by driving through snowstorms, along icy coastal roads, at a latitude of seventy degrees. How could we save the children if we crashed? How could we call to them if they couldn't hear? Earlier this year I'd wanted to be away so desperately, out of my house, away from my country. Today I regretted that decision and wished myself at home under the covers, a cat on either side, drinking cocoa, and reading about the adventures of some braver traveler than I—Olive Murray Chapman, perhaps, in her reindeer *pulka,* racing across the tundra with camera and watercolors.

Suddenly, swinging around a curve, the bus skidded to a halt, and the whole huge raft of us in this metal machine seemed to tilt to the right. There was silence. Eventually a man got up and peered out the window.

"*Ja,*" he said to the rest of us, with typical Norwegian understatement, "it's a long way down."

Then we continued on.

6. ON THE FINNMARK PLATEAU

I LAY ON MY BACK on a snow crust that barely covered the frozen, stony ground. My head was still ringing. Perhaps I had a concussion and wouldn't have to go on. The sky was palest eggshell blue above me. Earlier, when I was still upright and thundering behind my dogs over the northern plateau, the moon had appeared in the east, a luminous rose-gold flattened flower-head above the pink snow. Now, at eleven in the morning on one of the last days in December, it was as light as it would get.

Someone lumbered over to peer at my unmoving body. It was another dogsledder, Steve, from England. He had frost outlining his lashes, white crinkles inside his nose. Like me, he was wearing two hats, two pairs of woolen gloves underneath snow mitts, probably a set of long underwear, a jacket, thick pants, and over all that a quilted snowsuit. It was about thirty-five degrees below zero.

"Are you all right?" he asked.

Steve's sled, with its four dogs, was anchored to the ground with an iron grapple. That's the only way he could leave them to check on me. They howled with impatience. My team, who only understood what it was to go forward, had long since run off, but I knew that Sven would stop them. Sven had already stopped them twice today and four times yesterday. Yesterday, during the first hour of the six-day trip, I was flung off my sled and my knee hit a protruding rock. The knee was now swollen and stiff with an interesting ring of blue around the perimeter. Today, with my brain still shivering inside my cranium, I considered pretending I was dead, or at least unconscious. Perhaps I could be airlifted away. I'd come so far to see the Finnmark Plateau. Now I considered the possibility that I might be seriously hurt, and wished myself safely away.

I pushed myself up from the snow and stepped onto Steve's sled behind him. It wasn't easy in my bulkiness to take hold of his bulkiness. We careered off again, the dogs barking madly, to where Sven waited for us, a long-suffering look on his face.

"Sven," I said, "I think I have a concussion. My head is ringing. I believe I hit a rock."

He looked at me coolly from inside his fur ruff. He was a man not much given to speaking. He gestured to the sled he'd secured. My dogs didn't give me a second glance; they hardly knew I existed.

"We try again," said Sven.

Originally I'd wanted to be part of a long reindeer caravan crossing the snowy tundra or, failing that, to travel by sledge and reindeer as had the British travelers whose books I'd read. The Finnmark Plateau is the ur-landscape of the Nordic subarctic, and I'd wanted to see the frozen rivers and vast white plains up close. But strings of reindeer and baggage sledges no longer traveled the Finnmark

Plateau as they had decades earlier. The Sami went by snowmobile or even helicopter when looking for their herds. The nearest equivalent of a trek across the tundra seemed to be dogsledding. Dogsledding was of course not part of northern Scandinavia's past; it had been adapted from the Inuit in Greenland and Alaska. But it was said to be one of the fastest-growing winter sports in the world, so when I found a six-day dogsledding trip advertised for over New Year's in just the area I was interested in—around Karasjok—I made immediate inquiries, and was easily convinced that such a trip would get me as close to nature in winter as I could hope. I was especially thrilled that our group would be traveling from hut to hut every night and that we'd be staying in some of the same *fjellstuer* that Frank Butler and Olive Murray Chapman had occupied long ago.

When I was signing up for the trek with Engholm's Huskies, safely in front of my computer in Seattle on a warm September day, I'd asked if a fifty-year-old woman could learn to dogsled. "All you need is good balance," Sven Engholm had typed back. But even then I wasn't quite sure about how well I'd do. I was balanced enough to walk down the street and ride my bike without toppling over, but I was a mediocre skier. In fact, I'd never skied until I went to Norway as an au pair at twenty-one, and although I could get around on my waxed wooden skis, I had been no match for my young charge, two-year-old Knut. I hadn't improved measurably in the years since.

I persuaded my friend Betsy, outdoorsy and a longtime skier, to fly to Tromsø and join me for a Norwegian Christmas, followed by an exciting dogsledding trip in the polar winter. I painted an enticing picture—first, of Christmas cookies and cakes in Tromsø with my wonderful friends Ragnhild and Øystein, and then the chance to see wild animals on the winter tundra. Betsy was a

wildlife biologist for the U.S. Forest Service. In making the reservations, I'd queried Sven about the wildlife on the Finnmark
Plateau. Moose, wolverines, and lynx all inhabited the North, he
assured me. I didn't quite realize, and Sven didn't bother to remind me, that with only a few hours of daylight in winter the
chances of viewing wildlife other than reindeer were slim.

Christmas in Tromsø was all we'd hoped for. When not lounging
around Ragnhild and Øystein's cozy living room, Betsy and I walked
through streets packed with snow and lined with substantial wooden
houses, lit by electric candelabras and small lamps. In the center of
town we found evergreen garlands decorated with plump red hearts
strung across the pedestrian-only zones. Candles in glass jars or paper
bags glowed on sidewalks in front of the shops with their big gleam-
ing windows. There was a small-town feeling long absent in most
of America: Shoppers lingered in the center of the streets to chat;
kids stood in groups around the outdoor waffle stand that scented
the crisp air with sweetness. Children sledded on the hills and many
people took to skis to get around. No grating holiday music marred
the atmosphere in the shops. No Santas or reindeer were on display,
though this would have been the place for reindeer, certainly.

In front of the wooden church in the center of town was a
tasteful crèche; otherwise, nothing reminded passersby that it
was Jesus' birthday. Although Norway has a state religion—
Lutheranism—like most Europeans they're lax on church at-
tendance. The rituals seemed to be more about food than faith.
Ragnhild loved to make all the special Christmas dishes—pork
ribs, halibut, and creamed potatoes—and, as Christmas Day approached, we spent more and more time at the groaning table.
Breakfast, too, was enormous—four kinds of herring, six types

of cheese, and jams, jellies, and fresh butter with the *julekake,* a holiday bread studded with candied fruit, smelling of cardamom. When we visited Ragnhild and Øystein's friends or when friends visited them, plates of almond-studded butter cookies came out, along with fluted cones filled with cream, and *kransekake,* the tall almond-flavored cake made of rounded rings arranged in a pyramid, was passed around with the marzipan, chocolates, and strong black coffee.

The memory of those delightful, civilized meals would tantalize us in the week to come.

Two days after Christmas, Ragnhild and Øystein took us to the Tromsø airport and, with worried looks, hugged us farewell. We arrived forty-five minutes later in Lakselv and then were driven for an hour in a minivan to Sven's spread outside Karasjok: Engholm's Huskies. In the group were seven people from England and a French pair. Didi and Sara were alpine skiers; they had matching luggage and fashionable snowsuits that precisely fit their trim bodies. The Brits wore mismatched clothes and seemed shocked at the cold. One of the Englishmen, Tony, was only along because his wife had wanted to make the trip with her brother and sister-in-law. Cheerful Tony said he was quite nonathletic and had his doubts about the whole business. His sister-in-law, Josie, said, "Oh Tony, don't be a wet blanket. We're here to have fun." Another woman, Clare, spoke of her work as a costume supervisor in the film industry. Her film had wrapped and she'd suddenly called up a travel agent and decided to come to Lapland on the spur of the moment. None of them had ever been to Norway before, much less this far north. The mood was uncertain, but eager, when Sven and his girlfriend, Bodil, hustled us into two dorms with bunk beds and woodstoves. Half an hour later we all met up at a central building that included a kitchen and dining table.

Sven wasn't native to these parts. He'd been born in Malmö, in the south of Sweden. But he'd been living up here a long time, and had the look by now of a northern Norwegian: reserved and a bit somber. He was well over six feet, with a craggy Clint Eastwood sort of face and remote blue eyes. Although in his fifties, he'd entered some ageless-Scandinavian-male zone and would doubtless be skiing and hunting into his nineties. He'd won the Finnmark Long-Distance Dogsledding Race eleven times and had been a runner-up at Iditarod. Bodil, who'd also be a guide on the trip, was about twenty-five years younger, rounded and gorgeous, with thick, long blond braids. As we sat eating fish stew together, Sven answered questions about the week to come with genial ambiguity. "I explain everything tomorrow morning. In the corral."

The night was black, shot with stars, bitter, bitter cold, the temperature minus forty. Bodil took us to another cabin stuffed with snowsuits, boots, and thick caps, and helped us choose clothing for the trip. We wouldn't be taking much with us: a small bag was all. Cameras were to be kept inside our clothes, lest the batteries freeze, along with our food for the day. Bodil told us that in the morning we'd have breakfast at seven, then make our sandwiches and place them close to our hearts to keep them warm. Sometime during the evening, a truck pulled up with extra dogs from neighboring kennels to supplement Sven's own teams.

All through the night we could hear the dogs howling.

Before Frank Butler undertook his long trek across the tundra in 1914, the trip that forms the basis for his book *Through Lapland with Skis and Reindeer,* he'd already been to the north of Sweden a few times and had made the acquaintance of two men who would accompany him on his late-winter journey from Bossekop to Vadsø, in the north of Norway, and then onward to the Kola Peninsula in Russia. Butler traveled with two guides: Borg Mesch and Johan Turi. Mesch lived in Kiruna, where he'd established the town's first photography studio. His glass-plate images of mine workers, early Kiruna pioneers, and the local Sami and their reindeer are still housed in Kiruna in a city archive. He's considered one of Sweden's great early photographers, but he was also a violinist and alpinist and, because his English was excellent, he occasionally was pressed into accompanying tourists around the mountains. Turi, or "Johnnie" as Butler often called him, was the same Turi whom Laila Stein had told me about, the Sami wolf hunter and writer.

Butler crossed the Finnmark Plateau in March, so he had the advantage over us in both light and quantity of snow. He also had the advantage over us in provisions. Before becoming enamored of Lapland he'd been around the world a time or two. He'd traveled by elephant in India and by balloon across Europe. He'd safaried in Africa and thus he was equipped with "chop-boxes, the same I had used in Central Africa when big-game shooting." His provisions were abundant and included, along with fresh reindeer meat pro-cured en route, a store of delicacies: French sardines, Danish but-ter, Worcester sauce and piccalilli onions, potted meats, Yorkshire ham, bacon, sausages, tinned asparagus from Los Angeles, plum puddings, raisins and figs, dried fruits, and rice cakes, as well as "old Cognac brandy, port and whisky and kummel, tobacco and cigars and cigarettes."

In addition to abundant food and drink, he brought plenty of warm clothes: ". . . very astonishing is the number of articles nec-essary to keep out the cold. The following is a list of those I had to wear throughout the journey when driving in my *pulka:* thick flan-nel vest, khaki flannel bush shirt, waistcoat, Shetland wool waist-coat, collar and tie, coat, wind jacket, reindeer fur coat, belt round waist, wool scarf to wind several times round neck and over head, long knife, and bag containing matches, pipe, tobacco and chocolate, bear tippet over shoulders, cap filled with an eiderdown pillow, flannel drawers, knickerbockers, reindeer leggings, reindeer breeches, bands at bottom of leggings round the shoes, stockings, reindeer socks, dried grass, reindeer shoes, woolen gloves filled with hay and a long pair of reindeer-skin gloves over the gloves."

Olive Murray Chapman also wore a *pesk,* or "fur tunic," along with a leather flying helmet and shoes that were far too big for her. She carried her own food and cooking equipment, which was Spartan compared to Butler's. Tea, a boiled egg, sardines, and porridge seem to have been her daily fare except when her hosts prepared a dinner. Both were resourceful, but Butler had the advantage of wealth, which enabled him to travel, as he had everywhere else, with an entourage to help keep him comfortable.

There were many times in the days to come when I envied him.

The next morning the din in the corral was like something from a Fellini film. Sixty or more dogs yowled and yipped in the frigid darkness. It was −32°F, but the cold, surprisingly, didn't mask the horrid smell of dog shit and piss everywhere. Sven gathered us together and began to explain how to attach the short dog chains to our sled lines and how to stand on the sled and steer with our weight. Most of us could hear nothing he said, because he chose to make his explanations in the midst of the barking pack of dogs. He seemed to know his business, but he was clearly not the sort of leader Betsy or I had been used to from various excursions whitewater rafting and kayaking, where safety was the order of the day. In a land less preoccupied with suing, he never asked us for our next of kin or to sign any waiver. More worrisome, it seemed that this brief explanation of dogsledding, unheard by many of us, would be the sole lesson we'd receive on the subject.

"The first kilometer is the worst," was really all I remember him saying. That, and, "Don't let go the sled."

Each of us had four dogs; some of them were Sven's and some had arrived last night. The "rental dogs," as we began to call them, were in general scruffier and less predictable than those trained by Sven. His team of six was beautifully groomed, snow-white with blue eyes, alert and proud; they sat quietly and responded to his commands. They did not howl or make improper advances to each other. The rental dogs seemed to be a mix of terrier-sheltie-Lab-mutt, as different in size as they were in appearance. Sven explained that they didn't all look like traditional huskies, because they were selected on the basis of strength, not looks. Mine were all rental dogs. Although Sven's Web site had predicted that we would come to think of the sled dogs on our team as *our dogs,* I had a strange feeling right from the moment I saw my team that I might not feel that way. One of them was mostly white, with pale wolf eyes that seemed to look straight through me. She was one of the lead dogs; the other lead was shaggy and brown and melancholy, old in his movements and elderly in his heart. One of the back dogs was something like a large brindled pug, while the other was a little sheltie, delicate and feminine, something many of the other dogs seemed to appreciate from the way they were trying to nose her rear end.

The howling of the dogs was constant, but they all had their own howls: some were wolf-like, others ghostly; some yipped as if hurt, others jabbered in their barking. The thing they had in common was a certain single-mindedness. They'd been bred to run, and they were eager to be off. Once they were harnessed to the sleds, we had to stand on the runners, with the brake on, to keep them from dashing away. It was only then that I felt the power of the sixteen legs that were to be my locomotion over the snowy tundra. The sleds themselves were simple affairs, almost rickety. The rounded birch handle was attached to long runners on which we stood. In front of the sled was a long case, something like a body bag, where we placed our sleeping bags and simple gear. Attached to the sled—in addition to the brake, on which we were to stomp in order to stop the dogs—was a kind of iron grappling hook, the purpose of which was not explained at the time.

We set off in two groups: the British couples with Bodil and the rest of us with Sven. He gestured that I was to follow him, with Betsy behind me. I pulled my fleece balaclava up over my nose and lifted my foot from the brake. With unbelievable speed, the dogs were off, through a narrow trail in the woods where the snow-laden trees almost brushed our faces. I was too surprised to fall off that first kilometer, leading me to think, mistakenly, that this excursion might be exhilaratingly fun. Then we came to a steep riverbank, and Sven halted, the first six of us screeching to a stop behind him. Far behind us, there was a lot of shouting and laughing. The Brits had come to grief, as they often would, good-humoredly, and were in a dog-lead/sled/human tangle with a tree involved. But the Brits were Bodil's charge, and Sven decided to head down to the river. Turning to speak to Betsy, I must have lifted my foot slightly from the brake, for with a jerk, the dogs were off, and I was suddenly in a pile on the ground and had to get out of the way of the hordes of dogs, sleds, and bundled-up bodies stampeding by. I remember laughing, jumping up, and walking through deep snow down to the river. It was all so strange, so new, and, yes, so beautiful, that it didn't bother me that I'd been thrown. Sven had caught my dogs and the frozen river was stunningly white and smooth, covered with fresh, untracked snow. The light was just coming up, and the juniper bushes and birches were tricked out with gold embroidery thread, like the clothes the Snow Queen herself might wear.

We arrived at Ravnastua, the first cabin on our itinerary, around half past one, when it was already dark. These mountain huts were built decades before and are maintained by the Norwegian Touring Association, often caretaken by someone who lives nearby or on-site. The Ravnastua caretaker had been remiss. There was no toasty fire going. The rooms, in fact, seemed to be colder than outdoors, where it had been about minus thirty-two all day, colder when you were going a good five miles an hour, cold enough to freeze your eyelashes and crisp up your nose hairs and enter into your bones and blend with your hot blood and turn it lukewarm. Our hands were so cold that they hardly worked.

The dogs were finally separated, fighting- and sniffing-distance apart. We took our belongings from the sleds and staggered into the cabin, with barely enough energy to pull off our boots. We'd neither eaten nor drunk since about seven in the morning, and it was now after two. My peanut butter and jelly sandwich was squashed and battered from where I'd fallen on it. I ate it anyway. I put my boots back on and went over to the outside toilet. There had been no chance to pee en route; the body, understanding the consequences of pulling off any piece of clothing, agreed to hold it. Betsy and I sat on our bunks in a total stupor. She was so exhausted that she didn't even have the energy to upbraid me for getting her into this. The French couple with whom we were to share this room tonight came in. Sara was the only one of us who hadn't fallen today. She was used to the French Alps and, though delicate, was in excellent shape. Remarkably, she now began to brush her lustrous dark hair and to cream her face with lavender-scented lotion, while her husband tried to figure out why his camera hadn't worked today. Betsy fell over on her bunk and strange loud snores emanated from her pillow. "She has jet lag," I explained, hoping she wasn't really having some kind of attack.

Butler had stayed at Ravnastua in 1914 and had found it very comfortable. Of course, Turi would have secured the reindeer, and Mesch would have taken out his violin to play while they were cooking a dinner of reindeer or potted meats, with Worcester sauce and piccalilli onions. We eventually got some tea, after the water boiled on the woodstove. Later there was moose stew; Sven had shot the moose earlier in the fall. It was served with potatoes and bread, and juice for beverage. Clare, the vegetarian, had to make do with a cheese sandwich.

"Conditions are difficult," Sven allowed as we unthawed. "There is not much snow. It is icy and the rocks show. That is bad. Later, in the spring, there will be much snow. And light. It is very nice then."

The lack of sufficient snow had been a large part of the problem today. Our sleds kept knocking against rocks, and it had been very icy on the downhills. I'd had a difficult time with my dogs. The elderly, melancholy rental dog could simply not keep up with his coleader, the wolf with the cold blue eyes. But since they were linked together, they couldn't go at different speeds, and the wolf had to accommodate herself to the old man, though sometimes she dragged him faster forward. Their erratic, slowish speed was fine on the flat parts, like the river, but there were simply not as many flat parts as one might have liked. A certain amount of the time we were dashing through scrubby bushes, along rock-strewn paths. On the steeper downhills, when I was going faster than the dogs through sheer momentum, my sled had a tendency to swing in a wide arc. Sometimes when an especially large boulder loomed, I could avoid it; other times, not. That was how I'd been thrown off and banged my knee.

I recalled looking at Sven's Web site last September. The digital pictures were brightly lit, the snow white, the sky blue. Bareheaded, smiling people stood in groups having hot cocoa or mushing slowly—it had seemed slowly—across the plateau. The dogs looked eager and friendly. Pictures are static, of course. And quiet.

I'd tried to explain the dog problem to Sven during the day, but he'd had other things on his mind, like getting the eleven of us to Ravnastua before dark. Now, belatedly, he gave us some instructions in handling our dogs and sleds. Afterward, he asked if anyone would like to accompany him and Bodil out to feed the dogs. In big buckets, they'd mixed dry kibble with boiling water into a steaming brown, gravelly mush. Several of the British dog-lovers eagerly jumped up. They could hardly believe that the dogs were going to sleep out in the snow at these temperatures. Betsy and I sat on our bunks, each writing in our journals. I could practically hear her pen scratching out: "I paid hundreds of dollars to eat moose stew and freeze my butt off?"

Butler and company ate the biggest meal of the day in the morning before setting out. It was hard, he wrote, to eat so heartily at seven AM, although it made sense to fortify oneself against the cold early on, in case one couldn't find a time or place to eat until nightfall. I imagine that Turi got up and started the fire, then put some dried reindeer on to stew and served it up hot with bread and black coffee. Our own seven AM breakfast was only instant coffee and bread and cheese, and I could barely force myself to eat that. My stomach was in knots from exhaustion and fear. Sara looked at me with impatient compassion over the wooden table in our room. "You look so veree sad thees morning, Barbara. *Pourquoi?*"

Today we had to get an early start because we had some distance to go, over a high ridge to the next cabin at Mollesjok. Wearing headlamps, and once again in full gear, we stomped through the snow to where the dogs had curled up among the trees, each in his or her own tramped-down spot surrounded by yellow snow and lumps of brown. Tethered together as they were, they had to lie near their own excrement. Again, the smell was strong, given the temperature, which Sven had told us was close to minus forty this morning. The howling was excruciating. I felt fear along with re-vulsion looking at my "rentals" and again begged Sven to exchange the old and melancholy dog with another lead dog that could be faster. He decided instead to put the brown dog in the second row, and promoted the pug alongside the wolfish female. Betsy came over and helped me with my hitches, for Sven expected us to do everything ourselves today. I told her, "I'm dreading this." "I know," she said. There was something so kindly in her helping me that I felt even worse that I'd dragged her to Finnmark.

But how lovely it was, too, as we set off without too much mishap and began to traverse the snowy plain. I fell a couple of times, but so did others; and although Bodil continued to be frus-trated with the Brits' habit of stopping to take photographs and in the process falling off their sleds and temporarily losing their dogs, we seemed to be on a smoother course than yesterday. As we approached higher ground and began traveling along the ridge, which had no trees or bushes, the full moon began to show itself over the horizon. It was enormous, and silvery gold. It didn't look like any moon I'd ever seen. It was as close and big as something viewed from another planet than Earth. It was rising in the west, fast and fat in the baby blue sky; in the east was a sunrise without sun. A low bank of thin clouds blushed pink and then intensified to rose and yellow ochre, and the sky spread, like strawberry jam and orange marmalade, over the plain below us. It reminded me of how I've felt sometimes flying east to west from Scandinavia to Seattle and passing over Greenland. From the air, the snowy land often appeared so close that it seemed possible just to step outside and walk. Dogsledding along the ridge, with the golden moon on one side, and the pink and orange sky-plateau on the other, was just that roomy. For half an hour or so the view was so otherworldly—so strangely, lusciously technicolored—that I could hardly stand it, and my physical discomfort was as nothing.

Then my head met the boulder and the day suddenly seemed less enchanting. Even once I was up, I felt shaken and fearful that something like that might happen again. A sort of cold fog settled over the plateau, and Sven made us pause from time to time to keep us together. Again we could not stop to eat, and so drove ourselves onward with nothing in our bellies to sustain us. The extreme cold hour after hour grew next to unbearable: Breathing was breathing ice shards, ice crusted my lashes and made it difficult to see, my feet were cement blocks, and my fingers were frozen, cramped around the sled. Yet the beauty was part of the cold perhaps; the world could not be beautiful in any other way than through this terrible chill. We arrived at Mollesjok in darkness, our headlamps on, and again spent an hour fumbling to unchain the dogs and link them on their leads.

I hated them by this time.

Butler and Olive Murray Chapman had both stayed at the Mollesjok *fjellstue*. Butler's arrival was pleasant. He found nice beds of silver birch twigs and a good fire. Chapman's approach to

Mollesjok was more dramatic. The crossing of the high ridge had been difficult: "the wind moaned and screamed like a live thing and the snow whirled in wild gusts against our faces." As the blizzard raged, her reindeer lay down in the snow, and she thought it might be the end. Then came the welcome shout: "Mollesjok *fjellstue!*" It was one small room, not very clean, and bitterly cold; but they'd reached the cabin just in time because the snow increased in fury all through the night. In the morning, snow blocked the window and was half up the door. Yet the Sami caretaker kept bringing wood, and Chapman was not alone. A Norwegian forester and his dog, Sonia, had also taken refuge there.

That evening we were all giddy with exhaustion. Tony related that Bodil had called him "you stupid, stupid man!" after he lost his sled for the fourth time while trying to take a photograph of the moon. I showed anyone who was interested the lump on my head. Didi and Sara retreated to a separate room and spoke French. After a meal of stewed reindeer, potatoes, and bread, we lounged around our bunks while Clare told us stories of movie stars she'd worked with on different films. The incongruity of hearing how Tom Cruise behaved on set while we rubbed warmth back into our limbs and drank more tea and hot cocoa kept sending us into hysterics. The civilized world seemed a long ways away, much less the world of movie stars.

In the midst of celebrity gossip, a visitor appeared at the door: a fourteen-year-old girl, Inger. We'd believed we were out in the middle of the wildest wilderness, but no, Mollesjok was her 'hood. Her uncle lived next door and was the caretaker of the *fjellstue*. Nonchalantly, she told us that she'd skied several kilometers down the river from her house to take a look at us and practice her English.

Inger was Sami, curious, open, and absolutely self-possessed, with two black braids and a straight line of bangs across her forehead. She had the ear of a linguist, the eye of an anthropologist, and a notebook. She wrote down our names and where we were from. She noted that Tony spoke with an accent different than the other British—"Lancashire," she wrote down—and that Clare was "more like the BBC." Betsy and I were obviously from the United States, but she observed that we were not from the South or Texas, "like many people we hear on TV." We said it was perhaps because we lived in the Northwest, near Canada. She wrote it all down.

Inger stayed the evening, long after I fell asleep. I heard she interviewed the British thoroughly and sang them a couple of *joiks,* vocalizations midway between chanting and yodeling. Then, she put her skis back on and went home. She had to get up early in the morning to go to school in Karasjok. Her English teacher would be pleased to find she'd learned so much.

The next morning, my head still ringing a little from my fall, I was so stiff I could barely get out of my sleeping bag. I realized I couldn't take another day of trying to keep my balance behind the hurtling little dogs. I was getting more and more tired, and in tiredness lay a surefire recipe for a serious accident. I might be a coward, but I just couldn't get back on those runners that freezing black morning. Sven offered me a ride in the boat-like compartment of his sled. Tucked under a reindeer skin, like a baby in a cradle, I huddled against the cold, while Sven stood behind me, calling softly to his dogs. It's no mistake that Amundsen and Nanson, the Arctic explorers, were Northern men. Scott was an English romantic who could have killed his dogs and eaten them to stay alive longer but refused. Amundsen and Nanson killed their dogs and survived.

I could have killed my dogs too.

With an abrupt jerk, we set off through snowy woods, the rest of the dogsledders behind us. Soon enough, I heard the cries and thuds of others as they were flung off their sleds and staggered around in the snow or slipped on the ice. Eventually we came to one of the wide rivers and began to travel along it. Now the sledding was smoother, without rocks or tree roots, and all of us began to fly along.

Ice-crusted willows and junipers, lit pink from the sky, lined our passage. Up ahead, a herd of reindeer crossed the river, giving the dogs and us quick, distrustful glances as they scrabbled up the banks. From time to time Sven called out to ask if the cold bothered me. In truth, my thumbs and toes throbbed with pain until, ominously, like satellites in space, they stopped sending messages back to the control room. My breath was ice in my lungs whenever my fleece balaclava slipped down over my nose, and my eyeballs were round ice cubes in their sockets, fringed with lash-sicles.

I could not help but think of Butler in his "twenty-five separate articles of clothing, the only one of no use being the handkerchief, because in dry air colds are unknown." His description of travel also sounded so much more pleasant than ours. He spoke of his *pulka* as being "simply a skate, on which the driver sits, with sides and a backboard. . . . Often when crossing the lakes and long rivers, the deer are tied to the *vappus* [the guide's *pulka*] in front, and one can sleep for hours with the arms outside, keeping the balance subconsciously."

I felt as though I might be able to sleep, too, but I knew this would not be a very good idea. This is what had happened to little Kai in "The Snow Queen" when the ice empress stopped her sleigh and kissed him several times. These kisses made him hers; he forgot all about Gerda and his grandmother at home. After the kisses (she joked that if she kissed him anymore she would kiss him to death), she tucked him into a bearskin that "felt like a snowdrift" and let him sleep at her feet as she continued north to her palace of snow and ice. Andersen much preferred to travel to Italy in the warm South, but he must have remembered stories from his youth in Odense about farmers and traders who were caught in snowstorms and just lay down and let the snow cover them. The eroticism of the Snow Queen was the eroticism of sleep; of giving in to her desire to make you forget everything you'd ever thought was important. I was colder than I had been when driving my dogs, and yet I was more content. Sven could have been the Snow Queen cracking an icy whip behind me, carrying me farther and farther north. I closed my eyes and nodded off.

It took some time to get the feeling back into my fingers and toes when we arrived at the next *fjellstue* of Sjusjvarre, but nothing was frostbitten. And although my head still hurt and my knee ached, I could still manage to stagger into the cabin and take off my outerwear. This cabin was just off a road that led back to Karasjok; it was, as Sven said casually, our last connection with any sort of comfort. Tomorrow we'd set off for what Sven called "the primitive cabin," where we'd spend New Year's Eve and Day. In an offhand manner he now mentioned that there would be no caretaker to heat up the place before we arrived. It wasn't as if we were living in the lap of luxury now; the toilets were all outdoors and there were no showers. But so far there'd been water and light. The primitive cabin had no running water or electricity. "We will use lanterns," Sven said. "We will break a hole in the ice to get our water." Nervous laughter greeted his description over a dinner of moose stew and potatoes. Betsy had skipped this meal in favor of a cheese sandwich. "I've about had it with the moose," she said.

"What are we going to be eating at the primitive cabin? Are we going to have to go shoot something?" She lay down on her bunk and began writing in her journal, then put the pillow over her head in case the exhausted snores began again.

A young woman named Anna, who worked for Sven, had driven here to meet us with more food, and after sharing dinner with us, she started to get ready to leave again. Suddenly I saw my chance and took it. I told Sven that I wanted to go back with Anna, that my knee hurt and my head hurt, and that I wasn't up to another three days of this. I think he was a bit disappointed in me, but of course he couldn't say no. I went to find Betsy and woke her up. She had a glazed look in her eyes, but she said she didn't want to return with me. She had paid for this trip and she was determined to get everything she could from it. She'd spent years with the forest service in Oregon, camping alone in the woods at times, setting up remote cameras to catch sight of martens and bobcats. She'd traveled around Africa by herself. She'd worked in the Peace Corps in Argentina and been lost in the Amazonian jungle with a fellow wildlife biologist, looking for a jaguar while carrying a live chicken in a cage as bait. She didn't want to return with me. Grimly, perhaps, but with admirable curiosity, she wanted to follow this unexpected adventure to the edge.

In months to come she'd often show her slides of Lapland and the dogsledding trek. She'd talk about the final grueling days of the trip when, after a difficult day of sledding, they finally reached the primitive cabin in the dark and had to hack holes with an ax in the river and lower a bucket down for water. "And it turned out there was no wood at the cabin," she'd say, "and so we had to chop down birch trees, but they were damp and wouldn't burn well. And," she'd add, as the final, horrible insult, "all Sven and Bodil gave us to eat was hot dogs."

Tony wrapped his sled around a tree during that time and destroyed it; fortunately he was able to use my old one. My sad old brown dog was traded around for a day or two, but eventually Sven had to put him on his sled and carry him back to his kennel. All this Betsy would tell audiences as she showed slides. She ended by saying she hoped never, never ever to be cold in the way she was cold then. Her listeners laughed even as they shivered. No, they wouldn't be going to Lapland anytime soon either.

Back at Engholm's Huskies it was strange to find myself alone with nothing special to do. I slept a lot and took ibuprofen, sat on a sofa, and wrote up my notes and read. Anna took the young dogs in Sven's kennel out for a run every day riding an Icelandic horse. One morning I joined her. With a passel of playful, barking young pups all around us, we trotted down the same path my sled had taken me only a few days before, and came to the riverbank, then, instead of descending, followed a path along the river. I hadn't ridden for a long time, but it came back to me. My horse was short and stubby, with thick hocks and a steady plodding pace, and Anna and I went for a long ways by the Karasjok River, easily talking while we brushed under low, snow-laden branches. The sunrise-set blazed across the sky, the white world grew tropical, like mango syrup and grenadine poured over a drink of white rum and ice. It wasn't as cold as it had been during the last few days, and the air was tonic to breathe, crisp and immensely fresh. The young dogs ran and ran, down to the river and up again, mad with energy. This puppy spirit seemed so normal and happy that it was hard to think that humans would want to bend it for their own aims, to make the dogs run on command and carry us around.

❊

On New Year's Eve, Anna and her friend made me a delicious dinner, served with wine, by candlelight. Then they went into town to party. It was a cold, clear night, and I slipped outside many times over the course of the evening to see if the Northern Lights would make an appearance.

Every tourist brochure I touched, every postcard rack I pawed through, had magnificent views of the Aurora Borealis, and, like many visitors who come north, I'd expected that the displays were a nightly occurrence. Didn't the travel articles and tourist propaganda practically promise that? I had seen the Northern Lights several times while in Tromsø over Christmas, but the displays were brief: fifteen minutes or so, and then gone. You had to be in the right place at the right time, and given the cold, it wasn't always possible. In Tromsø, Øystein had shown me the most common direction to look, for the area around Tromsø was a prime place to see the Aurora, and thousands of Japanese tourists flew in during the winter to do just that. The dilemma was that Tromsø, although a smallish city, kept its lights on all night, and that could interfere with viewing.

But that night, New Year's Eve, outside the dormitory, in a clearing surrounded by evergreens on the Finnmark Plateau, I saw the Northern Lights and they took up half the sky. First, pale green fans unfurled, and then they turned darker green, and green-blue, and rippled against the night sky. They pulsed in waves, faded, began again in the same place, larger perhaps, or thinner. You had the sense watching that there was a pattern, but it wasn't so much a visual pattern you could count or predict, but some underlying rhythm, the universe pulsing in a way that made you stand stock-still, freezing and reverent under the black sky with its thin flying green banners.

I felt the rhythm of something huge that night, and it comforted me, unexpectedly alone on New Year's Eve in a foreign country in the middle of darkest winter. The sadness I'd been living with for months began to shift. Perhaps it would continue to pulse for some time, but it would thin and change meaning. My future was different than how I'd imagined it; the world was different too, a sadder more frightening place. But all that—my own aching sorrow, even the shock and tragedy of 9/11 and the wars that would follow it—was small under the waves of green and blue light. The universe was larger, stranger, and more beautiful than we were.

Then the long display was over. The moon seemed brighter and its glow gave the trees shadows on the white snow. However cold the winter, the trees were still alive, their sap still ran.

7. SANTA'S POST OFFICE

IN KARASJOK BETSY AND I TOOK endless hot showers and ate big breakfasts at our hotel. We visited the Sami Museum and Sami Parliament buildings, and then headed east across the Norwegian border to Inari, Finland. We took another bus down to the ski resort of Luosto for two days of relaxed cross-country skiing on empty, well-maintained trails, before traveling farther south. On the bus ride from Luosto to Rovaniemi we came across something unfamiliar. I'd been staring out the window at the transparent golden sheathing around the snow-laden branches of passing spruce trees, wondering, a little abstractedly, why the snow looked so very *golden*, when I turned my head in the other direction and caught a glimpse of a yellow sphere sitting like a child's toy on a white chenille bedspread.

The sun.

How unexpected, shocking almost; and what a relief, as if a long-lost gold watch had suddenly materialized on the kitchen counter. It was January 11, and the first time I'd seen the sun for six weeks. I understood now, from the deepest part of me, why the Sami and the Scandinavians celebrated the return of the sun in January. Because it meant the end of darkness, the beginning of life returning. *You could see again.* From now on, the sun would rise higher and higher every day, until, for two months in summer, it would seem to swing in the sky all day and all night.

Although travel in the far North had been difficult, always cold, always dark, and often complicated, I found I missed the silence and clarity of the sweeping white plains of inland Scandinavia. Rovaniemi, southeast of Kiruna, was of course chill and snowy, but it was a real city, with traffic, big hotels, shopping centers, and public buildings, many of which had been designed by Alvar Aalto. Rovaniemi, like all of northern Finland and Norway, was burned to the ground by the retreating German army. The towns were more devastated than Berlin or even Hiroshima in terms of net loss of habitable structures. In Rovaniemi, only seventeen buildings were left standing. Aalto was among several great architects who contributed to redesigning and constructing the city after the Second World War.

One of his famous buildings is the library, where Betsy and I went often, to get away from our cramped hotel room near the railway station. Aalto's design was open and spacious, built on several levels, with blond woods for shelves, trim, and tables that softened and brightened the circular shapes of the rooms and curving stairways. Betsy and I arrived the first time in the evening and found the place packed. In that peculiar Finnish way, it was also intensely silent as everyone went about his or her business working on a computer or choosing books. Even the children were industrious and respectfully quiet. I'd been in Finland before and had felt it was like watching a film with the sound turned down low.

As well as for its functionalist, inviting architecture, the Rovaniemi library is notable for its Lapponica Collection, which contains two further specialized libraries: one of Sami material and one of Greenland-Inuit. Their rare books include the 1555 first printing of Olaus Magnus's *A Description of the Northern People* and Johannes Schefferus's *Lapponia* from 1673.

The Lapponica Collection specializes in reindeer husbandry, the Laestadian religious movement, and Christmas, but I found dozens of volumes on the shelves about the Northern Skullcap, the Barents region, northern Finland and Norway, works of geography and anthropology and history, as well as tales by mountaineers, botanists, astronomers, and photographers. I found more books by foreigners about Lapland, so many of whom used the same phrasing about the Lappish people: *primitive, peace-loving, naive, fascinating.* I thought of Inger, the young girl at Ravnastua, writing up her notes on us sorry dogsledders based on an evening's talk. Would she call us *naive* and *fascinating? Peace-loving,* she could not.

The Lapponica Collection had a copy of *Turi's Book of Lappland,* the English translation of *Muitalas sámiid birra,* published in 1931 by Jonathan Cape. There was an introduction by Emilie Demant Hatt. The Sami journalist in Tromsø, John Gustavsen, had said enough about Turi and Demant Hatt to make me curious. "Emilie's book about the Sami, *With the Lapps in the High Mountains,* has been out of print for a long time," he'd told me when I asked about her, "but it's considered quite important by the Sami themselves and those who study this culture. Because, of all the ethnologists who came to the North—and are still coming, I might add—she was one of the only writers to put the lives of women and children in central focus. When living with the Sami, she stayed behind when the men went hunting."

What caused a Danish painter to come so far north and ensconce herself in a Sami community, only to leave again? What had she done the rest of her life? What had her relationship with Turi been? What did her paintings look like? And where were they? I hardly knew it then, but I was at the beginning of my curiosity about those two unlikely friends and collaborators.

Restful and engaging as it was to sit in a comfortable Modernist chair at the Rovaniemi Library looking through books by the Sami and by travelers to Lapland, that wasn't the reason I'd wanted to come to Rovaniemi. The real reason lay just outside the modern city, in a place called Santa Village. When I'd arrived above the Arctic Circle last November, I'd discovered there were divided opinions about Santa Village and the adjacent amusement center, Santa Park. Tourist officials vigorously promoted the site as an example of successful winter tourism, while most other people suggested I skip it. But I knew I wanted to go there as soon as I heard Santa Village had a famous post office.

Like many children, I'd once written to Santa with a list and had dropped the letter in the mailbox, perfectly confident it would end up at the North Pole.

The day after our arrival, then, Betsy and I took a bus fifteen miles outside the city to see why thousands of people come to Finland every year, especially in November and December. In the deep snow, the log-cabin-style buildings of Santa Village were dark brown, heavy, and solid. The first structure was originally built for Eleanor Roosevelt, who visited Finland in 1952 as part of a goodwill trip to see the results of the Marshall Plan. The Finns were so pleased about Mrs. Roosevelt's visit that they constructed a log cabin, right on the Arctic Circle, for her to stay in. The cabin is there yet, filled with Roosevelt memorabilia, and around it has grown Santa Village, a collection of shops, cafés, and restaurants. The day we arrived the snow was falling softly on evergreen branches and frosted windowpanes, and Christmas music played in the buildings. Everything still looked like Christmas in January, but then, at Santa Village it's Christmas 365 days a year.

Betsy and I had mushroom soup with rye bread in a brightly decorated Russian café stuffed with icons and dolls for sale, then poked our noses into a room where Santa Claus was still hefting children up to his capacious lap to listen to their wishes while they were photographed. But this Santa didn't look like the ones who inhabit the malls of America in December. And in fact, the Finns didn't try to pass him off as Santa; instead he was Joulupukki, "a good friend of Santa's." Although Joulupukki also sported a curly mass of white facial hair and a long cap, he wore a more Russian-like tunic over trousers and boots.

The post office I'd come to see was off in a large timbered house, divided into two rooms, one of which had a counter stacked with all the usual postal paraphernalia for sale. The other room had a fireplace, a wingback armchair, decorative sacks of "mail," and a large wooden desk. All of these were props for photos, and over the course of the hour, I saw a few dozen Japanese tourists run in, put on a floppy, fur-trimmed red hat, sit at the desk or in the armchair, and be photographed, before dashing out again. During the rush period before Christmas, there can be four thousand people a day coming through, as a hundred planes land at the Rovaniemi airport and transport groups from all over the world. England, Poland, and Japan are the top countries of tourist origin.

Postal worker Tuija Pulju greeted me wearing a red elf hat, red felt skirt, and red reindeer-pattern sweater. Since 1986 she'd been one of two permanent employees; in high summer and during the Christmas season, they were joined by temps. Most of her work was at the counter. Santa's post office is self-supporting through the sale of stamps, postcards, and stamped envelopes, all canceled with an image of Santa peeping up from over a globe spanned by the Arctic Circle. The post office's real function, however, is less overtly commercial and less visible to the busloads of tourists: It is to take in, process, and respond to the hundreds of thousands of letters that arrive yearly, from 184 countries. The letters are sorted and shelved in cabinets with glass doors, locked against those who would rifle them for stamps. They're labeled A–Z, Antigua to Zambia (Afghanistan hadn't yet been added). Tuija unlocked the cabinets and I looked briefly at the letters, resolving to come back in a day or two and read through them more closely. Some of the letters were aerograms, some cards; some were scribbled on lined newsprint. Children had sent photographs of themselves and siblings, of their dogs, of their houses. Some had careful pen-and-ink drawings in the margins; others included wild crayon scribbles from imagination. Some letters asked for long lists of toys, CDs, and PlayStations. Others only sent greetings to Santa and Mrs. Claus, or requested less tangible presents: *Please Santa Claus, Pray to God to bring peace once more to Sri Lanka.*

After I'd been reading a little while, the manager of the post office sat down across from me. Like Tuija, Taina Ollila was dressed in red: smart red suit, with a red feather boa around her shoulders, and bright red lipstick. She introduced herself as "Chief of the Elves."

I asked her how Finland had gotten the monopoly on letters to Santa. St. Nicholas started life as a desert father in Smyrna, after all. One legend had it that a family with three daughters and no dowries was prepared to sell one of the daughters into slavery to raise money for the marriages of the other two. Hearing of this, the fourth-century bishop came to their house one night and tossed three bags of gold down the chimney—or alternately, into the open window of the house. I could have liked St. Nicholas for that alone, but he was also the patron saint of orphans and sailors, which endeared him to me even more. The date of his death, December 6, eventually marked the start of Christmas celebrations in medieval Europe. Children set out food for the saint and were rewarded with gifts and sweetmeats. Even after the Reformation, this one saint's day continued, and he became Father Christmas in Merry England, Père Noël in France, and Weihnachtsmann in Germany. The Dutch who first colonized New York in the 1600s brought with them Sinterklaas, who became our American Santa Claus.

In 1808 Washington Irving described this Dutch Santa as a jolly fellow with a long clay pipe in the Knickerbocker stories, and gave him an airborne wagon with horses, from which he dropped gifts down into chimneys. But it was in 1822, when "The Night Before Christmas" appeared in newspapers, that the man with a belly "like a bowl full of jelly" turned up with eight tiny reindeer. Dr. Clement Clarke Moore's poem was illustrated in 1883 by Thomas Nast; here, for the first time, Santa's reindeer and sleigh came straight from the North Pole.

In pagan times, Finns believed in an evil male goat who demanded gifts at the winter solstice, but eventually Finland adopted the tradition of Joulupukki, the Father Christmas who brought presents on Christmas Eve. Yet no one seemed averse to taking on Santa as well. In 1927 a Finnish radio personality called Uncle Marcus announced that Santa's home lay in the Finnish province of Lapland, near the Russian border; by the 1950s Mr. and Mrs. Claus had migrated slightly south to the log cabin built for Mrs. Roosevelt on the Arctic Circle. Even though Norway or Greenland could reasonably have staked out Santa and the North Pole for themselves, no one jumped on it fast enough. Local and government officials in Finland saw an opportunity to create goodwill and tourism jobs for the north of the country in laying claim to Santa's home and marketing it to the rest of the world. The Finnish Board of Tourism has twenty branches in different countries and sends out press releases to newspapers. Articles follow, and people read the articles to their children. Teachers tell their students, and letters to Santa become class projects. Tour companies have naturally jumped in to assist those who decide to make the trek to Finland in winter.

Not all letters addressed to *Santa, North Pole, Mr. and Mrs. Claus, Snowflake Lane, Reindeer Land,* or even *Mr. Santa Claus, Lapland,* end up in Finland. For instance, Taina told me, when a child in England or France sends a stamped letter to Santa, the letter doesn't even leave the country. Instead, it goes to a special sorting unit where it's dealt with by a corps of volunteers. But when there is no stamp, or the letter originates outside of Europe, the post offices of the world direct it first to Helsinki and then up to Santa Village. "It's good for us in Rovaniemi," Taina said. "But it's quite an expensive proposition for Finland. A lot of children would never think to put a stamp on a letter to Santa. We have to pay all the postage no matter where the letter originates."

I was fairly sure I'd never stamped my letter to Santa when I mailed it long ago on a hot December day in California, asking for a pair of roller skates and more Laura Ingalls Wilder books. I always assumed it arrived, and my mother, who had helped me spell a couple of things, assured me that it had.

A little more than a mile away from Santa Village is Santa Park. Betsy and I walked over and found ourselves standing in front of a large door leading into a mountain. According to the sign at the entrance, Santa Park shares this man-made cavern with an enormous shelter, which has 2,000 beds and can handle 3,600 people in an emergency. The shelter, 129,000 square feet, was blasted out of granite and gneiss in 1997, a belated response to Chernobyl, perhaps, or maybe to the fact that Russia has a number of decaying nuclear submarines up in the harbor of Murmansk. All of northern Scandinavia worries about those subs, and Tromsø, too, has bored into one of its mountains to make a shelter. But Tromsø's cavern only doubles, during nonemergency times, as a parking garage; Santa Park is a far more lucrative business, opening out of a long, windy tunnel into a large ventilated space with shops and cafés and old-fashioned, simple rides. In spite of the bright lights, the rock walls gave off a chill, cavey smell, and the sight of rough-edged dark corners leading deeper into the mountains made my predator-prey alert system tingle. Behind doors here and there are first-aid stations and dormitories. The sign at the entrance said it takes twenty-four hours to convert the amusement center to a shelter with medical facilities.

Santa Park was set to close in a few days until the summer holidays, and it felt even more post-seasonal than Santa Village. A few families wandered about, and when Betsy persuaded me onto some rides, we were the only customers, mildly self-conscious in small cars that chugged farther into the mountain to look at the homes of the elves.

Santa Park had its own Santa, a big guy, over six foot three, who sat at a wooden desk in his office, working on his list of naughty and nice, and who spoke English with a twist of in-character irony. He asked where we came from and when we said, "the Pacific Northwest—Seattle and Port Townsend," he nodded his white beard and white flowing locks.

"Beautiful place, Seattle."

"Oh, have you been there?"

Reprovingly, he smiled: "Santa has been everywhere," adding, "My reindeer enjoyed your forests and mountains."

He then grilled us on our behavior over the year. Fortunately it was only January, so we still had a chance to make up for some of the naughtiness of the last two weeks.

Using the royal we, he told us of his travels. Betsy and I were astonished, when a Japanese family appeared, to hear him chatting in Japanese to the children, and we asked about this after they left. Had he studied Japanese?

"Santa speaks all languages," he said, again with the mild, reproving smile. "Even Finnish, which is quite difficult."

He encouraged us each to draw a picture of Santa at a small table with paper and crayons, and when we did, he autographed them for us with a flourish:

Merry Christmas. From Santa.

On the last day of our stay in Rovaniemi, Betsy set off by herself by bus to a zoo south of Rovaniemi. In a few days she'd be flying back to Seattle from Oslo, and she was determined to see some northern animals, even if she had to view them in captivity. There she finally saw a lynx and a snowy owl. I returned to Santa's Post Office on my own, to spend the afternoon reading letters and talking more with Tuija and Taina. I seated myself at the table in front of the cabinets and began taking out stacks of envelopes from the previous year. The ones from this year hadn't begun to come in yet.

Dear Santa,
Do you remember you I am? I am Prasana, which I
expect was computer. So, I know your problems and
please try to get it.

Prasana, Uzbekistan

Dear Santa:
I wanted to write to you for a long time ago. At first I
didn't believe than you were living in Laplandia. Then I
read a very interesting article about and wanted to talk
to you. Do you have parents? What are there names? I
am ten years old. I would like a small alive puppy.

(Uzbekistan)

Again there were few people, except when a Japanese busload
of tourists pulled up and everyone rushed out to buy souvenirs
and stamps. Today Tuija was wearing a red-striped, long-sleeved T-
shirt. She handed out long red caps and took photos of the visitors
with their cameras. She also could take more formal portraits for
a fee, which were then printed onto sheets of stickers. I was struck
by how many solemn Japanese men seemed to want to buy stickers that showed them in red hats with shy smiles. Taina, the manager, came out to chat. She was again in a red suit and red boa.

Although Santa's Post Office now has a Web site that has received millions of hits, so far Santa doesn't read or respond to
e-mail. The letters come in the ordinary way: in envelopes, scribbled, badly spelled, illustrated, heartfelt. Sometimes whole schools
write and send a box of letters. The schools may be in Manchester,
Warsaw, or Saudi Arabia. One batch came from a Japanese school
in Jeddah. Every season a team of students studying tourism at the
University of Lapland in Rovaniemi turns up to open and answer
the letters. Forty thousand form letters go back to people who
give full return addresses, while the volunteers respond to one or
two thousand letters with handwritten responses. These are the

letters that form the emotional core of the post office, the ones that can wrench the soul. They are the ones asking for medical care for a dying parent, or for a new limb to replace one blown off by a land mine in Bosnia.

Taina told me, "We don't answer letters that ask for material things. The ones that come on an Excel spreadsheet, or the ones that have advertising pictures cut out and pasted on the page with clear instructions about which model of electronic gadget Santa should bring." I saw a few of those lists in the cabinet, but most of them had been turned over to the tourism faculty at the university for the purposes of calibrating what kinds of letters came to Santa's Post Office and where they came from. There was an ongoing project in which the university was investigating what images of the North and of Finland come up. Their study would focus on winter tourism, a fast-growing sector of northern Finland's economy. Already about 20 percent of Rovaniemi's population was connected with the tourism industry. Taina had told me that she frequently traveled with the Finnish Board of Tourism, seeking out new markets. Recently she'd joined a delegation to Poland that included a couple of Santas. They went to Krakow and Warsaw spreading the word about Santa Village and the post office. "The Polish economy is growing fast, and they're a good market. The Poles are a religious people. They *admire* Santa's goodness. After we visited Poland, charter flights increased. Now Poles are some of our most frequent visitors, along with the English and the Japanese."

Children are not the only ones to write to Santa. I was surprised at how many letters were from adults.

> Dear Santa,
> Give my sister a new boyfriend. Her old one was no good.
>
> (Japan)

Dear Santa,
I would like some children.

(Japan)

"They're not sure who or what Santa is," Taina said. "Especially some of the people in Asia and Africa. They write about their hobbies and dreams as well as what they want for themselves. They don't usually want material things. They want someone to talk to." These letters are in English, sometimes long, filled with stories of misfortune and displacement. "I don't know if they really think Santa can do something," said Taina. "Maybe they just need some hope."

Dear Santa,
Can you help me find a pen pal? I am twenty-three and still living with my parents because I am not married. Our village was burned and we are in exile.

(Uganda)

"People think of Santa as the last person they can call on," Taina went on. "After a crisis, people always write. After Bosnia, we received many letters. We can see everything that is going on in the world through the letters. September 11, that will be in the letters. There will be people asking for peace, an end to destruction. That is so often what they ask for."

"What's it like to work here?" said Tania. "It's busy, it's fun—people are so happy when they arrive here. Just delighted. As a marketing tool for the north of Finland, it's marvelous. And now we're working with the tourism department at the university to really analyze what people are drawn to about Lapland, so that we can more effectively meet people's expectations.

"We're a small country spread out over a large space. Not everyone can work for Nokia or in high tech or computers. Tourism employs many of us. We're learning to make our long winters work for us, to make people see snow and ice as an exciting thing. We've been successful beyond our dreams in creating media coverage. Last year, something like 180 film crews from around the world turned up here to film the baskets of letters coming in: CNN, BBC, the Italians, Koreans, Brazilians, they were all here."

Taina adjusted her boa and looked at the letters that lay open in front of me. I'd been looking through a small pile from Iraq.

> Dear Santa,
> Please send information on your services for children.
>
> Mohammed, Baghdad, Iraq

"Sometimes," she confided, her tone changing from upbeat to thoughtful, "I get fed up with the film crews. All they want is footage of the letters or of the addresses. They don't care what's inside. But all of us who work here and who read the letters, we're affected by what we read. The sadness of children's lives, their hopes and dreams. It's not all jolly and fun here, you know. There's a deeper story. People used to have the saints to call on when they felt they couldn't reach God himself. Now, some of them think, 'If God can't help me, maybe Santa can.'"

I hadn't written a letter to Santa since I was about eight, but before the day was over I'd written two, on special paper provided by the post office. "Dear Santa," I wrote on the first one. "I need a new laser printer, preferably an HP LaserJet. Thanks! Barbara."

And on the other card I wrote simply, "Dear Santa, please bring peace to the world if you can."

Then I mailed them, before stepping back out into the falling snow.

8. BRAZILIANS AT THE ICE CINEMA

NAKED YOUNG MEN painted with red clay leaped into the murky tan waters of a river somewhere in the Amazon jungle. They splashed each other, crawled up on the muddy banks, and daubed more red warm earth on their bronzed bodies. They had bones in their ears and loincloths over their privates, and they were in the midst of a male initiation ritual. Through the gauze of warm greens and ruddy browns of the digital pixels, a granulated crust of icy snow sparkled.

It was January, outdoors, ten o'clock at night, −31°F in Inari, Finland. Bundled up to roly-poly roundness and seated on tiers of packed snow covered in reindeer skins, we watched *Initiation,* the last movie of the day here at the Indigenous People's Film and TV Production Festival, projected onto a screen of hard-packed snow. Behind a bar shaped of snow, a woman dispensed hot lingonberry juice and rum with steaming-hot water. Our freezing exhalations made clouds around our thickly padded heads. Some clouds smelled of rum. A crisp full moon blacked out the constellations.

The heat from the Styrofoam cup in my hand lasted only a minute or two. I was conscious of the intense cold, of my body doing all it could to keep my core warm, but I was also aware of the black night, the frosty moon, the crunch of boots in the snow, the white branches of the spruce illuminated by lanterns of ice set at regular intervals around the walls of the ice cinema.

This outdoor theater with its icy screen was a purely aesthetic experience. Most of the films at this yearly festival were screened inside the eighty-seat auditorium of SIIDA, the museum of northern Scandinavian nature and of Sami culture and history, a short snowy walk from where we sat and shivered on our ice benches. Every January the museum puts on a two-week festival called Skábmagovat, the Sami word for "endless night." The weekend of films showcases work by and about the Sami, as well as productions by other indigenous filmmakers from around the world. The first year of the festival, Aborigines arrived from the baking heat of central Australia. The following winters brought directors from northern Canada, Siberia, and the Pacific Islands. This year three Brazilians had come from their summer to Finland's winter to show their work.

Divino Tserewahú, the leader of the crew who wrote and filmed the video *Initiation,* is a Xavante Indian from Mato Grosso in the interior of Brazil. A beautiful young man with warm brown skin, eyes that missed nothing, and bones the size of a little finger through his elongated ears, he didn't speak English but knew some Spanish, so he and I had been able to talk earlier today. He was amazed to find himself transported here from the humid Amazon jungle; he'd never seen snow and had never heard anything about the Sami. He didn't know what a reindeer was until two days ago, but today he'd been pulled by one of the antlered creatures in a sleigh. Everything thrilled him; some of it made him laugh. He went everywhere with his camera, taking photographs of these pale, often quite short Northern people in their blue and red Sami dress, reindeer leggings, monstrously large four-cornered hats, and lace-trimmed bonnets—Northerners who were probably too shy to photograph him, however much they'd like to get a good look at those bone-riven ears. Divino learned his trade through the *Video nas Aldeias,* or "Video in the Village" project, begun by Vincente Carelli and Mari Corrêa, two Brazilian filmmakers who were also attending the festival and showing films they made for TV. Divino told me, "Making videos is my profession. I was born for it."

On the surface, Inari and its surroundings, with a population of only five hundred, seems an unlikely venue for an international film festival that takes place in January. Aside from a couple of hotels, one Nordically clean and the other Nordically drunken and smoky, the village has a post office, a couple of grocery stores, and several handicraft stores, all except one of which is closed in winter. During the summer months busloads of tourists stop at the museum en route to the North Cape. Lake Inari is an attraction, too; a large sign near the shore, now covered in snow, advertised cruises and fishing-boat rentals. Frank Butler slid into town in 1914, noting "the large open squares, a Russian post office and of course Russian stamps and money." He didn't pay the village much heed, however, being more interested in the Finnish "vapour-baths," or saunas, attended by pure young girls who would beat a man with birch twigs, then wash him with soft flannel, and dry him with a large towel. "It is a cheap bath to make, and could easily be erected at the bottom of a small London garden," he noted, adding a bit wistfully that relations between the sexes would make this a difficult proposition in Edwardian England.

Norah Gourlie made Inari her base while traveling about Lapland in the winter of 1938. She found it "a small straggling village at the western end of Inarijärvi [the lake] . . . Here are the parish church (Lutheran), school, hospital, post office and two small general stores." From Inari, Gourlie set off to explore Finnish Lapland for a couple of months, with reindeer and *pulka* and guides, with a stash of Ovaltine and dried milk (which did not freeze), some potted meats, and ten frozen oranges (which became "nasty"). She wore a "knee-length chemise of reindeer skin" over her Burberry ski-suit and slept inside a down-filled sack inside a reindeer sleeping bag on an inflatable Li-Lo mattress. The latter was the wonder of all the Sami adults and children who offered her hospitality.

Inari still had the post office, though it sold only Finnish stamps now and offered a computer terminal for Internet access. The village was the kind of place that a reindeer *pulka* could traverse at speed in ten minutes, and that a car could drive through in two, yet Inari's history goes back millennia. Lake Inari once formed part of the Arctic Ocean, but gradually the coastline up north filled in, and the lake became the third largest in Finland. Hundreds of rocky, pine-studded islands dot the lake. Inari pines grow very slowly, and date back to the Middle Ages. For some time now a coalition of Finnish environmentalists, Greenpeace activists from Finland and abroad, and local Sami have been fighting a difficult battle with the Finnish state and its logging company Metsähallitus to stop the destruction of this important old-growth forest. The Sami depend on the habitat for their reindeer's winter grazing; and dozens of other endangered species also are affected. The logging company mainly sells the pine forest for pulp.

Lapland has been inhabited between eight and ten thousand years, but the Inari Sami and the Skolt Sami (on the other side of

Lake Inari, across the border in Russia) seem to be some of the few who've stayed in the same place all these centuries. Unlike the nomads who followed the reindeer migration from summer to winter pastures, the Inari Sami fished and cared for small herds of reindeer. Only about a thousand people speak the Inari dialect now, most of them elderly. Although the population of Inari is tiny, everyone who lives here seems to be an artist, politician, teacher, or media worker—sometimes all four.

Inari is the center of Finnish Sápmi. The Sami Parliament of Finland meets in Inari, Sami Radio broadcasts from Inari, and the Sami Training Institute teaches Finns and Sami alike screenwriting, filmmaking, and traditional handicrafts. There's also the improbably large and brilliantly conceived museum, SIIDA, with its elegant, intelligent displays of Arctic natural history and Sami life through history. *Siida* refers both to the community of people themselves and to the permanent village that served as winter quarters. The museum SIIDA opened in 1998, constructed with funding from the European Union, and the Skábmagovat festival began a year later as part of a plan to bring people together in the dark winter months. Other Northern cities like Tromsø had experimented with winter film festivals and found them successful, but the Inari committee had an even more innovative idea. Why not invite filmmakers from other parts of the world, specifically from one indigenous country or culture a year, and showcase their films in conjunction with films about the Sami?

I'd first found out about this festival a few weeks ago when passing through Inari by bus from Karasjok to Rovaniemi. Betsy and I had stopped off for a night to see the museum and have a dinner at the hotel that offered a Finnish menu very different from what we'd eaten in Norway: smoky mushroom soup, sour rye bread, whitefish, and sour cream with pickles. At SIIDA I talked with Sari Valkonen, a woman in her early thirties who looked more Irish than Sami-Finnish, with fair reddish hair and lightly freckled skin. The film festival particularly intrigued me, because it was such a different way of presenting Sami life than much of what I'd seen in the North—by which I mean that the concept of it was sophisticated and international. Tourists were very welcome, but Skábmagovat wasn't for them: It was for the Sami community, as a means of both fostering self-recognition and making connections with indigenous peoples around the world.

Sari had taken us out behind the museum to the site where the ice cinema was being erected, more or less on the same plan as the Icehotel in Sweden. An architect in Rovaniemi had designed the structure and given them forms for the walls and the screen. A bulldozer piled the snow between two forms, then volunteers climbed up and jumped up and down to tamp down the snow. I felt a pang of longing when I saw that big upright rectangle of snow under the trees. I imagined being in Helsinki on the last leg of my journey when the film festival would be taking place. To get back to Inari, I'd have to fly north again to Ivalo, then take a shuttle for half an hour. Just to sit outside at night in freezing cold and watch a video being screened on snow.

"All over Finland they speak of Lapland Sickness, saying how once the spell gets hold of a man, he must return," wrote Gourlie.

No sooner had I arrived in Helsinki than I found myself at the counter of Finnair, signing yet another credit card slip—this time for a plane ticket north. I was still under the spell of Lapland.

Madness.

I'd arrived yesterday and had been absorbed in films for two days. Half were Sami and the other half Brazilian Indian. One of the

short videos I watched earlier today, *Who Are They?*, featured in-
terviews with Brazilians from the heavily populated coast, most
of whom seemed to think that either Brazil had no more Indians
left, or that the handful remaining were either drunks or hopeless
protesters in the jungle. In fact, there are 180 different tribes of
indigenous people in Brazil, and their population is steady, even
growing. Much traditional tribal land has been appropriated; many
Indians have been exploited and victimized; but other Indians in
the Amazon continue to exist in relatively intact ecological and
cultural systems.

After the film, Vincente Carelli, a handsome man with salt-
and-pepper hair and a bronze leather jacket, told the audience
something about the video we'd just seen. He'd come to this
project after being asked to make a ten-part series about the
Amazonian people for the Ministry of Education, to be shown initially in schools around the country. The series eventually was presented on Brazilian TV to millions of viewers. After this success,
Carelli came to realize that he didn't just want to make films about
the Indians, he wanted to find a way to empower them to make
their own films about themselves. "The point is for us to see what
they see," he said. "It is their culture. The films they make are ones
we could not make. They see from the inside, not the outside." He
went on, "To explain and give information is not the same as making people feel an emotion."

In the auditorium, we watched Brazilian films about the loss
of language and the loss of ancestral territory, about assimilation
versus stigmatization, about missionary work and the old be-
liefs, about what it means to leave the village and get educated,
about what it means to return. Although some of the Indians were
exotic-looking, like the Zo'é, who sported large wooden tubes in
their lower lips and were seen plunging whole spider monkeys into

boiling pots of water, the issues they were dealing with weren't so different than those of the Sami. They also struggled to preserve rights to land the state claimed it "owned" and to maintain and honor their traditions.

The Sami documentaries that interspersed the videos by Carelli and the Video in the Village project were made by both men and women, but a surprising number had women at their core. Funded by Norwegian or Swedish public broadcasting, the films had higher production values than the Brazilian work. Sometimes the people in the documentaries wore Sami dress, but most often they were in jeans and sweaters; frequently they were light-haired, with blue eyes. Not all spoke Sami. When they did, the subtitles were almost always in English. Few films were directly political—most dealt with the complexities of identity. What was a Sami identity anyway? One film followed a young woman of Sami heritage who'd grown up not speaking Sami as she headed off to Swedish university and discovered her Sami heritage by getting to know other students with the same background. Another delightful little video, shot right here in Inari, told the story of a single woman who worked at Sami Radio and had adopted a Chinese girl and was raising her as Sami.

The film with the most resonance for me was *Lesbian in Kautokeino,* which told the story of a young woman who'd grown up in a Laestadian family on the Finnmark Plateau and who had to move to Oslo to find a partner and social acceptance. The Laestadian faith has long been an integral part of Sami culture, but its emphasis on sinfulness and often-rigid morality leaves little room for individual choice and creative freedom. The documentary focused on the young woman's return to Kautokeino and her sometimes-painful encounters with family and former friends. A bright spot in the film was her meeting with a young, blond, reindeer-herding tomboy who announced that she too was lesbian—and that they should get together. It was a surprise to me how much applause the film received, for it cast an unflattering light on the church, a pillar of Sami society. But perhaps it wasn't unusual that a critique of the Laestadian church would inspire so much discussion. Sami society had become far more sophisticated in recent years, and a new generation rebelled against old ways of thinking.

A number of the people in the audience today had on winter finery: white rabbit jackets and dark reindeer-skin boots, everything trimmed with blue, yellow, and red. Each Sami area has its own distinctive dress, but I could not yet tell them apart. I only knew, from the displays in the museum, that the *gákti,* the belted tunic over leggings, probably had its origin in Italy—the style resembles Renaissance figures from frescoes in Florence. Like the silver jewelry so prevalent, the clothes were a reminder that the Sami were never so isolated as some historic and contemporary reports would have them be; they were always, usually via Russia, traders with the South. The hats, especially those of the Sami from around Karasjok, were later extravagances; the women's inflated bonnets resembled outsize prairie schooners from the American westward migration, and the men's four-cornered caps, twice as big as a head, are based on the uniform of Russian sailors.

These Sami lived in Scandinavia, however, and many of the people here were indistinguishable from Finns or Norwegians in their jeans and sweaters, and in their rectitude and tolerance. Quietly, only gasping a tiny bit, they watched the spider monkeys going into the boiling water, the bloody tapir carcasses being chopped up, the manioc beer made and consumed. Yet, although this was fascinating, they were willing to be critical. After several films, all of which were about men, with women seen in the background, as figures of lust or derision, a Sami woman in a red bonnet stood up and asked pointedly, "Where are the women?" The Sami had a matriarchal past with less gender division than many traditional peoples. The Nordic countries also emphasize equality in education and mandate and encourage parity in public life. "I like the films very much," she said. "But do no women make films? Are no women's lives being recorded?"

"Not enough women make films," answered Mari Corrêa, the other half of the Video in the Village project, a chic, outgoing woman who lives in Paris half the year and in the Amazon the rest. "That's something we're trying to change."

Nobody wore Sami clothing out at the ice cinema when we gathered to watch another film the second night of the festival, or if they did, the tunics and dresses were invisible underneath heavy jackets and snowsuits. It wasn't quite as cold as the previous night. It was snowing and had been all day. The moon was a pale, smudged thumbprint in a soft sky devoid of stars. The snow on the ground was luminously soft, illuminated by candles set in the walls of the open-air cinema and the electric bulbs that made the ice lanterns glow. The first year of the festival, one of the Aboriginal filmmakers was asked how he would describe the experience of being in Sápmi in the winter to his friends at home. "I would ask them to open the freezer and put their hand in, and I'd say, 'That is what it is like.'"

Sari introduced me to Jorma Lehtola on the first day of the festival. A short, gentle man in his forties, with an amused look and something still in his luxurious moustache and long dark hair of the global hippie he once was, Jorma wore a black festival T-shirt and *komagers,* the heel-less reindeer boots with upturned toes. He was a journalist at a popular magazine in Helsinki and the author of the first and only book on films by and about the Sami. He was also one of the main organizers of Skábmagovat and the artistic director of the film festival, the one who had chosen most of the films.

We shook hands briefly, and I asked if I could talk to him later, when he had a few spare minutes. A few spare minutes in the midst of the hectic festival were rare, but over the next few days I talked with Jorma whenever I could: in the cafeteria, in the lobby, and en route to Ivalo and the airport at the end of my stay. Eventually I'd spend time with him in Helsinki too. He was the person I'd been looking for: someone who spoke English fluently, whom I could bombard with all the questions growing in my mind about Sami culture and politics. Someone with a reindeer-shod foot in two worlds—that of Inari, where he'd grown up, and that of the wider world, so much of which he'd seen in his travels to seventy countries.

Jorma had lived in Helsinki ten years, but "it's not home." Inari wasn't completely "home" either, even though his father and one of his two brothers lived here. Home was perhaps the village of Karigasniemi, northwest of here, a Sami village on the Finnish side of the Norwegian-Finnish border, not far from Karasjok. In 1944, during the war, Jorma's mother was evacuated to the middle of Finland. She didn't speak a word of Finnish. "She left home with Sami clothes and returned with Finnish," Jorma told me one afternoon, as we sat in the cafeteria over lunch. His mother also met her husband, a Finn from Inari, and returned with him there to start a family.

"My mother tried to hide her Sami origins outside the family," Jorma said, "but"—he paused, looking for the right word—"*Sami-ness* was strong in our family. In the summers we'd go visiting our relatives in Karigasniemi. They had reindeer and spoke Fjell Sami. My mother didn't speak Sami with us, but we absorbed the culture from her."

"Why didn't you speak Sami at home?" I asked.

"What was the point? You were forbidden to speak it in school. They didn't teach it either."

Finland, like Norway, had discouraged the use of Sami as a language for the whole of the twentieth century. In Sweden the situation had been somewhat better; instead of forcing Sami children into boarding schools, the state had tried a policy of bringing the teachers to the mountains in the summers. Eventually, both Sweden and Norway allowed classes in Sami up through high school in the areas that were most heavily populated by Sami, such as the Finnmark Plateau. Finland maintained a single-language policy, however. Next to Russia, where perhaps only a few thousand Sami still lived, Finland had the fewest numbers—only about six thousand.

Jorma said the issue of language continued to be debated. "'Why teach Sami?' a lot of Finnish people ask. Well, the same could be said for Finnish. When the language of the globe is increasingly English, why would you keep alive a small language like Finnish? After all, only five million people speak it." He smiled. "That's a line of questioning that would enrage most Finns."

His brother who stayed in Inari now runs a contracting company. It was his bulldozer that piled up the snow for the ice cinema. Their mother was dead, but their father still lives here. He had always taken a great interest in history and in Sami Studies and now ran, with help from his sons, a small publishing company called Puntsi. Jorma's older brother, Veli-Pekka Lehtola, had decided to study Sami literature and history and had attended the University of Oulu, the only place in the country where the subject was even on the curriculum. Veli-Pekka now had a doctorate in Sami Studies, the first ever given, and taught at the University of Oulu.

"My political awakening began in 1982," Jorma told me. "I noticed stereotypes in old travel books, and later the same stereotypes in film. The directors in Finland who made films were all from Helsinki. The script was written in Helsinki. They shot the films in the North, then returned to Helsinki. This is what we know about the Sami from those films: All Sami are reindeer herders. All Sami like drink. All Sami wander around in the mountains—we don't just wander around! It is hard work to prove otherwise. These old films are funny to watch today, but many new ones also repeat these stereotypes."

Every year Skábmagovat airs some of those old films, and they are some of the most popular offerings of the festival. The Sami roared to see Lapland and the Lapps portrayed as dirty and grizzled old people standing, often with a pipe in the mouth, looking off into a landscape of mountains and lakes. In spite of the irony, there was nostalgia too. In the films shot around Inari, for instance, people recognized their relatives and ancestors.

I wondered what Norah Gourlie would make of this gathering, taking place sixty years later in a village that looked not much different on the outside, but that had changed immeasurably in every other way. *A Winter with Finnish Lapps* would have described the grandparents of some of the young people in black jeans and leather jackets attending the film festival. Doubtless there were Sami here related to her guide Juhani and the families that she'd stayed with as she traveled around the North.

Unlike Frank Butler and Olive Murray Chapman, Gourlie didn't take a steamship to Oslo and another one up the Norwegian coast to the North. Instead she embarked for Helsinki by ship, on the twenty-ninth of December, 1937. "I found myself the only woman passenger on board, and the general opinion regarding my journey, as expressed by the four other passengers and the captain, did nothing to raise my spirits, which towards the end had been falling rapidly." Arriving in Helsinki, she boarded a train for Rovaniemi and then an orange post bus to Ivalo. "The snow was very deep," she wrote. "The firs stood like great pillars of salt."

Of the three British travelers whose books had accompanied me on my travels north, I was most fond of Gourlie. Like Butler and Chapman, Gourlie had a sturdy sense of adventure. Although she wrote of reindeers running away with her, and of being dumped from her sled, of "gripping my courage and repressing a desire to scream" as her reindeer made for the woods, she had pluck and grit. *She* would probably not have been deterred by the dogsledding fiasco, I suspected. From the black-and-white photographs of her in her book, she seemed to be strong and hearty, a blond Scottish-born Amazon. She had more of a sense of humor than Chapman and Butler. Although both of her predecessors were also excellent observers, Gourlie put herself into the picture in a way that they didn't. She wasn't afraid to show that Lapland moved her in a sometimes inexplicable way.

I was rereading *A Winter with Finnish Lapps* at night and over breakfast in the Inari Hotel, which was where Gourlie had stayed when it was a Tourist Inn and much smaller. She'd arrived by bus in early January at ten in the morning, when it was still dark. Here in the lobby she'd met with Herr Stenbäck, the General Secretary of the Finnish Tourist Association, who seemed to have traveled especially to Lapland to make sure she had everything necessary for her journey, and who helped teach her to drive a reindeer *pulka*.

It is the work of pages of clothing description to get her dressed for her first driving lesson, and when she looked in the mirror, "I saw a strange furry object which I hardly recognized." This *peski,* a "long fur tunic," weighed fifteen pounds, and with it she wore a huge fur bonnet, leggings, boots, and gloves. At one point during her trip she lost a glove: "I was like Hans Andersen's little Gerda who 'lost her glove, yet dared not stop the reindeer, as she drove for the sake of her dear love Kay [*sic*], through the middle of dreary icy-cold Finland.'"

Her first guide was a local lad called Juhani, and with him she traveled for about a week, 127 miles in a radius around Inari. She stayed with Lapp families, visited schools and orphanages, took photographs and extensive notes on what she saw. She was alive to the beauty of Lapland in winter, of the "North wind's masonry" in sculpting snow along the riverbanks, and of the Aurora Borealis, sometimes a "softly pulsing flood of radiance," sometimes a sky lit by fire, "like being in an immense illuminated cupola." That experience, lying outside in a biting cold night, on her Li-Lo mattress, wearing her *peski* and fur bonnet, was strongly spiritual for her: "It was dumbfounding; it roused a longing in one that was pain, one was so utterly alone, so insignificant."

Some passages made me laugh, as when she disrobed for a wash in front of some Sami women, who were as interested in her as she was in them, "especially in my brassiere, a French affair of pink ribbon and lace." Some passages filled in gaps in my understanding of Lapland, especially in this Finnish region. I didn't know much about Gourlie and wondered if she was a teacher back in London because of her habit of visiting schools. Invariably she found the schoolrooms and dormitories clean and neat, the young students, both Lapp and Finn, washed and eager to make a good impression.

She evidently had little sympathy for the fact that these children had been separated from their reindeer-herding families and sent to study in Finnish, a language few would have known from home. In England and Scotland, after all, many children (and perhaps Gourlie herself) went to boarding school. Here, Gourlie's lack of comprehension of what she saw merged with her habit of amused, usually unconscious superiority, and made me want to shake her by the shoulders. In this, however, she was only like most travelers to Lapland—and I wasn't excepting myself.

We were all like film projectors, really, beaming our habitual ways of thought and prejudices onto the frozen screen of ice that was the North.

During the festival I also found time to slip into the library one day to look for more work by Nils-Aslak Valkeapää.

I'd wanted to know more about this multimedia artist who'd so recently died. I had heard of him before Laila Stien showed me his books in Alta. I knew that he'd composed music and sung it in performance, that he'd been an artist and poet, and that he'd also been one of the most visible political figures during the fight to save the Alta River during the '70s and '80s. I'd seen him on TV when he'd performed a *joik* for the opening ceremonies of the Winter Olympics in Lillehammer in 1994. Surrounded by reindeer and herders, Valkeapää—in his bright clothes, with a clear, resonant voice—made a strong impression on the television screen. I didn't know that his way of being an artist, in the world and as a Sami, had had such a profound effect on all of Sami culture. The film festival and this museum came from his vision of what had been and what could be.

Here in the library at SIIDA I discovered a copy of his early manifesto from the '70s, translated to English as *Greetings from Lapland* and published in 1983. In the preface to the English edition, Valkeapää called it "a book that was originally meant to be an exclamation mark, punctuating a certain moment in time." Written in short segments, a page or two long, the book had a tone that was fresh, real—insouciant with a desperate sincerity, a rallying cry. Under sometimes bludgeoning irony was youthful hopefulness. In its cobweb-clearing call for seeing and revolutionary action, it reminded me of other tracts from the late '60s and early '70s, by Abbie Hoffman and Stokely Carmichael, by Robin Morgan and Jill Johnson.

Valkeapää was born in 1943 in Finnish Sápmi. His mother was a Sami from Kautokeino. His father, he wrote, came from "far in the south of Sweden, near the Arctic Circle." He grew up in a reindeer-herding family, with a Laestadian background, in a culture that in the '60s was stagnant and had little use for artists, especially of the sort that he was: eclectic, innovative, and highly political. But after 1968, when Valkeapää first released a recording of Sami *joiks,* he came to represent in many people's minds the changing face of Sápmi.

In 1975 the first world conference for indigenous peoples was held at Port Alberni on Canada's Vancouver Island. Valkeapää represented the Sami of the three Nordic nations. "It was unforgettable," he wrote in *Greetings from Lapland,* "strenuous. For me at any rate it was an experience. A privilege. The fate of the indigenous peoples who were gathered there was so similar, that at the end of the conference the assembly stood up and passed a resolution to found the World Council of Indigenous Peoples (WCIP). The ninth Sami Conference at Inari in 1976 ratified the rules of the council, and thus associated itself officially with the

World Council. In summer, 1977, the second world conference of indigenous peoples was held in Samiland, in Kiruna."

But *Greetings from Lapland,* in spite of some stirring quotes from Nat Turner and James Baldwin and references to postcolonialism in Africa and the situation of North American Indians, wasn't a history of Sami political organizing; it was more than that. Writing about the environment, about the overharvesting of forests and the changes wrought by roads, tourism, and snowmobiles, he managed to touch on almost every issue that is still being discussed and quarreled over in Lapland today. It was a measure of what had changed and not changed for the Sami people that the book seemed dated, prescient, and current all at once.

> When people are so keen to make Samis into museum pieces— live in tents, herd reindeer—then something is wrong somewhere. When in addition to that they want Samis to reproduce old things which no longer have any practical function, it's not very stimulating to do anything. This eagerness to keep an eye on folk and keep them "genuine" seems revolting. Just as though everything which was done in the past was good, and nothing can be improved upon, and people aren't capable of creating anything completely new.

> It also seems dubious when the Samis become aware of their culture only after the preservation experts have become interested in homecrafts, and demand that they be thus and thus. Once rules and regulations start coming, the decline will soon be underway too. The sign of a living culture is precisely flux and constant change. It seems as though the adherents of preservation want to express our culture the way one presses plants, in order to admire them later in a herbarium.

It was inspiring to read Valkeapää here at SIIDA, which combined historical displays meant to educate and inform, with a festival that brought other indigenous cultures to Inari and encouraged the production of art that explored and interrogated Sami identity. It seemed the embodiment of the "living culture" Valkeapää had envisioned for his people thirty years ago. Skábmagovat was a living, breathing, intellectual and artistic world that had allowed me to glimpse, through the scrim of my ignorance, a Sami community in the process of discovering itself, making itself known, and changing.

Putting down *Greetings from Lapland,* I thought of Gourlie again and how terribly old-fashioned her travelogue seemed now. It was already outdated when it was published by Blackie and Son in 1939. In the 1930s, worried about the designs of the Soviet Union on its territory, Finland had developed ties with Nazi Germany. Less than two years after her trip, the Russians invaded Finland in November of 1939 while the rest of the world was preoccupied with Hitler and the coming world war.

This so-called "Winter War" lasted only a hundred days before the Finns capitulated, but they were days of −40°F temperatures that claimed the lives of thousands, though far more Russians than Finns. That was the beginning of long years of hardship for the Sami. During the Second World War, Germany came to Finland to fight the Soviet Union. The Sami's reindeer were killed or confiscated; their homes were burned as the Germans retreated north; and even after the war, those Sami caught on the Soviet side of the border were forcibly removed from their homelands and collectivized.

I left the museum and walked back to my hotel room to lie down a little before the evening films. Snow had fallen earlier today, and all was white and peaceful. Only a few children were sledding and building snow forts. The moon was bright above, though it was only four in the afternoon.

"I realized the loveliness of Lapland more than ever that night," Gourlie wrote about a walk she took when "pale silver streamers of aurora played over the sky," and she put on her frozen leather boots and went off down the silver river. "There, where Nature is so strong, so merciless, one had not to be afraid of one's fellow humans, think of air raids, gas masks, and the distant rumble of unrest that undermines our so-called civilized life of to-day."

I felt the same, about the loveliness of Lapland, about the distant rumble of unrest in the world. I wished I had a Li-Lo mattress and a fur sleeping bag, so that I could nap out under the stars this afternoon. Instead, I reached the hotel, lay down on my twin bed, and fell into a deep and dreamless sleep.

9. POSTCARDS FROM LAPLAND

JORMA LEHTOLA HAS the world's largest collection of Sami kitsch. This isn't saying much, perhaps, since he's most likely the only one in the world who collects it. Still, the array of colorfully dressed Lapland dolls, miniature reindeer boots, tiny shaman's drums, ashtrays and toothpick holders carved from reindeer horn, playing cards imprinted with drunken Lapps, and tea towels decorated with Lapps lassoing reindeer was impressive, as well as ridiculous in bulk. The dolls and souvenirs, many of them gathered at garage sales and tacky "Arctic Circle" gift shops, spilled over the tops of several bookcases in his apartment in Helsinki.

Jorma had told me about his collection of Sami kitsch after the film festival was over and we were en route to the Ivalo airport with the Brazilians. Leaving Inari, we'd stopped at Sami Radio and the technical college, then had gone on to a high school in Ivalo where we joined students for lunch in the cafeteria. Divino Tserewahú was a great hit in his bright-yellow down jacket and ear-bones. Jorma had gone to school here, and it was clear it had not been a happy time. Jorma still looked out of place on campus, with his long dark hair and reindeer boots.

While the Brazilians gave their talk, Jorma and I walked Ivalo's main street and entered a large souvenir shop. We wandered around the aisles, looking at all the familiar tourist detritus of Lapland, the useless items carved in reindeer antler or sewn from reindeer skin. More than half the items were made in Chinese factories and imported into Finland. It was there, surrounded by ashtrays, shot glasses, teaspoons, stuffed reindeer toys, miniature Sami caps and bonnets, and racks of postcards, that Jorma told me about his collection.

"I have a thousand postcards too," he said, spinning a rack of postcards that showed Sami who puffed on pipes and looked pensively off into a distance of mountains and lakes or sternly at their reindeer. Some of the postcards were jokingly offensive, cartoons of dirty or drunken Sami, but most were romantic: how Finns wished to portray their indigenous population and what tourists wished to see. It reminded me of my family's trip through the Southwest in our 1956 Chevrolet when we'd visited the Grand Canyon and driven through some Hopi and Navajo villages. Along the highways we saw souvenir shops with tipis out front and shelves stocked with moccasins, dolls, bows and arrows, ashtrays, and probably many postcards just like these. In the United States much of that Native American kitsch had been replaced by tasteful shops full of jewelry, pottery, and original art. The exploitation of the Sami in Finland jolted me; and yet I knew that era had barely passed in my own country.

Jorma plucked out one of the cards from the rack. "It's certain that some of the people in these photographs aren't Sami at all; they're just dressed up to look like it. Others, like these people in wedding clothes, had their photograph taken without realizing that it would end up on a postcard or a tourist poster. My mother stopped wearing her traditional clothes to church because she was tired of people taking photographs of her."

I thought of Olive Murray Chapman and her insistence on photographing and filming the "primitive" people of the North. "Just as I was focusing my camera," she wrote once, "an old woman ran hastily out of an adjoining hut and, shaking her fist at me, angrily drove the boy inside. She was evidently one of those who feared the camera, believing it to be an invention of the evil one. After that I was careful to hide my camera when visiting Lapps for the first time, especially those with babies, as I noticed the mothers sometimes looked rather scared, covering the cradles with shawls."

Now, in his apartment in Helsinki, Jorma brought out shoe-boxes full of postcards, some quite old and others more contemporary, welcoming tourists to Lapland. If you looked at enough of these cards in sequence you couldn't help laughing, as well as feel embarrassed and ignorant, which was, perhaps, part of Jorma's intention. The title of Valkeapää's book *Greetings from Lapland* referred specifically to the postcards that tourists sent home from the North. Jorma, whose great interest in life is representational theory, had taken the notion literally and actually collected the postcards. He used them in presentations about stereotypes and had displayed many of them in exhibits.

"One of the things that's consistent," Jorma told me as I thumbed through the postcards, "is that there are never any signs of modernity. The Sami people are always in tents or with their reindeer, or sitting on a rock smoking a pipe, looking out over the tundra. They're never in jeans, always in costume. There is never a house on the tundra, never a car in the background. Not even a telephone wire! It's not just the Finns who want this fantasy—

Italian photographers are very fond of Sami subjects. They love to take portraits of Sami smoking pipes, close-ups, and without permission naturally. Then they sell the rights, and the next thing you know, your grandfather is for sale in the souvenir shop."

I recalled my own surreptitious camera work at SIIDA, during a break between films. I'd *wanted* pictures of those people in their traditional clothes; I had wanted the Sami in juxtaposition with Divino. How else could I remember them, how else could I show them to my friends? How else could I capture for others at home the sense of the bright colors and beautifully worked embroidery, the strangeness of the scene? And yet what the film festival had meant to me was far more complicated than what would appear in an envelope of prints. How could I convey that to anyone? I barely grasped it myself.

I told Jorma something of my travels around northern Scandinavia. I mentioned my growing interest in how winter tourism was being reconfigured to attract new travelers above the Arctic Circle by promoting Sami culture as part of the Lapland package. Hesitantly I spoke of my experience in Jukkasjärvi during my first week in the North, with Ailo and the bachelors, the tent, and the reindeer. I cast myself as wiser about such frivolities, though I'm not certain I was. I asked him what he thought of such ventures, especially when they were operated by Sami people themselves.

"The Norwegians and Swedes at least have some regard for the Sami. A tourist thing like you tried, at least that's owned and run by a Sami person and exists to give a sense of Sami culture from the Sami perspective."

"What about the multimedia theater they have in Karasjok?" I asked. This was attached to a huge shop very near the Rica Hotel, where Betsy and I had stayed after leaving Engholm's Huskies. Called Sápmi, it had been designed by a firm that also created theaters for tribal museums in North America. Betsy had decided it wasn't worth the $15 to enter, so I'd been the only visitor on a mid-afternoon in a room that was clearly set up to move busloads of tourists in and out within a 30-minute time frame. It was done professionally, even sensitively, in the way of such things in the modern world, treading a politically correct line between *the Sami have always been here in the North* and *you too can experience the mysticism of their culture without having to actually encounter a real Sami who might feel disenfranchised.*

"That, too, could not have been created without input from the local Sami. Karasjok is the center of Norwegian Sami life," said Jorma philosophically. "Are tourists spending the afternoon in Karasjok going to the parliament building and library like you did, or even the museum? No, they're going to the multimedia theater and getting a small taste of Sápmi. The Norwegian Sami are the largest group of us," he reminded me. "They have learned to work with the government; they get more respect from Oslo.

"But the Finns! The Finns feel like they own Sami culture," Jorma went on, gesturing to the box of postcards between us on the couch, "so they can use it however they want. When we complain, we're told it's good for us, it gets us more attention. The Finns use the Sami people in a different way than the Norwegians or Swedes do. For instance, the design of Sami clothes signifies important differences in region and language. I come from the Fjell Sami group, and our clothes are different from those of the Lule Sami living across the border in Sweden. But the Finns think they can put on any sort of Sami costume when they compete internationally in ice-skating or beauty contests. They have so-called Sami dances, people dressed up in Sami clothes, performing for tourists. The Sami don't even have a tradition of dancing.

"And then the Finns tell us that tourism *saves* our culture." Jorma gave a half-smile. "All we can do is laugh at them. That's a traditional Sami response. We don't have a word for 'war.' We withdraw and make a joke. That's how we've survived all these centuries. The Sami were never fighters. We did not go to war to protect our land. We simply retreated. Our way is to appear to accept the status quo and yet to resist through keeping our traditions alive and remembering who we are. Our way is to make fun of our situation—and of the people in power. Irony is our way of dealing with pain. In laughter is resistance."

I had often heard this comment about the Sami being not at all warlike, and it's true that the Sami throughout history had been more likely to withdraw from an area than to fight over it. After all, they were a nomadic people, and few in number. But I wondered if it could truly be said that the response to aggression had always been irony and laughter. Valkeapää's book had certainly been ironic, but it had also been angry—he'd quoted a Finnish scholar, T. I. Itkonen: "It is depressing to read the *ting* [parliament] books from this time. Samis often sat in the courtroom weeping and complaining over the injustice they had suffered at the hands of the colonists." Itkonen, born in 1891, had grown up in Inari, the son of the pastor, and had, as the head of the Department of Ethnology, recorded Sami folklore and customs. He'd been one of Gourlie's resources.

There are many forms of resistance, however. One of them is to keep one's culture alive. Even after the land is taken, the language suppressed, and the religious customs banned, there is still music. While I continued looking at the postcards, Jorma got up and began to rummage through his collection of vinyl albums, tapes, and CDs, then put on some music. In this bachelor pad of the working journalist, the smiling dolls in Sami dress struck an incongruous note, but not the hundreds of books or the sound system and piles of CDs. Jorma claimed to have every note of music ever recorded by a Sami, beginning with the plainest of *joiks* captured by ethnologists decades ago.

Joiks are not exactly songs, nor is *joiking* quite like chanting. *Joiks* are sometimes composed with words that make sense, sometimes not. They often are highly emotional, but they are not tuneful, rarely melodic. They range across several octaves, from the guttural to the falsetto, from gargling to yodeling. *Joiking* is more similar to Inuit throat singing and to American Indian chanting than to any European model of song; yet it also has elements of jazzy scat singing. *Joiking* isn't choral but unaccompanied solo vocalization. To see a *joik* written down is not to understand it at all:

> I tended the reindeer
> On the slopes
> Valev vale vala
> Nenne nanna

ran one transcription I'd seen. Another, from Johan Turi had been translated:

> Voia voia voia, nana nana nana, the finest reindeer in
>   the land running like a flock of birds,
> Voia voia voia, nana nana nana, big, high-legged; when
>   they start to run,
> Voia voia voia, nana nana nana, then they spring till
>   you can see nothing but smoke,
> Then they spring like the boiling falls, voia voia, nana
>   nana nana nana nana.

Joiks usually make no clear distinction between the prose of words and the poetry of song. Some *joiks* are improvised on the spot—to describe a feeling of great joy or sadness; some *joiks* are handed down through generations. *Joiks* can describe a place on the river or the way two mountains come together. They are also song maps, a way topography could be remembered and passed on to others. They are a form of long-distance communication. Sami would *joik* over the snow in winter and could be heard from a long way away. In this way they could locate other herders and hunters, their families, their reindeer. Animals are often the subjects of *joiks;* or, put in a better way, they *are* the *joik*. In the Sami section of the Tromsø Museum, you can put on earphones and listen to *joiks* of wolves, bears, and reindeer.

People also have *joiks* composed about them, but these are not physical descriptions. They are more like Gertrude Stein's "portraits" of people, composed of words in the way that the cubists composed paintings of simple things that were taken apart and put back together again. Stein's famous portrait of Picasso begins:

> One whom some were certainly following was one who was completely charming. One whom some were certainly following was one who was charming. One whom some were following was one who was completely charming. One whom some were following was one who was certainly completely charming.

Joiking, wrote Israel Ruong, a Sami professor of language, "is the art of recalling other people. Some are remembered in hatred, some in love, some in grief." He noted that *joiking* has a "great depth of feeling, which is intensified by repetition and by varying the order of the words . . . so it has a strong element of improvisation."

In Alta, Laila Stien had played me a CD of modern *joiks* by Jon Anders Baer, amplified with a keyboard, drums, and, in one cut, a haunting baritone sax. One of the pieces was named after her; it was *her joik,* and consisted of many variations on Laila-la-la, with a steady drumming in the background. Curiously it did manage to capture something of Laila's spirit, a certain square-shouldered, steady warmth, a light-stepping quickness. "You must earn your *joik,*" Jorma told me.

In the past, *joiking* was connected with shamanic practices. Lutheran missionaries in seventeenth- and eighteenth-century Lapland had tried to put a stop to both drumming and *joiking,* calling it witchcraft. There were those who were hung for *joiking.* Later the Sami themselves began to abandon the practice. Laestadianism, to which many had converted, frowned on *joiking,* believing it had the ability to call up evil spirits from the netherworld. Yet, in spite of this, *joiking* had continued as long as reindeer nomadism was still an integral part of Sami life—that is, through the mid-twentieth century. Some scholars have noted that *joiks* often have a double meaning that is only intelligible to the Sami themselves and helped them resist their colonizers. "I was told an amusing story of a Lapp," Chapman writes, "who had composed what sounded a very fine *joik* in honour of the Lensmann [sheriff] of his district. On the words being translated into Norwegian, they proved to be all about that gentleman's bald head!"

Once, the Sami wouldn't have *joiked* in the presence of strangers. Tourists to Lapland sometimes gave the Sami drink to get them to *joik*—not that most tourists enjoyed the sound of *joiking*—but because it was strange and primitive. Gourlie wrote of bringing out schnapps at a Lapp home to encourage an old grandmother to sing. The woman drank plenty, but refused to *joik.* In the middle of the twentieth century, Nordic ethnologists went out into the field to record Sami *joiking,* much the way that American anthropologists recorded the chants of Native Americans. The researchers believed these cultures were dying and wanted to capture their sounds and sights before they disappeared forever. Yet, the archiving of the *joiks* in museums in Helsinki and Stockholm didn't make up for the fact that *joiking* had almost lost its social meaning by the '60s.

Joiking didn't die, and one of the main reasons was Nils-Áslak Valkeapää, who released an album in 1968. Valkeapää turned what had been private into performance art. He also transformed the traditional form into something more innovative. He gave permission for the *joik* to begin to develop in conjunction with rock-and-roll and world-fusion music. His example encouraged a generation.

Jorma first put on a record of traditional Sami *joiking*. This was pure sound, like the *cante jondo* of Andalusia in Spain. Some of it was melodic—long, rolling notes over a drumbeat—and some of it was stranger, jumpier—notes strung together in a kind of humming/growling vocalization. *Joiking* uses the pentatonic scale with no half tones. It can take some getting used to.

After that he inserted a CD of Mari Boine's *Gula Gula*. Like Valkeapää, Boine grew up in a Laestadian family in which *joiking* had long been discouraged. She always loved to sing, however, and the pietistic hymns of the religion played a major role in her musical upbringing. Her childhood home was in a small village outside Karasjok. She was born in 1956 and, like most Sami children at the time, she didn't want to identify herself as Sami. She said in an interview, "I was taught in elementary school to hate what I am. I was ashamed of my language and my culture. It was impressed upon us that we were somehow inferior."

It was only when she entered teachers' college that she began to learn the language and something of her culture. She decided to enter a song competition in the north of Norway where the contestants had always sung in Norwegian. She decided to sing in

Sami. After two years of being a runner-up, she won the competition, which led to appearing on Norwegian television.

Her first album was based on Western rock, Jorma said. They were protest songs about the Alta dam conflict. "Then she began to create her own world."

Her second album, *Gula Gula,* or "Listen, Listen," was released in 1989 when she was thirty-three. The themes were ecological, the voice haunting, and the global music community took notice after Real World Records became her distributor. Jorma told me that *Gula Gula* was based to some extent on shamanic ritual. Like most of the Northern nomads that circle the Arctic, the Sami had once placed the welfare of the community in the hands of their Shaman, or *noaidi,* who left his or her body to travel to another world and learn from and parlay with the spirits. The *noaidi* usually undertook this soul journey on behalf of a sick or troubled member of the *siida;* it was not the pilgrimage of self-knowledge that it's become in countless Western weekend workshops. The *noaidi* worked for the *siida,* to heal a single body or heart and, in doing so, to heal a people. Boine wasn't a Shaman, but she used song "to make a picture and to heal that picture," as Jorma said. Her work had been transformative for her, but also for everyone who listened to her, who heard in her voice a powerful link to an animistic past when all the world was alive.

In the years since *Gula Gula,* Boine has performed and recorded ceaselessly. She married a Senegalese musician and lives part-time in Paris. I realized I'd heard her voice before, on two albums with Jan Garbarek, the Norwegian ambient jazz musician. The voice was unmistakable, deep and strong, but full of high notes that wound through time and space: calling, questioning, returning.

The ambient, electronic music of Wimme Saari was quite different. Born in 1959 in Kelottijärvi, a tiny community in the northwest of Finland near the border to Sweden, Wimme (who is usually known by his first name) was raised, like Boine, in a fundamentalist, non-*joiking* family, or so he thought. After moving to Helsinki to study sound engineering, he went to work for the Finnish Broadcasting Company in 1986. While looking through the archives of recorded *joik*s, in search of his roots and inspiration, Wimme found that an uncle of his had been recorded by researchers from 1956 to 1963. Like most Sami of his time, Wimme hadn't learned Sami in school, but now he began to sing in Sami and to create his own style of *joiking,* which has been called "free *joiking,*" and which marries ancient vocal techniques—the scale, the throat singing, the imitation of animal sounds—to modern techno sounds.

Even more than Boine's, Wimme's music transported me somewhere else. His childhood was spent in nature, for his community by a lake consisted of only a few houses, and something of that emptiness was in his remarkable voice, which was both deep and wide. I was reminded of the Norwegian word for the plateau—*vidda*. Breadth. Broad. Wimme's voice filled Jorma's apartment, yet I was back on the Finnmark Plateau, one of those evenings when I'd gone outside and been caught up in the stars, the moon, the wisps of the Aurora. Wimme's *joiking* was pure yearning, huge as the wide landscape under the night sky.

By this time, it was very late. I said farewell to Jorma and took the tram back to Hakaniemi Square. Then I walked along the half-frozen lake back to the Villa Kivi.

Some years ago when I was in Helsinki to promote a book, my guide had pointed out the Villa Kivi and told me the former summer home of a wealthy manufacturer was now owned by the Finnish Writers Union and that authors could stay there. I'd long cherished a dream of spending a week or two writing in the big pleasure villa on the shores of the lake, surrounded by birches.

The reality had turned out to be somewhat different. The space for authors to stay was a small annex with three tiny bed-rooms, a shared bath, and a kitchen. As I found out, it was un-usual for a foreign writer like myself to stay there, and for so many days. Most of the time it was empty, but several times, par-ticularly very late at night on weekends, I could hear stumbling footsteps in the foyer. Once, a man rattled my locked doorknob, mumbling something. When this didn't stop, I said clearly in English, "If you try to come in, I'll kill you." Dead silence after that, and whoever it was went into another room and closed the door and locked it.

The man left early in the morning, and it reminded me that *all* the guests seemed to leave early in the morning, no matter how late they arrived.

In the office of the Villa Kivi the next day, I voiced my suspicion that the authors' annex was actually a sort of literary flophouse for Finnish male writers who might have had too much to drink and were unable to make their way home. Embarrassed laugh-ter enfolded an admission of "yes, that might be so." Afterward I knew I was probably safe enough, but having gotten the word one Saturday that the house was to be occupied by Finnish writers from out of town that night, I took myself off to a nearby hotel and luxuriated in a large room with a giant television before returning late Sunday evening after the authors had left.

※

Every morning at the Villa Kivi I got up and went to my laptop, with my small journals propped open on the table, and tried to describe dogsledding, the voyage to the North Cape, the Icehotel, my own emotional trek through a desolate and yet strangely beautiful winter. Outside my window I saw the stately, modern Opera House glimmering through a stand of white birch on the shoreline. Some days the lake was frozen, with ducks waddling across the ice; some days it was open, the water black, wavelets rippling in the breeze. Some days it snowed steadily; other days a whiff of spring swept through the barren trees. Up north the heavy snows and bitter cold would linger for many more weeks, but Helsinki was subject to thaws and freezes. The city was on the Baltic, so the air had a salty tinge at times. The sun was still low but dependably there, radiating more light and heat each day. Many evenings I felt lonely—it seemed I'd been gone from home a lifetime—but every morning I woke eager to open my laptop, and I wrote looking out the window at the lake, marveling at the return of the sun.

Around noon, those brightening days in Helsinki, I'd stop writing, put on my heavy coat without worrying overmuch about layers underneath, and slip my notebook and camera into my bag. I'd walk a couple of miles along the lake into the city, then have a lunch of soup and salad in my favorite café on the Esplanade, a long, narrow park lined by tall apartment buildings and arcaded shops that wouldn't have looked out of place on Paris's Right Bank or in St. Petersburg. Surrounded by students and office workers, I'd read the *Herald Tribune* or *The Guardian,* easing my way back into the mind-set of my country and its critics. I'd write a few last postcards, mindful not to choose any that pictured Sami people, or reindeer, or anything but the stunning art and design to be found in Helsinki. Then I'd spend an hour or two just walking, no matter what the weather, exploring every part of the city, from the docks where the giant ferries crossed the Baltic to Estonia and Latvia, to the parks, to the museums, of which there were many. If I grew tired, I'd hop on one of the trams that rattled so pleasantly up and down the streets, through districts that blended nineteenth-century apartment blocks with 1930s functionalist buildings (including a fabulous railway station with statues plastered against the exterior, the entrances half Abyssinian palace, half Hollywood set) and modern Scandinavian architecture, like Alvar Aalto's Finlandia Hall. Many streets still had their old Swedish names alongside the Finnish ones, for Finland was once part of Sweden, and Swedish is the minority language.

What surprised me most was the high-tech aspect of Helsinki, grafted so seamlessly onto its old-fashioned charm. It was almost futuristic, with free Internet terminals in stores, cafés, and railway stations. Finland is the home of Nokia, and 95 percent of Finns have one or more cell phones. Either because Finns are quieter in general or because they're more used to cell phones, these little devices seemed more harmless than at home. There were no conversations on the trams that took place above a whisper; the ringing was muted, too. The cell phones were most visible in the slightly hunched manner that most people walked, hand cupped to jaw as if for toothache.

This wasn't my first visit to Helsinki. I'd been here twice in the early 1990s, the first time invited by my publishers when two of my books were published. I was apparently the first lesbian writer ever to be translated into Finnish. The first visit, I sat in my suite at the Hotel Torneo and was interviewed hour after hour by journalists—fourteen of them. I was on Finnish television, being asked questions I felt unprepared for—the history of Gay Liberation, for instance—and found my picture on the front page of the arts section of the *Sanomat,* the country's main paper. The following year I'd been invited back to an international conference outside Helsinki, in Lahti. Now I walked past the hotels where I'd stayed, the restaurants where I'd been taken (far fancier than what I could afford now), and I was amused at the difference. Those visits ten years ago had been scripted and short. I'd never been alone, and hadn't had the time or opportunity to explore on my own. On those visits, flying from New York, Helsinki had seemed far north to me. Now, traveling down to the city from the true North, it seemed southern, European, luxurious, with its central promenade and squares, cafés and cyber-libraries, the Akademiet bookstore and Marimekko shop, and of course Stockmann department store, with a food hall that rivaled Harrods in London.

Mid-afternoons, when the light began to fade, I went into the university library off Senate Square. The square was one of the loveliest old sections of the city, modeled on St. Petersburg. To get into the library itself, I walked through the great hall, under painted ceilings. Along the walls were ancient leather volumes in bookcases that traveled up two floors, with a wooden balcony around. The library itself was computerized, and there was an inexpensive modern café in the basement, but every time I came through the great hall, built in the eighteenth century, I felt enchanted. I usually went upstairs and found a table by a window that looked out over rooftops.

I browsed through many books in that library, but the only one I read, slowly and steadily each afternoon, with a Danish-English dictionary beside me, was Emilie Demant Hatt's *With the Lapps in the High Mountains*—the story of a year spent in two distinct Sami *siidas,* a record of living in tents and trekking over the mountains on the spring migration from Sweden to Norway.

It was easy to tell she was an artist from her visual and sensual connection with the North. She wrote of the gray clouds of mosquitoes, the tents with their distinctive smell of spruce boughs, smoke and damp reindeer pelts, and the taste of hot coffee on a freezing day. Later in her narrative, as the winter cold and snow returned, she wrote of endless deep snow and the "hyacinth blue light." Of puppies who pushed their noses up to her face while she slept so that they could warm their noses on her breath.

I now knew that some of her paintings were at the regional museum of Skive, Denmark, and that others, the so-called Lapland paintings, she'd given to the Nordiska Museum in Stockholm before her death. I felt I'd like to see those canvases. Demant Hatt offered me, her reader, a different model of traveling through Lapland, not as a tourist dashing through with a camera and note-book, on a reindeer sledge, but as someone who cared about where she was, who didn't send back postcards, but paintings.

I looked out the window of the library's upper floor and saw the light fade into darkness, but now it was five o'clock, not one or two. In a week, I'd be back in rainy Seattle, back to my house with all its familiar comforts, back to my cats, my books, my friends, and my new life. I'd listen to my new CDs of Boine and Wimme and pin up two maps in my house: one the long map I'd fallen asleep under my first night in Kiruna at the Vinterpalatset, the other a reproduction of Magnus's *Carta Marina,* with its depictions of wizards and reindeer and monsters in the northern seas.

Only three months ago, northern Scandinavia in winter had been a mystery to me, the names of the towns and villages strange and sometimes unpronounceable, the climate and travel conditions unknown and impossible to completely imagine. Hans Christian Andersen had been my first guide when Lapland was a cold fairy tale—when I'd decided to come here to explore a dream of ice and snow, to walk into the frozen palace of the Snow Queen and see if I could read the shards of ice on the ground. Later, Frank

Butler, Olive Murray Chapman, and Norah Gourlie had been my travel companions, and I'd often turned to their descriptions and compared them with my own. Now that had changed. I'd begun to exchange their travelogues for the works of Laila Stien and Nils-Aslak Valkeapää, for Emilie Demant Hatt and Johan Turi.

Often, as I read *With the Lapps in the High Mountains* by the light of a desk lamp in the library, I wished, oddly, that I didn't have to go home, even though I was homesick and tired of living out of a suitcase. I wished that I could be back up in the North, the far North, in Lapland, Lapponia, the Northern Skullcap, Samiland, Sápmi. I wanted to learn more, to see more, to feel more. It had been that desire which had made me buy a plane ticket back to Ivalo for the film festival just days after arriving in Helsinki. I remembered how, when I'd stepped off the plane in Ivalo and felt the cold, sharp air in my lungs again, and seen the diamond-bright dusting of the newly returned sun on the birches and pines, I'd felt, so vividly and unexpectedly: *I'm in the right place. I'm home.*

Leaving the university library, I'd sometimes take a tram in the direction of the Villa Kivi, or just walk, over the bridge to Hakaniemi Square, past the Swedish-language theater, up the hill past other villas, and along the shore of the lake, sometimes white, and sometimes black. The alternating freeze and thaw of Helsinki mirrored my own state of mind. Sometimes I believed my heartache was gone, that travel had knocked all the pain from memory. Open water beckoned as the ice broke up. Some mornings I still woke numb under mounds of painful, snowy memories that had fallen in the night. But other mornings I was—almost—joyful. That pattern of freeze and thaw, of dreams dashed and hopes revived, would go on for a while longer. But something had shifted during this journey north, during these months of darkness and icy cold. Back in Seattle I'd take up my life again with renewed energy, and the North would eventually become my subject.

Helsinki, that city of cell phones, trams, and libraries, of Jorma's collection of Sami kitsch and my room at the Villa Kivi, is where this visit begun in grief and loneliness came to an expectant close, and where I resolved, walking back to my little room on a sparkling cold evening, my feet crunching on snow, that one day soon, I would return to Lapland—to Sápmi.

In winter, of course.

II

Mid WINTER

10. MACBETH ON ICE

FLICKERING CANDLES IN foot-tall pillars of crystalline ice lined the path across the snow to the Ice Globe Theatre, which sat on the banks of the frozen Torne River, a perfect replica in snow and ice of the Globe Theatre in London. With flaming torches on either side of the door and a brazier burning in front, along with electric searchlights shooting into the sky, the building had the appearance of a space station designed by a Renaissance architect. The lights had turned the circular walls of the theater, embossed with octagonal snow moldings, into a golden shell against the black night, while the open door glowed blue and eerie. The production this January evening was *Macbeth,* the temperature was −13°F, and it was snowing lightly.

Two years after my first visit to the Icehotel, I was back in Lapland. I'd been yearning for deep snow and freezing starry nights all through the drizzly-damp green and brown days of a Pacific Northwest November and December. A few days ago I'd dug through my closets and pulled out my long quilted parka from

Lands' End, my thick-soled boots, and plenty of long underwear and hats and mittens. I'd flown to Tromsø to visit Ragnhild and Øystein and then had taken a bus south to Narvik and the train east over the mountains to Kiruna. As soon as I could, I came out to see what the Icehotel looked like in its finished state.

The Ice Globe hadn't existed my first time here in Jukkasjärvi; this was its second season. Earlier this afternoon I'd talked with Rolf Degerlund, who'd come up with the idea of the theater. Big and blond, with a furrowed forehead and neatly trimmed beard and moustache, and wearing a beat-up black sweater with a neck-enveloping cowl, Rolf was the longtime director of The Norrbotten Theater in Luleå, a Swedish city on the Gulf of Bothnia. We sat at a wooden table in the bar across the street from the Icehotel, and he told me that some years ago he'd had a vision. He'd visited London and had seen the newly restored Globe Theatre on the Thames. *Why not re-create the theater in snow and ice back in northern Sweden?* he thought on the plane. Back home he painted a watercolor of how such an ice theater might look, and hung it up in the living room.

About five years later Rolf was invited to speak at a conference on tourism in the North. After talking for a while about the role of theater in attracting tourists above the Arctic Circle, he ended by lightheartedly describing his vision of a Globe Theatre built of snow and ice.

"I told them that my greatest dream was to become the world's first director of an ice theater," Rolf said. "Fifteen seconds after I was done speaking, a man popped up and said to me, 'I'll build you that theater. When do you want it done?'"

The man was Yngve Bergqvist, the Icehotel's CEO, probably the only person in the world who could have realized Rolf's dream. A year later, *Hamlet* was on the snow boards, and this year it was *Macbeth,* playing two nights a week, alternating with a short version of Verdi's opera *Falstaff,* a concert evening, and one night devoted to showing films.

The Globe Theatre in London didn't look all that massive in photographs, but this replica did, looming up in front of me across the snow like a glacier in the dark. Designed by Åke Larsson, its construction was similar to the Icehotel's: It had been created by jamming snice into large forms, letting below-freezing temperatures do their work, and then removing the forms. Perhaps the Ice Globe was simpler—it had no roof; it also, on the side less visible to theatergoers, had a wooden dressing room attached. The stage lights had to be kept on day and night, so the bulbs wouldn't freeze.

At the entrance to the Ice Globe, we were handed silvery quilted ponchos with fur-trimmed hoods. Most of the audience were guests of the Icehotel next door and were already warmly clad in the fashionable black snowsuits, padded hood-hats, and boots that the management provides. Moving clumsily, we stumbled up narrow stairs cut of hard-packed snow into the open-roofed theater. The tall, curved walls of snow around us were bathed in pale-blue light, and the stage, with its backdrop of crackled ice blocks, glittered with the same cool blue. Snow drifted down onto our heads. Our tiered seats were of snow; we each had a small polystyrene square to sit on. Behind us, more theatergoers crowded into boxes shaped of snow. Their silver ponchos made them look like wraiths floating above. Murmurs of awe and delight (teeth-chattering would come later) rumbled from within the hoods. We'd entered an enchanted space, and in such a setting found it easy to be transported to Shakespeare's world of ambition and madness, a world not so different from our own. Rolf Degerlund had chosen *Macbeth* deliberately, he told me, and had compressed the play to highlight its central theme: power run amok. My country was just ending its first year in Iraq.

"Mac-bet. Mac-bet . . ." The witches glided through the theater from behind us up to the frozen stage. They wore white, tightly bodiced jackets with sleeves that draped down over their gloved hands; their long skirts belled out into hoops over their feet. The material for their costumes was a white felted overlay that resembled frost rime or spiderwebs. Their headdresses were of the same material and covered their ears—warm to wear no doubt, but also spectral, viewed from the audience. Their makeup was white. They glistened up there onstage. Vapor issued from their mouths as they hissed Macbeth's name. His name was all I could understand, for this production was all in Sami, North Sami to be exact.

Although *Macbeth,* like *Hamlet,* could have been performed in Swedish—or English, given the number of foreign guests—Rolf had made an unusual decision when he first came up with the notion of doing Shakespeare in Jukkasjärvi. He asked the national Sami theater of Norway, Beaivváš Sámi Teáhter, to direct and act in *Hamlet.* This year, he'd called on the Swedish Sámi Teáhter, based in Kiruna, to produce *Macbeth.* The actors would come, as they had before, from all over Scandinavian Sápmi.

"People objected to *Hamlet* in Sami, of course," Rolf had told me earlier, "saying, 'We won't be able to understand!' but I told them, 'If you go to Japan, wouldn't you expect the play to be in Japanese?' What we're after," he said, "is the whole spectacle. The chance for people to experience something unexpected."

Of course the main issue in producing a play at night in the deep midwinter was the cold. Tonight the temperature was slightly milder than it had been, and that was because of the snow falling. Sometimes it could go down to −40°F (if it went much colder than that, they had to cancel the performance). "Costume design is crucial," Rolf had told me: furs and woolen tunics and dresses, hats and headpieces, gloves, wigs, boots, layers of long underwear underneath it all. The designer was the talented Sami artist Berit Haetta, whom I'd met in Tromsø with her husband, writer John Gustavsen.

The male actors in their rough but cunningly designed garments of fur and skin, with bone and iron ornaments, moved around the stage with sturdy grace. Macbeth himself had on a wig of dreads that slipped over the fur band around his forehead. They wore reindeer boots and carried whips made of heavy chain, and this combination of gliding over the snow and clanking their chains was very threatening indeed. Lady Macbeth, a tall beast of a woman with a long mass of dark curls halfway down her back, wore a red leather corset, the sections over her breasts cut out, so that the red leather formed pinwheels radiating out from the nipple. That this corset was worn over a black woolen shirt with a turtleneck up to her chin, and a black woolen skirt didn't detract from its radiating sex appeal. I had never seen a Lady Macbeth so sexy. The icy steam coming from her bright red lips seemed, again, perfectly and scarily appropriate. After this it would be hard to see a production of *Macbeth* where frost did *not* waft in a cloud around an actor's mouth and to feel the play was historically accurate.

In Shakespeare's time, the earth's climate was colder. The Little Ice Age, which stretched from 1300 to 1850, was known for erratic temperature swings. In addition to killer frosts and violent snowstorms, floods that swamped low-lying farms, and gales that scattered ships at sea, there were plenty of hot, dry summers through the centuries that turned wooden cities to kindling and burned the crops. But the general trend was chill winters in Europe, and some periods were particularly severe: 1570–1610, for instance, 1680–90, and 1805–20, when Charles

Dickens, creator of many unforgettable wintry scenes, was grow-ing up. William Shakespeare lived from 1564 to 1616 and *Macbeth* is dated to around 1606; the winter of 1607 was one of record cold. Extreme frosts split England's grand old trees where they stood, and the Thames froze meters thick. During the weeks of below-freezing temperatures, pageantry and trade flourished on the river. Booths were set up, masques performed; an atmosphere of carnival prevailed even as the poor froze to death in droves.

> The Great Frost was, historians tell us, the most severe that has ever visited these islands. Birds froze in mid-air and fell like stones to the ground. At Norwich a young countrywoman started to cross the road in her usual robust health and was seen by the onlookers to turn visibly to powder and be blown in a puff of dust over the roofs as the icy blast struck her at the street corner. The mortality among sheep and cattle was enormous. Corpses froze and could not be drawn from the sheets. It was no uncommon sight to come upon a whole herd of swine frozen immovable upon the road.
>
> . . . But while the country people suffered the extremity of want, and the trade of the country was at a standstill, London enjoyed a carnival of the utmost brilliancy. The Court was at Greenwich, and the new King seized the opportunity that his coronation gave him to curry favour with the citizens. He directed that the river, which was frozen to a depth of twenty feet and more for six or seven miles on either side, should be swept, decorated and given all the semblance of a park or pleasure ground, with arbours, mazes, alleys, drinking booths, etc., at his expense.

At least, this is how Virginia Woolf re-created those winter days in *Orlando.* One can also think of Brueghel's paintings of fairs on the ice and hunters in the deep snow to imagine the barbaric festivities that the chill climate gave rise to. The cold of the North suited *Macbeth,* and so did watching the play under the night sky as snow drifted down, for *Macbeth* is nothing if not a play about dark-ness. "Stars, hide your fires. Let not light see my black and deep desires," whispers Macbeth in Act I, when he recognizes who must be removed if he's to attain the kingdom. In Act II, the chilling scene between Lady Macbeth and her husband, when he prepares her for Banquo's murder later, includes these lines: "Good things of day begin to droop and drowse, Whiles night's black agents to their preys do rouse."

It didn't matter that the well-known English lines were absent here; that the actors spoke another tongue heightened the strangeness. Rolf had told me that directing actors in temperatures below freezing posed some challenges. "We became very good at quick, direct instructions: *Go right. Turn left.* We had no deep discussions about motivations or characters' actions—at least while we were rehearsing onstage!"

The first act was thirty-two minutes long. After about fifteen minutes, my toes and fingers were numb. In spite of my own long underwear, fleece balaclava, woolen gloves, and the thermal poncho provided by the theater, I was chilled sitting in place. Riveted but chilled. When the first act came to an end, everyone made a beeline out of the theater and into the Absolut Ice Bar for an intermission of twenty minutes. The bar wasn't exactly warm, but, like the rest of the hotel, its temperature of 23°F was tolerable. Soon I sat on a banquette of snow with my drink before me: vodka and elderberry juice, a mixture red as fresh blood in a square-cut glass of ice.

Around me, silver poncho hoods were pushed back and I heard a variety of tongues. Next to me, a Swedish couple was discussing the play. They were Stockholmers, up specifically to see this theater. It was the first time they'd ever heard the Sami language, it seemed.

"But their acting is so fine, you wouldn't know they're speaking Sami," said the well-coiffed matron judiciously.

"It's like Finnish, isn't it?" said her tall, serious husband. "Just like Finnish really."

I thought about Rolf's comment that if you went to Japan you'd expect the play to be in Japanese. That seemed to me a bit disingenuous, like comparing apples and oranges; after all, Japanese is the language of Japan, while Swedish is the language of Sweden. No one, not even the most radical of Sami activists, expected that Sápmi would revert to Sami ownership. Sami, a Finno-Ugric language, had almost faded away this century, like Welsh and Gaelic. But while a more activist generation has reclaimed the language for themselves and their children, it has little status within Swedish society and is hardly known to foreigners. By making it the language of these performances, Rolf told me, "We could give these fine actors a larger audience, with huge media attention. We could allow a space for them to be seen and their language heard."

The Sami language is made up of nine dialects, some so distinct from each other as to be almost separate languages. The dialect with the largest number of speakers, North Sami, is still only spoken by probably no more than ten thousand people, most of them in Norway and the majority reindeer herders. Sami, even today, is the language of weather, snow conditions, and reindeer breeding; some scholars estimate that a quarter of words in Sami have something to do with reindeer.

Sami hasn't been, until the twentieth century, a literary language, and few translations in or out of the language exist. Why would a Sami bother to read a Swedish or Norwegian novel translated into North Sami? Yet language visibility is crucial for the larger struggle of the Sami to not only hold on to their culture, but expand it. By producing *Hamlet* and now *Macbeth* in North Sami, Rolf had helped the Sami theaters of Norway and Sweden immeasurably in their goal, as Rolf said, of "strengthening Sami identity." There was another interesting level of politics involved: Swedes might have objected if the play had been performed in English; while English speakers would not have flocked to see Shakespeare in Swedish. A Sami production rendered the experience artistically avant-garde, politically correct for the Swedes, and exotic for tourists. Even in Sweden, few Swedes would attend a Sami performance; only the cachet of the Icehotel—and the fact that there wasn't much else to do except drink in the bar—made a cold performance of *Macbeth* the place to be.

Back in the blue-glazed icy theater for the twenty-nine minutes of Act II, the familiar speeches ("Life's but a walking shadow" and "Out, damned spot!") took on new life in Sami. The story evolved with sinister simplicity, and Lady Macbeth's madness was strangely heartbreaking, as was Macbeth's certainty that Burnham Wood would never come to Dunsinane. What else is live theater for but to break down clichés and make us feel the story as if for the first time? Through Sami I had experienced Shakespeare in a way I wouldn't have thought possible. My body might have been frozen, but my attention was thoroughly engaged. We clapped hard at the end, our thick gloves making a muffled thunder in the theater.

The snow was still falling, and outside the theater everything was quiet as death; the audience handed in the silver ponchos, and we slipped into the darkness or the bar. There was now no putting it off: It was time to tuck in for the night. I thought of the cozy cabin where I'd stayed in solitary splendor on my first visit to Jukkasjärvi. Then I'd had my choice of eight bunks. This time I had a bed of ice, a few reindeer skins, and a thermal mummy bag.

It was my choice to sleep tonight inside the Palace of the Snow Queen, just as it had been my choice to return to Swedish Lapland in January. My earlier winter in the far North was a wide-ranging reconnaissance that left me feeling I'd departed too soon, just when the light was returning and the season really coming into its own. This time I'd waited for high winter to make another visit. The North was now associated in my mind with snow and ice, with the polar blue night, the moon, and candlelight, and that was how I preferred to know it. I'd come for a month and expected to spend most of that in a relatively small radius around Kiruna. I wanted to learn more about winter tourism and about Sami life and customs. I wanted to consider the ways in which tourism energized and clashed with tradition.

I'd been low-spirited when I first arrived in Jukkasjärvi two years ago; these days I was much happier. I was, in fact, in an expansive, independent period, unattached, living alone, traveling a great deal. I could have gone anywhere this winter. But I'd wished—no, I'd *longed*—to come back to a dark cold world where I'd been despondent, because that time was also mixed with magic.

My fascination with the North wasn't shared by many I knew at home. Although I showed photographs of the trip and raved about the polar light, the beauty of the Icehotel, and the strangeness of my journey up to the North Cape and over the Finnmark Plateau, I couldn't seem to make it real to people, much less enticing. That seemed to be an ongoing problem of the tourist industry all over northern Scandinavia: to find the right words to evoke what was compelling about the North. "What we are trying to do," a tourism official had told me, a little desperately, two years ago in Tromsø, "is to create a *positive* sense of winter."

Even Betsy, who'd enjoyed her Norwegian Christmas, if not the "action holiday" that followed, tended to emphasize to everyone how cold she'd been, how incredibly *dark* it was up in northern Scandinavia. I couldn't explain the compulsion I had to return, and when friends gasped, "You're kidding, you're thinking of going again?" I could only nod. I had the Lapland Sickness: Arctic Fever.

The Icehotel and the Torne River at Jukkasjärvi were part of my illness. My craving for the North was as much a physical craving as an intellectual one, and that sometimes surprised me, because I didn't otherwise live in a snowy city or appreciate snow when it fell on rare occasions in Seattle. There it overwhelmed the few snowplows and made the freeway undriveable; it turned quickly to slush and ice, flooded basements, and caused massive traffic tie-ups. But snow in the far North wasn't just a thick white layer over the sleeping earth, it was a way of life. I remembered in my bones the long dark nights and cold, the moon and Northern Lights, the way the colors of the low sun stained the snow honey and raspberry, the metallic crunch of my boots, the crisping of my nose hairs, the taste of snowflakes caught on my wool muffler.

I had wanted, more than anything, to walk through the icy corridors of the Palace of the Snow Queen again. The Icehotel was as close as I would ever get to inhabiting that favorite old fairy tale. Yet from the moment I arrived this January I had to realize that it would never be the same as my imagination had recalled. Mainly because I now had to share it with other tourists. I couldn't have an experience quite like the one I'd had before, when the hotel was unfinished, and when, late in the evening, I would sometimes be the only one still flitting from room to room, a solitary child like Kai.

Although the Palace of the Snow Queen looked much the same from the outside this year, a series of molehills by the vast frozen river, the interior was different from two winters ago, and this was of course as it should be. Every year the main hall, the bar, the chapel, and the twenty or so suites were designed with new architectural and design elements. Earlier today, on first arriving at the Icehotel, I'd picked up my press pass and made straight for the reindeer-skin-covered main door with its antlered handles.

Two years ago I'd only glimpsed how the suites might look when finished. Now, as I entered each room through a narrow doorway that opened out into an illuminated hollow, I glanced at the title of the room and the artist's statement. Once I'd had to use my imagination, as had the artist, in seeing the possibilities of a chunk of ice, a blank white wall of snice. Now I had to judge whether the effort was successful. Sometimes I couldn't grasp the concept or found it shallow or forced: a pair of carved ice aliens, mother and child, with open horns for faces, for instance; a school of ice fish, one large flounder with a hook in its mouth. Many rooms were simplicity themselves: a wall of ice bricks broken by a large star shape, which opened into the sleeping chamber; a low, curved ice wall around a bed, to be entered like a labyrinth; another bed sitting like a fur flower between two large wings of ice. One artist had carved into the floor to set the reindeer-skin-covered bed in a rounded indentation, as if it were an animal Jacuzzi. On the wall above this bed was an arch of snow whiter and smoother than the snow into which globes of ice were set; the colored lights behind each ice ball gave the impression of bright moons circling a larger planet, Jupiter perhaps. I thought that Arne Bergh, the artistic director, must have made an exception for this room, given his usual ban on any color in the Icehotel.

The room in which I lost myself was a long hall where two lines of blocky ice figures promenaded parallel to the walls. The figures at one end were half-buried in snow, so only their torsos marched forward; each body was a little more exposed and free, and the fifth and last figure were walking upright. The figures had been etched along the sides, and the cuts filled in with snow, so that they seemed to have white lightning running along their bodies. If you stood away from them, the eye played a trick: It *saw* the white lightning first and best and gave a calligraphic movement to the figures.

I missed the camaraderie of the building when it had been a construction site. Now I kept passing Europeans and Japanese in glamorous ski clothes in the halls; I competed with them and their cameras on tripods or videocams in the suites for the right angles to shoot the ice furniture and beds. Most of the suites had been designed by people I hadn't met. Mats Indseth, a fixture at the Icehotel who worked realistically and often wittily, was the exception. All the other names were new. In spite of remembering how lost I'd been at times during my first visit to Jukkasjärvi, I couldn't help longing for the days when the Icehotel was just being constructed and every face was known to me.

Like the other tourists preparing to spend a night in the Icehotel, I'd left my bags in a locker in the warm luggage room, which also doubled as an escape hatch for those who simply couldn't make it through the night. "Almost everybody has a very good night's sleep," the young staff had reassured us as they took away our things, "but *just in case.*"

I went to the bathroom for the last time and brushed my teeth, then walked down a corridor to Room 312. My room was simple as a monastic cell, lit by a candle in the corner, with a faint glow from inside the ice blocks that made up the bed. The walls weren't as rough as I remembered them from the early stages of construction. Weeks of use had given them an icier patina from having melted and refrozen. Leaving my fleece cap on, I jumped as quickly as I could out of my clothes and into the mummy bag. So far, so good.

In spite of knowing all about the insulating properties of snow, I was still surprised that I couldn't hear a sound from elsewhere in the hotel, even though the only thing between me and the corridor was a thin cotton drape imprinted with the Icehotel logo. It was quiet. Very, very quiet. Eerily quiet, in fact, as if I were the last person left in the world. Even when you camped out on a backpacking trip in the wilderness, it was not this quiet. There were trees creaking, animal sounds, the wind. I tried not to think about the thirty thousand tons of snow that surrounded me and that hung over my head. I knew logically, with absolute certainty, that there was no possibility, none at all, of the hotel collapsing on me, burying me as if in an avalanche.

I would not think about avalanches, or earthquakes for that matter; I would think about being a nun. I would think of this as a spiritual experience. I would think about it briefly, and then go to sleep. I was certainly warm enough in my mummy bag. Of course my face was frozen, but I could cover my face. Now I was hot. Now I couldn't breathe. I stuck my face out again, pulled my balaclava up. I thought about how I'd blithely told friends, "Cold doesn't bother me. In fact, it's not as cold as you think, because it's a *dry* cold." Sheer lies, now that I was lying on an ice bed, in an ice hotel, with my face turning to a slab of ice.

I slept, and then I woke up, heart pounding. Where *was* I? Everything was white and cold; the candle fluttered and cast strange shadows on the wall. Lady Macbeth was walking, wringing her hands. I had to go to the bathroom; that was what had woken me up. I thought about the prospect of getting out of my sleeping bag and putting on all my clothes and my boots and walking over to the restroom. I thought about it for fifteen minutes. Still not a sound, anywhere. I knew now why the workers at the Icehotel found yellow snow in corners of the rooms in the morning. But that was out of the question. Helena Sjöholm and everyone who worked in reception would hear about that if I gave in to the temptation. Twenty-three degrees with no clothes on is colder than 23° when you're wearing a snowsuit. It makes for rapid dressing. My room was just down the corridor from the main hall. I was shocked to come out into this central place, only a few feet away from where I'd been sleeping in deepest silence. A blue light suffused everything, and here was a sculptor chipping away at something, a trio of black-snowsuited Japanese watching him and talking and another group of Spaniards wandering around with ice glasses full of blue and pink liquid. I felt as if I'd risen from the grave into a celestially blue waiting room full of people chatting in different languages, all of us thrown together before the gates opened to paradise.

I lingered a long time in the warm toilet annex before I forced myself to suit up again and trudge through heaven's waiting room back to the grave of my dark room and thermal sleeping bag. From time to time during the night, I woke up and felt as if a frozen mask had been placed over my face, only to realize that *was* my face. I burrowed down into the bag again over and over until finally I fell into a dead sleep.

Many things distinguish this hotel from other luxury hostelries, and one of them is that you can't put a Do Not Disturb sign on your door. There is no sleeping in. However late you stay up, however restless your sleep, you're still awakened at seven AM by a cheerful young woman with a thermos of hot lingonberry juice who pours you a cup and tells you, "It's minus twenty-five [–13°F] outside, quite a bit colder than in here, so dress up warmly before you go outside."

Outside? But of course that's where the sauna was, across the street, upstairs from the dining room with its breakfast buffet. I didn't feel like getting up, but there was no choice, and the room certainly didn't invite lounging around in with my journal and books. As soon as I finished the rapidly chilling lingonberry juice, I walked out of the hotel into a very cold world. The sauna was a blessing and so was the breakfast room. Those of us who'd spent the night in the Icehotel were recognizable; we had a stiff walk and bleary-eyed gaze.

I overheard several conversations along the lines of *How did you sleep? Me either.*

"Once is enough," said a British man to his companion, who had white reindeer hair all over her black sweater. "More than enough," she said grumpily.

Other visitors looked not only cold and chilled, but red-eyed, unshaven, hungover. Still others were silent, drinking cup after cup of hot black coffee. Only a young German pair at the table next to me seemed lively and awake, in a dreamy way. They couldn't stop smiling and looking at each other, and I caught a few words about, "Absolutely magical."

Yes, in spite of everything, it was.

And once was enough.

11. IRON MOUNTAIN

EARLY EVERY MORNING, at one thirty precisely, explosive charges are set off deep below the granite mountain of Kirunavaara, and an underground vibration rocks the town of Kiruna. The shaking lasts just five seconds, and the first time I stayed in Kiruna I never noticed the slightest rumble. The blasting of the magnetic ore vein is always done when there are fewest people down in the mine. The rest of the day is spent removing the rubble from the blast site and whooshing the lump ore up to the surface in superfast elevators to be processed into pellets on-site or transported to other pelletizing plants nearby. Twelve times a day trains leave for the Norwegian port of Narvik: fifty-two cars, each with eighty tons of ore. Slowly the mountain yields up its deep, almost vertical streak of phosphorus-rich ore—"toast in a toaster," they call it. In the late 1800s, when miners first attacked Kirunavaara with pickaxes, the mountain had eleven peaks; those peaks are long gone. For about sixty years, from 1903, when dynamiting and drilling commenced in earnest, the mine was an open pit. Now the extraction continues to a depth of 2,600 feet below the earth's surface—3,400 feet below the old top of the mountain, which no longer exists.

This is the largest underground iron ore mine in the world, and plans are under way to excavate to the next main haulage level, 4,500 feet below Kirunavaara's former summit. Drilling has shown ore veins down to 5,000 feet, and magnetic measuring indicates ore to at least 6,500 feet. One billion tons of ore have been taken from Kirunavaara in the last hundred years.

The iron mountain lies across a small plain and what was once a large, marshy lake from Kiruna's hillsides. Lake Luossa has been partially filled in. From my room at the Vinterpalaset, the Winter Palace, I'd looked across the railroad tracks at the snowy, flat-topped, terraced mountain many times before I grew interested enough to take a tour. Lars Aile met me around noon in the lobby of the mining company LKAB's main building, jokingly referred to as the "skyscraper." On the upper floors of the twelve-story building, well-paid white-collar employees look at computer monitors and wiggle joysticks, guiding the movements of the automated machinery far below them. Only five hundred people now work underground, where thirty years ago there were three thousand. Outside, in the bitter cold of a snowstorm, we got into a van and Lars drove into the opening of the mountain at ground level. It was very dark, lit only by occasional lamps and the headlights. The road wound steadily downward. An unexpected, queer kind of claustrophobia pressed in on me. Lars asked how I felt.

"Some people panic," he said, "or physically just don't feel well."

"I feel okay," I said, and tried to calm myself. After a moment I did feel calm.

There are 250 miles of paved road through and below the mountain. About a third of a mile down, at an earlier main haulage level, we parked near a science fiction–size metal door into sheer rock. The air was much warmer than outside, a little humid. But the interior of the mine is ventilated up to the surface. I tried not to think of how far away that was. Lars led me into a small auditorium and showed me a fourteen-minute film. It began, lyrically, with photographs of the landscape and uplifting music meant to evoke the past. There was a long shot of Kirunavaara with its peaks intact and of a lone Sami with his reindeer; the English voice-over spoke of a timeless past when nomads wandered the land ("We don't just *wander around*," I remembered Jorma Lehtola saying). Then, the music assumed a faster pace, and images flew by—paintings and old photographs, accompanied by narration. Mineral wealth was first discovered in northern Scandinavia almost four centuries ago. Swedes and foreigners alike dreamed of making fortunes, first from silver and copper and then from iron ore, and the Swedish state, always in need of funds, encouraged them. "In the north, within our own boundaries, we have our own India, if only we understand how to use it," wrote Axel Oxenstierna, chancellor to King Gustav II Adolf in the seventeenth century. But capital to develop mines and transport minerals fell short. In Svappavaara was a copper mine; in Kengis an ironworks run by a German. Mining in the North didn't really begin in earnest until around 1800, when Samuel Gustav Hermelin began producing pig iron from his mines at Malmberget, about eighty miles from Kiruna.

Compared with the ore coming out of mines in central Sweden, Northern production remained minimal. One problem of earlier times—that of extraction—had been solved by Alfred Nobel's invention of dynamite in 1866, and in 1878 two Englishmen figured out how to produce steel from high-phosphorus iron ore; yet the very serious issue of how to transport the ore over mountains or across marshy plains to harbors in the Gulf of Bothnia had to wait until the 1880s. English business interests created the North of Europe Railway Company, and from 1884 to 1888 the company employed thousands of navvies to build a railway from the mines of Malmberget to Luleå on the Gulf of Bothnia. When the English company went bankrupt, the Swedish state took over the railway line and, after acrimonious debate, decided to continue laying track in the North. The rail line reached Kiruna in 1900, and in 1903 the navvies, working day and night, winter as well as summer, under almost impossible weather conditions, finished the last section of the 143-mile track through the mountains to the village of Victoriahavn, which later became Narvik. The Narvik connection was important, for Norway's fjords were ice-free year-round due to the mitigating effects of the Gulf Stream, while the Gulf of Bothnia froze over five months of the year.

LKAB, incorporated by its owners in Stockholm in 1880, delivered ore to its two main clients: England and Germany. So far so good, the film's music intimated, in spite of a war and a strike or two; but as the Second World War approached, the soundtrack grew somber. A few shots of bombed ships in Narvik and some brief comments about that harbor becoming unusable for some years touched on what was in reality far more brutal. One of the most contested sites of the war's early days was Narvik's harbor. Germany invaded and occupied Norway in 1940 for several reasons: as part of its proxy war with the British, who fought alongside the Norwegians to keep Narvik from falling into German hands; because Norway had a border with Russia; and because Norwegians, after all, were blond and Aryan, just the sort of people who should embrace Nazism. But Narvik's great importance was its ice-free harbor. It was the main port for Sweden's ore, and ore for steel was crucial in building tanks and bombers.

During the war, Germany was LKAB's main customer, and trains full of ore rumbled through northern Sweden. If you talk to any Norwegian of a certain age, that's something he or she still broods about—Norway's heroic resistance, neutral Sweden's profiteering, or at best craven acquiescence to the Reich's bullying. In fact Norway was also neutral until it was invaded, and Sweden ended up providing a crucial haven for 44,000 Norwegian refugees, as well as thousands of Jews from Norway, Denmark, and—through Swedish diplomat Raoul Wallenberg's efforts to grant protective Swedish passports—from Hungary. History is never simple, but the film did rather gloss over the war years and LKAB's role in supplying Germany with iron ore.

After the war, the harbor of Narvik was rebuilt and Luleå's port facilities modernized and expanded. In 1957, the Swedish state became LKAB's majority owner with 96 percent of the shares (in 1976 the state took total ownership). Now the film's music turned upbeat and energetic, as the welfare state took wing and proved that industry could be both efficient and caring. The film ended with shots of robots in the mine and of employees using remote controls to direct the excavation, neatly skipping over the fact that as automation came in, the workforce had been considerably downsized. In 1961, LKAB employed 8,297; in 2002, 3,150. LKAB has only about 2 to 3 percent of the global ore market, but the company has competed successfully with companies in other countries by making pellets of its high-quality ore, for "added value." They sell primarily to Europe these days, but the industrial giant China has become an increasingly important client. Some mines in the area are worked out, but Malmberget still produces, and the riches under the iron mountain of Kirunavaara are vast.

After the film Lars walked me around the exhibits, most of which were highly technical. He gave me a pellet, very heavy for its pea size, as a keepsake, and opened up the cafeteria for coffee and cookies. We had our snack in the echoing room, surrounded by blown-up black-and-white photographs of miners from earlier times, and he told me that he'd become a guide after working below for many years. A lot had changed in his lifetime, and I felt his sadness, unexpressed, at the demise of the underground culture. The photographs around us told a story of fellowship and goodwill, of a Kiruna society that existed below the town, yet sustained and reflected it. "In winter we woke up in darkness, worked in darkness, returned home in darkness. But everybody wanted to work in the mine. The pay was good, the company took care of you, and it was warm inside the mountain. There was a lot of camaraderie." Nowadays it's different. Young people aren't being hired in great numbers by LKAB, and most of them don't want to work in a mine anyway. The best and brightest go south to college and don't come back to Kiruna.

Lastly, Lars let me into the historical museum, with its displays of old pickaxes and jackhammers and drills, its re-creation of a pioneer miner's shack, and a great deal of information about LKAB's first managing director, the larger-than-life Hjalmar Lundbohm, nicknamed "The Uncrowned King of Lapland," who was the founder of Kiruna. After I was back up on the surface again, I was surprised that there was still a pale light in the world. I went over to Lundbohm's original home, now a museum. The brown-log building stood in a small park, surrounded by birches loaded with snow, next to a cabin that had been LKAB's first storage shed. Over the two decades that Lundbohm lived here, he added on and remodeled his house into a home to host visitors and display some of his large art collection. Most of the art was dispersed (some to city hall and the town library) now, but in every room black-and-white photographs hung above the

wainscoting: miners, gentry, visiting aristocracy, pioneer settlers, and navvies.

Lundbohm was born in 1855 in the south of Sweden. He
dreamed of becoming an artist and studied art in Göteborg before
switching to technical chemistry, in which he took his degree. He
landed a job with the Geological Survey of Sweden, mapping out
bedrock and collecting samples for a mineral museum. As part of
his work he went to the mountains around Kiruna and surveyed
earth layers for apatite, valuable in the production of fertilizers.
He traveled abroad, particularly in the United States, to promote
Swedish stone as a building material; this fueled his interest in
architecture as well as introduced him to how mining was done
elsewhere. In 1898, LKAB asked him to become Kirunavaara's local manager and to oversee what was fast becoming the world's
most technically advanced mining operation.

Lundbohm was an excellent manager for the company, but he
was fired up by more than capitalistic zeal. The prospect of found-
ing a pioneer town and influencing the lives of the miners came
to interest the new manager most. In his travels in the United
States, he'd attended union meetings of miners and he'd toured
mines in Pennsylvania as well as the north of England. He'd seen
some of the slums that had developed around the mines, and he'd
also watched as neighboring Malmberget turned into a rowdy pioneer shantytown more reminiscent of America's Wild West with
its bordellos and saloons than a proper Swedish village. Kiruna
seemed poised at first to go the same direction; the navvies and
miners were living in tents and barracks, in shacks cobbled together from salt-pork crates.

In 1899 LKAB bought land around Kirunavaara, and
Lundbohm set to work with Stockholm architects Gustaf
Wickman and Per Olaf Hallman to design a town of beauty and

utility. Although the local Sami apparently told Lundbohm that the west-facing mountain of Haukivaara, where he proposed to situate the town, would catch the wind, he pressed ahead on the theory that the breezes would keep the buildings cool in summer and free from mosquitoes. His city planners tried, in fact, to work with the wind, designing streets with sudden turns and keeping the town decentralized, with stairs up and down the hillsides, following brooks and the natural land forms. In addition to the town on the mountainside, Lundbohm worked with his architects to design affordable, attractive company housing for the workers, the so-called "inkwell houses" with their mansard roofs and spacious gardens, each one holding two to six families, each with a modern, electric kitchen.

Once the housing problem was solved, Lundbohm began to put into practice some of the ideas of his hero Robert Owen, the Welsh manufacturer who, in the early 1800s, turned the cotton mill and the mill town of Lanark, Scotland, into a model of how industry and the health and welfare of workers could coexist. Long before the Swedish welfare state roared into action in the '50s and '60s, Kiruna's miners and their families experienced the benefits of Lundbohm's utopian plans and paternalistic benevolence. Lundbohm wanted Kiruna to be a place that attracted and kept workers, and he was always looking for ways to make life easier. He installed one of Sweden's first streetcars to carry the workers from the town to the mine and let the children ride free. Kiruna was also one of the first places in the country to have electricity apart from the generators; Lundbohm had cables laid from a new hydroelectric plant at a dam to the south. He created a laundry-bathhouse outside the mine for washing and cleaning up, so that the wives of the miners didn't have to do all that work themselves. The miners in Kiruna were the first in Sweden to get a two-week vacation—in 1911. He built the first elementary school and laid the foundation for a vocational training institute that was the most advanced in Sweden. He sent the miners' children to summer camp. He built a hospital and employed a midwife. He also, on behalf of LKAB, commissioned Gustaf Wickman to design an enormous wooden church that still stands, in a style that married Jugendstil with the interior of a Sami tent, and filled it with art by some of Sweden's best-known artists, including Prince Eugen and Christian Eriksson.

Lundbohm believed firmly that if his workers were treated well, and if Kiruna became a proper town, then that would be good for the company. Although he himself was wealthy, due to investments and mining claims, he prided himself on making things better for the common folk of his adopted city. Unmarried and a romantic, he appreciated women as lovers and friends, but couldn't settle down. His moods fluctuated; he was a man of strong passions and a drinker; a capitalist, a social visionary, and an arts patron. His well-preserved study in the museum, which had been his main habitation before the house was extended in various directions, didn't look like the office of a mining engineer, but of a well-read man of means who played host to hundreds of people every year.

The Lapland Maecenas, they called him, but to the Sami he was "Lid-eye," for the heavy lids that made him look perpetually sleepy. Over the years Lundbohm became a good friend to several Sami in the district, including Johan Turi, the wolf hunter, writer, and guide. Spurred on by Emilie Demant Hatt, Lundbohm published Turi's book about the Sami, *Muitalus sámiid birra,* in a bilingual edition with her Danish translation. The book was the first in a series called *The Lapps and Their Land,* which eventually also issued *With the Lapps in the High Mountains.* Like Demant Hatt, Lundbohm was among a small but influential number of Scandinavians who felt the need to speak out on behalf of the Sami, and who struggled with questions of how to put their case before the public.

"Lapps should stay Lapps," ran the liberal slogan of the time, which reflected a conflicted view of the Sami situation in the early years of the twentieth century. Should the Lapps be allowed to participate in Swedish society as equals—that is, should they also be able to work, buy houses, and send their children to school—or should they remain nomads living in tents and tending their reindeer? Lundbohm wouldn't hire them in the mine because he believed it was better for them to continue their traditional ways. He didn't want them to give up reindeer nomadism and in his paternalistic fashion tried to help by funding schools and books for Sami children. At the same time, the mining operations and the railway, the very town of Kiruna, brought thousands of new settlers and workers to the region, which had once been used solely by the Sami for winter grazing of the reindeer. The title of Lundbohm's book series, *The Lapps and Their Land,* was unintentionally ironic. The funds to publish it came from the mining that was taking away their land and livelihood.

Photographs hung throughout Lundbohm's house, most of them by Borg Mesch, the Swedish alpinist who accompanied Turi on the 1914 trek across the Finnmark Plateau with Frank Butler. Mesch was another of Kiruna's local legends who documented the world that was being built on the shores of Lake Luossa, and the one that was being displaced. Nicknamed Fjällkråkan (mountain buzzard), Mesch had come to Kiruna in 1900, when the town was hardly more than a scatter of wooden buildings. Having worked as a photographer in other studios in the north of Sweden, Mesch decided that here in this rough-and-ready pioneer town was an opportunity to create Kiruna's first and best atelier. Today the town of Kiruna still archives his many glass plates, including single and group portraits, many of them posed against a studio backdrop of a snowy forest clearing. But Mesch became something far greater than a studio portraitist. From the quantity and breadth of his photographs of settlers, Sami, tourists, and children, it's hard to imagine him ever stepping outdoors without his camera. In particular, his powerful photographs of the navvies are elegant, powerful documents of working-class life. Stiff and unsmiling the men stand, shovels in their hands, railway ties at their feet, mountains looming all around them. It's with these shovels they created one of the world's most northerly railway lines. Mesch's photographs of the Sami at work and at play along the shores of the lake are even more unsettlingly beautiful, especially when seen against the backdrop of the iron mountain behind them. Men in heavy fur tunics, or *gákti,* stand in the foreground with strings of reindeer and sledges, while mining operations go on at full speed in the distance. Later, it's just the mine: The Sami have been displaced.

Photographs of Mesch himself suggest the louche elegance of a rock star (or perhaps, given his expression of wry intelligence, a moustachioed Lyle Lovett). An experienced climber, Mesch also had an ability to convey the soul of the high mountains and the subtleties of Northern light in his photographs. The mountains were Mesch's natural home, and after the railway was finished and tourists began to appear in large numbers, spurred on by campaigns to "Know Your Country," Mesch found himself increasingly in demand as a guide and interpreter. He knew English well from a year he'd spent as a young man visiting relatives and making photographs in America and was at ease out of doors.

Butler's *Through Lapland with Skis and Reindeer* has a photograph of Mesch, Turi, and himself taken in Kiruna. They're on skis, in completely different sorts of dress. Butler wears plus fours, a vest and tweed jacket, a tweed cap. He looks as if he's headed for a golfing range in Scotland. Mesch is in a suit, with a high-collared shirt and a tie, and tall, black woolly hat (this adds to the Lyle Lovett effect). Turi is in the traditional Sami tunic, with leggings and reindeer-fur boots, a tall, tasseled cap. The photo was doubt- less taken just before the three departed on one of their journeys around the Northern tundra.

Some of what I found out about Hjalmar Lundbohm came from wandering around his museum home and some from a biography in Swedish, but some details—the spicier ones—were told to me by IngMari Lundmark. A former mineworker, IngMari had cre- ated LKAB's history museum. One cold, sunny afternoon we met in Kaffe Koppen, a place I'd lately been frequenting for its chicken salad and fragrant teas. The Swedes, while still strong coffee con- sumers, have a soft spot for what they call *blandnings,* or "blends": China and India teas mixed with all sorts of flowers and herbs, often sweetened with honey. I was systematically trying all Kaffe Koppen's *blandnings* and today had one that smelled of Darjeeling, roses, and cherries.

Like many Kiruna old-timers, IngMari called Lundbohm "Hjalmar" and thought of him fondly for everything he'd done for the town, especially the washhouse, the streetcar, the summer camps. All the same, he was a complicated man. Some (like the guide at the Lundbohm museum) maintained that Emilie Demant Hatt was the love of his life and it broke his heart that she married someone else. IngMari said he was a great womanizer. More than one housekeeper had been let go, pregnant, with a nice yearly sti- pend. And for all his identification with Kiruna, his primary resi- dence was Stockholm, where he lived at the Grand Hotel. "It's not easy to find a photograph of Lundbohm in Kiruna in the winter," IngMari told me with a wink.

He struggled with his Utopian ideas and with the needs of the miners and the board of LKAB. In 1909 miners struck for the first time, part of a general agitation all over Sweden. About a thousand people emigrated out of Kiruna that year, most to Brazil, which they'd heard was teeming with riches. It was Lundbohm who paid for the survivors to return to Kiruna, broken in health and heart. LKAB often felt that its manager didn't have his eye firmly enough on the mine and diverted too much of the income to the welfare of the workers and the town. In 1920, when he was sixty-five, they asked him to retire, and didn't give him a choice. But to recognize his many years of service, they arranged for a delegation with an orchestra to send him off at the Kiruna station. Bitter and angry, Lundbohm bribed the train conductor to pick him up elsewhere. "He left the fancy delegation waiting at the station," said IngMari. "And he never came back to Kiruna until he arrived in a coffin six years later. He left everything here, all his art and books and furniture, which was mostly auctioned off."

IngMari was in her early sixties, young-looking, with strong shoulders and a self-possessed calm. She was the third generation to work at the mine; her grandfather had started in 1903. He was a driller, one of those who removed the top of the mountain. His drill used compressed air from an electrical generator, but he had to crank the handle himself. She brought out one of his notebooks and showed it to me. The miners in those days had to keep track of how many meters they drilled; they were paid by the centimeter, no matter whether the rock was hard or soft. But his notebooks were also filled with personal entries: love poems to his fiancée and notes about a Socialist meeting he'd attended in 1909, a year of strikes that rocked the country.

IngMari's father started at the mine at fourteen; his first job was keeping the dynamite warm with hot water. In those days, they were still mining at the top of the mountain down in an open pit but had begun to sink shafts, in part to lower the ore to ground level to be loaded onto the trains. Her father worked on the shafts until he developed lung problems; then he switched to the job of testing out various explosives.

IngMari also started at LKAB at fourteen, as an errand girl in the office. Soon they sent her to school—their own school—to learn technical drawing. After a few years she moved down south and worked in a steel mill "for a change of pace." She had a daughter, and soon after returned to Kiruna, to LKAB and to office work, so that her mother could help with childcare. The year 1978 was the first that the miners' union agreed to let women work underground. "They were afraid women would take the 'easy' jobs set aside for the aging miners. So I felt I had to take a 'hard' job. I was given six months of underground training—blasting, loading, charging, drilling. I chose drilling in the end, because it was really easier, for a woman, to drill than to reach up to load the explosive charges. At first I thought I'd just try it out. Then I realized they were all waiting for me to quit. I wanted to challenge the expectation that I wouldn't make it."

She challenged it for eight years. Two more women drillers were hired in 1980, but were soon laid off. LKAB had a downturn in the early '80s, and the women simply didn't have enough seniority. "When I look back on it," IngMari said, stirring her coffee, "the drilling years were my best time with the company. Of course, doing shifts made it hard to have friends other than my coworkers, and, since they were all men, and married, I couldn't exactly socialize."

In the '90s she worked as a guide in the mine and persuaded LKAB to put some real money into designing the current display mine and museum. But a later director wanted to get rid of the hands-on stuff for kids and de-emphasize the history. The tour became more business-oriented and the emphasis was on LKAB's automatization. "They make it sound like the work is all done by robots, but there are still a lot of people underground." She decided to retire early, at fifty-eight, and take a reduced pension. Two months after she'd handed in her resignation, a month before her date to leave, she and her granddaughter had some time on their hands and went into a store where IngMari bought a simple scratch lottery ticket. As she scraped off the film, the numbers grew clear: One Million. One Million. One Million.

A million Swedish crowns.

I'd met IngMari through her daughter, Anneli Lundmark, when I contacted the Sami Parliament about a visit. A former journalist (and not a Sami), Anneli was one of about twenty employees for the parliament. She worked in the information office, creating content for the Swedish Sami Web site (www.samer.se). I'd gone over to its offices one day to see what such an institution did and what it looked like. I found it in a former high school building near the Kiruna church. Anneli, dark-haired, with a careful but mischievous way of speaking, grew up in Kiruna with her mother and has traveled widely in Central America, especially Nicaragua. She has a daughter with her former husband, a Chilean refugee from Santiago, who now works at LKAB.

The Swedish Sami Parliament was created in 1993 by an act of the Swedish Parliament, or Riksdag. It was the last of the three parliaments in Nordic Sápmi. The Finns had created an elected body first, in 1973; the Norwegians in 1989. In Sweden, thirty-one members of the parliament are elected every four years and meet three times a year. Surprising to me—though it shouldn't have been, with my past political experience in various grassroots movements—there's fracture and dissention even among this relatively small elected body. The Swedish Sami number approximately twenty thousand of whom seven thousand are registered voters, but there are nine political parties, ranging from the largest, the "Samiland Party," to several small parties. Since the establishment of the parliament, the question has raged about whether the majority party should govern, or whether it should be a coalition government. All this dissention is to some degree moot on the practical level, because the Sami Parliament can't create policy, make laws, or enforce them. It is neither independent nor self-governing; it exists at the behest of the Swedish government, essentially to rubber-stamp and carry out the government's various decisions and financial appropriations for the Sami people. While the Sami Parliament can put forth suggestions and try to make sure Sami needs, especially around issues concerning reindeer, are taken into account by the government, it's an advisory role. It's one thing for the Sami Parliament to request assistance for a cultural event or funding for Sami textbooks, but regarding large and controversial policies, such as land use for reindeer, mining, and hydroelectric power, Sami views that aren't in line with the government's go nowhere.

Norway's Sami Parliament has some of the same constraints. Unlike Sweden, however, Norway has gradually come to view its own indigenous population as one of the many other indigenous peoples around the world. So, although historically Sweden was said to have treated the Sami better, Norway is surging ahead.

The hardworking and charismatic Norwegian Sami, Ole Henrik Magga, was not only a spokesman for his people, he'd been appointed the chairman of the UN Permanent Forum for Indigenous Issues and represented three hundred million aboriginal people around the globe.

For all of the problems within the Swedish Sami Parliament, all the frustration over its lack of power vis-à-vis the Riksdag in Stockholm, most of the Sami I spoke with saw the parliament as an important symbol, a recognition of their separate legal status as a minority. Members of the Sami Parliament who traveled abroad to conferences organized by indigenous peoples—in Guatemala, or Brazil, or even Canada—realized how unusual their position was, as both Scandinavians and as Sami. Few indigenous peoples anywhere had had as much impact on their governments, and none had a separate elected body outside the government. Making connections around the globe only strengthened the Sami in the Nordic countries; for they were few in number, and other indigenous peoples were in the millions.

I had begun to see some of Kiruna's charm this visit, not just its drawbacks. I was developing connections with people who weren't part of the tourism scene and starting to have some routines: reading in the library, drinking tea at Kaffe Koppen or lattes at Café Safari, shopping for food in the local grocery store. I'd left the Vinterpalaset and had taken a room in a house about a mile from the center; it was spartan but had its own entrance and a kitchenette. It wasn't far from a place called Samigård, a building that housed a modest hotel, conference areas, and a basement museum. Remodeled over the years, the hotel dated back to the early 1900s. It had offered lodging to the Sami when they came into town from the land. The Vinterpalatset wouldn't have accepted them as guests then, nor would any other hotel.

I walked about the exhibits in the museum for a long while, the only visitor. The spirit of the place was about as far from the self-contained world of the Icehotel as an Indian reservation is from Disney's Frontierland. By now I'd seen the excellent collections of Sami artifacts in the Sami museums of Karasjok and Inari, as well as in the Sami departments of museums in Tromsø and Stockholm. These rooms had many of the same objects—*pulkas,* reindeer harnesses, wooden milking bowls and cups carved of birch boles, reindeer-skin gloves and boots, colorful embroidered blue tunics and hats. What the Samigård exhibit had that the other museums didn't was a palpable sense of outrage. The indignities and discrimination that the Sami had faced throughout history were often muted in other museum displays, something to read between the lines, downplayed in favor of stressing the long and rich heritage of Sápmi. The dominant cultures of the Nordic countries, like dominant cultures everywhere, believe in working together for the benefit of all, and if it benefits some more than others, that's regrettable but not really worth discussing. Just as in the United States, the majority white population believes that minorities shouldn't whine too much about what they don't have or what was taken from them. Here, in this out-of-the-way museum that probably few tourists ever visited, the general feeling of pride in the past had a tinge that was more confrontational than celebratory.

The LKAB film I'd seen down in the mine had made it seem as if the Sami played no role in the history of Kiruna and none at all in the mining industry of the region. In fact, the Sami of old were reluctant to show the newcomers and prospectors where minerals might exist. Spirits slept in the mountains, they said, and were not to be disturbed. The Sami have numerous tales of beings who live "underground" and who come out from time to time to snatch people and take them back down. According to Johan Turi in *Muitalus sámiid birra,* these beings were the "Uldas . . . descended from the race that our first forefathers bound under the earth. Uldas are strange folk of whom it is not good to know what they are, nor from whence they came in the beginning, or if they are human beings or not, but they too are Adam's children."

The Uldas have reindeer, just like the Sami, only better and more beautiful animals. They like to exchange their old parents for young Sami children. They are awake at night and asleep during the day and don't like Sami people to put their tents over their dwelling places. If you wake them up they tell you to go away. "And if you obey they don't do anything, but if you don't obey, they won't give you any peace to sleep in, they rumster about in the night till you don't know what is happening, but you won't get any peace to sleep in, and sleep won't come although you don't see anything. And they come in dreams and talk."

The Sami who lived around Kiruna, which they called Giron, the word for snow grouse, had other reasons for not wishing to encourage mining exploration. At the beginning of the seventeenth century, when Sweden had need of increased income to fight the Thirty Years' War, silver was discovered in the Nasa Mountains on the border between Norway and Sweden. The Sami and their reindeer were forced into service transporting silver and copper from the mountains 250 miles east to the Gulf of Bothnia. Many of their reindeer died, and in order to escape their own enslavement and the destruction of the reindeer, they crossed into Norway and disappeared. But at other places and other times, the Sami and their pack animals had been pressed into service to transport ore from the mountains to the sea.

The Sami had been displaced from their traditional herding grounds by dams and logging as well as by mineral exploitation, for the North was abundant in rivers and forests—or had been—as the last exhibits at the museum made clear with a series of black-and-white photos of deforested landscapes and houses and woods submerged by the rising waters of a dam. To make sure the point was clear, a chainsaw had been jammed into the wall of the museum.

Here at the Samigård was where I first came across the work of Paulus Utsi, a Sami poet and teacher of *duodji,* or handicraft, at the Sami Folk High School in Jokkmokk. A line from one of his poems, a poem I would come to know well, was used as part of the display: "Their needs have no limit," it read. Although Utsi had died in 1975, his poems were often quoted in Sápmi, in part because they were political but more because they expressed an important aspect of the Sami attitude toward the environment: that nature has a soul.

> I don't understand anything
> My heart is heavy
> Just look around
> Whole villages are gone
> The strangers have fooled us
> Their needs have no limit
>
> I stand by a shore
> A shoreless shore
> Just look around
> Old shores are no more
> The strangers have robbed them
> Their needs have no limit.

The land up north, this land that contemporary tourist brochures called "the last European wilderness," had once been called "the America of the North" or—something of a stretch—

"the California of the North." In 1867, a terrible famine year in Sweden, the government had tried to entice people not to leave for America, but instead to move to "Norrland" by naming it "The Land of the Future."

I was beginning to understand how the use of the land continued to be contested, inch by inch, by industry, by tourism, by hunters, by homeowners. Utsi ended up living most of his life next to a hydroelectric plant south of Kiruna. In those days, when Sweden's vast Northern river system was being converted into dams, there was no possibility of mounting an effective protest. Utsi became a poet in part to voice his anger and sadness at the loss of lands and waterways traditionally used by the Sami.

Without a car, I walked a lot, through snow-packed streets and up and down hills, and in walking, Kiruna became ever more familiar to me. In the library I found a special collection of Lapland materials and spent several afternoons reading through some of the precious old volumes of travel and hard-to-find accounts of Kiruna life through the decades. By the church I found Lundbohm's grave, with its memorial: "For the benefit of the nation he laid bare the treasures of the mountain and founded this town."

One morning I visited Kiruna's Picture Archive to take a more extensive look at Borg Mesch's many photographs. His atelier and house, once located down by the train station, burned a long time ago, but his glass plates are still here, along with boxes of prints: Finnish settlers, miners, navvies, and of course Sami—hundreds and hundreds of pictures of the Talma Sami, including Johan Turi and his extended family. Many people he took full front or in profile, and I was curious at the style of these pictures, which looked like good-quality mug shots.

"Borg Mesch liked the Sami," said Mats Spett, the director of the Archive. "You see all those pictures he took of the families and their reindeer—it was part of his documenting Kiruna life. But these headshots and full body shots of them full face and to the side? Mesch was paid by the Uppsala Institute to take them." The quasi-scientific Uppsala Institute collected information and photographs of human "types," a form of research that had its basis in racism and the eugenics movement of the first decades of the twentieth century. The widespread acceptance of the racial ideas behind the Uppsala Institute vanished abruptly when Hitler came to power. What's left are thousands of skull measurements and haunting photographs of those who once had a claim on the lands around Kiruna.

It was sunny and clear when I came out of the Picture Archive. I went over to the dining room of the Scandic Hotel, where you could get a substantial inexpensive lunch and sit looking out at the mountain of Kirunavaara and the reduced lake. In 1931, when Olive Murray Chapman finished up her spring trek through Lapland in Kiruna, she paid a visit to the mine with a guide. Unlike me, she didn't travel into the mountain, but up its side by funicular to the open pit. The blasting took place at noon then, and she and her guide had to make sure to get away by then. "A little later," she wrote, "all the windows of the town were shaken as the thundering sound of explosion after explosion rent the air."

When I went to bed that night I would be thinking of the mine, and of the Sami folktales of the underworld, where the Uldas live parallel lives to ours and don't like to be disturbed. Tonight, for the first time, I would feel the rumble at one thirty AM and from then on I would feel it every night.

12. A DAY AT THE REINDEER RACES

THE VINTERPALATSET WAS about a third of the way up the small mountain of Haukivaara, not far from the lake and railway station. In between the hotel and the town center higher up was Railway Park. Here ten massive cubes of hard-packed snow stood in preparation for the three-day snow-sculpting competition that was part of Kiruna's annual Snow Fest.

The competition was something the artist Barbro Behm had helped inaugurate and foster, but now she didn't bother to attend. She was over in Finland working on another ice chapel. "They don't do a very good job here in Kiruna taking care of the artists, promoting them, making sure they're recognized," she told me from her cell phone. "2000—*that* was a good year. Then Kiruna put up real money to bring twenty international teams here. *Then* we saw some real art."

One day I walked through Railway Park and the snow cubes were square no more. With hand tools only—saws, shovels, and chisels—the teams from Poland, France, England, and Sweden had attacked the blocks. Within hours rough curves and angles appeared. I thought of what Barbro had told me two years before—that ice was about light, and snow was about shadow. The white cubes had developed blue inlays that followed the shape of the cuts.

Because of the three-day time limit, the teams of two had to work fast and many of them had ambitious plans, whether realistic or abstract, to make three-dimensional in snow what was only a design on paper or in their heads. The weather—shifting temperatures especially—would play a role in what happened with the eventual sculpture. A sudden thaw, even a few days of sunshine, could make a hash of plans, and so could a heavy snowstorm. Today the climate seemed perfect for the task: sunshine on a cold day, but not so cold that it wasn't exhilarating for spectators to stand around admiring. I took off my mittens, fished out my camera, and took shot after shot. In the tiny view-screen, figures, dark against the dazzling snow, hacked away at their blocks, clambering up on top with ladders, circling with shovels. The Polish team, a man and a woman, was working on a grandiose monument called *The Slaves:* three enormous, thick-shouldered, big-headed bodies straining outward from each other, all in the process of breaking chains.

Kiruna's Snow Fest was conceived in 1986 as a way of celebrating winter and bringing some attention to the town. The festival had existed before the Icehotel, but was little-known among foreign tourists. There was no marketing budget, for one thing, and no glamour. To my mind, that was something of a relief from the Icehotel's relentless hype. Although I remained just as impressed by the architecture and the artists out in Jukkasjärvi, the narrowness of the tourist experience there left me yearning for more. The Icehotel was, for most visitors, a trip of only a few days, if that. The experience was constructed for them. They arrived by plane, were transported by van, taxi, or dogsled to the hotel, had a wonderful meal in the inn across the street, a few drinks in the bar. They could visit the gift shop and load up on tasteful souvenirs, sit in reception and write postcards, wander around the site. Now they could see a concert or play in the Ice Globe, and if they had a room in the newly constructed hotel annex, they could watch TV. If they stayed a day or two longer, they could go skiing or snowmobiling or dogsledding, or spend some time in the Sami tent down the road. All of this cost money, a lot of money, and all of it was for tourists, not locals. My first visit to the site had been endlessly interesting because every day there was someone new to talk to, something different to observe. This time I'd run out of things to do in Jukkasjärvi pretty quickly once I'd walked through the Icehotel a few times.

Kiruna's Snow Fest was free, except for some modestly priced musical events. Most of it was homegrown entertainment. Aside from hanging out in the park to see the snow sculptures take shape, you could watch the snowmobiling competitions or the "Strongest Man in Kiruna" event. You could observe the "junior snow sculpting" uptown, in which kids working alone or in groups made their own sculptures: pigs, chairs, giant heads. Children could take rides around a small track on Icelandic ponies, or be drawn in a sleigh pulled by reindeer.

Across town, the parking lot in front of the Folkets Hus had been cleared of cars, and snowplows and bulldozers were in the process of turning it into a racetrack for the reindeer races on Sunday. I was in and out of Folkets Hus several times a day, as Yvonne Niva at the tourist office was kind enough to let me use its copy machine and a computer for e-mail. I couldn't help noticing that the racks of tourist literature seemed to have more brochures for local dogsledding companies than I recalled from my first visit. Now my memories of hurtling over the Finnmark Plateau, barely hanging on to my sled, and of all the times I had not managed to hang on, returned in force as I read the descriptions in English:

> We pick you up at your hotel at 10 Am and go 12 KM outside of Kiruna. Then we put 10 eager dog's in front of the sled and get under way to the sound of snow sliding under the sled as the dogs carry you into the northern wilderness!

> Welcom to a evening trip with sleddogs. We pick you up at your hotel at 1800 and go out 30 km outside of Kiruna where you have the chance to meet friendly Alaskan huskies face to face. A few minutes later 10 eager huskies whisking us into the night. Head lamp from the guide light the trail. Everything else are dark and still then we will have the chance to see the famous northern light. This is an experience not to be missed…we continue to a lavo (lapish tent) for a break where we will have coffee or tea and cookies.

The brochures had lovely photographs of attractive, well-groomed Siberian huskies, all of which looked to be ambling peacefully along through fluffy, pristine snow. In spite of knowing what I knew about dogsledding, I was taken by the language of the brochures: "A travel for your senses and your soul where time doesn't exist" sounded particularly pleasant in this overstressed world, but I also liked the firmness of "There's only one reason to visit—your own."

"Northern Nature Experience—a little bit more, a little bit better," another company offered modestly, while Abisko Mountain Tours took the elk by the antlers: "We offer you . . . Sparkling white snow . . . Northern lights . . . Moonlit nights . . . Snowstorms. Nature is our attraction!" Not every company had the nerve to advertise snowstorms.

In the middle of these paeans to nature that invariably involved staying over in a "Lappish" hut or tent and eating reindeer "meet," was a small brochure with the decidedly nontouristy invitation: "To Jukkasjärvi guests" offering them "information you need to know about reindeer husbandry in this area."

In straightforward language the brochure explained some basics about reindeer herding in the area. Sweden is divided into fifty-one Sami reindeer herding communities, and the one around Jukkasjärvi was the Talma Sami village.

> Maybe you have plans to travel by dogsled or snowmobile. Dogsledding is a new activity here, primarily done by tourists. Historically the reindeer was used to transport people and goods. Dogs can be very disruptive to reindeer. **Reindeer need to be left in peace while grazing during the winter months so they are not unnecessarily stressed.** It is not only the barking and the howling that can scare reindeer away from an area. If a dogsled has traveled along a movement path during the day it is impossible to move the reindeer along that path.
>
> We use dogs in our daily work with the reindeer because reindeer are intuitively afraid of dogs. We especially use dogs when we gather and move our herds. It is very important that dogs are under complete control when in contact with the reindeer herd. Because the reindeer are afraid of dogs, we would like to see that all dogsled teams travel on or next to the river. **The closer to the river you stay, the better for the reindeer.**

After I finished reading this brochure, I was intrigued and a little abashed that I had never thought of dogsledding in any other context than my personal Waterloo. Had never stopped to consider what effect it might be having on the wildlife or the communities where dogs went through.

Yvonne in the tourist office sighed when I showed her the brochure and asked if I could get hold of the Sami who produced it. I would be interested in talking to them, I said, about reindeer grazing and dogsledding. Her normally sunny expression clouded. Yvonne had helped me with many, many things, but clearly putting me in touch with Talma Sami village hotheads was not something that she relished. She went on a rant, in fact, the import of which was somewhat lost on me at the time. "We all have to live here together," she said. "It's not the old times anymore. Do they want us to leave? Kiruna has made life better for people—roads and schools and jobs. We can't go back to the old ways."

Yet the brochure was couched in the mildest terms, suggesting only that, "As a guest to this area you play a part in shaping the natural environment," and "We would like to see that you request activities that take reindeer husbandry into consideration." And it ended, with great calmness, "Thank you for your thoughtfulness, Talma Sami Village."

I had to seek out another telephone to make my call to Börje Allas, the contact name on the brochure. When I got hold of him he sounded like he was in the middle of a reindeer roundup, and in fact he was up in the mountains somewhere. He said it would be best if I talked to the woman who lived with his brother, a woman named Lillemor Baer. I called her, and we arranged to meet during the last day of the Snow Fest.

Meanwhile I decided to go to the town of Gällivare about an hour and a half away by train, to talk with Lennart Pittja, who owned a tourist business called Vägvisaren, or Pathfinder. I wanted to meet a Sami who was involved in tourism and hear something from his perspective about how he presented himself and his culture to foreigners. The pathfinder is a figure in Sami lore; it's also the title of an award-winning Norwegian-Sami film.

Gällivare is a mining town somewhat older than Kiruna. The mountains are lower here, the aspect more open. Scandinavians know it for the skiing at Mount Dundret. "Visitors from Aspen weep at what we have here," I was told. "No lines at lifts. Fantastic powder from November through April or May. We take it for granted."

Lennart and I had spoken by phone, and the plan was that he would meet me at the train station and take me to his Sami camp on Mount Dundret, but things changed the night before. A number of reindeer were being shifted out of the mountains, where they'd been grazing on moss under the snow much of the winter. In older times, the nomad reindeer herders in this Sami community would have been moving with their reindeer, but these days the reindeer were herded together in the mountains and trucked down to corrals outside Gällivare, so that the individual owners could find and claim their own animals. Lennart needed to be there and said that if I'd like to see the reindeer roundup, his colleague Anders could pick me up and bring me over.

Anders and I drove about twenty miles outside Gällivare. The sun filtered through the snow-laden branches of the candle spruce on either side of the road. It was a sparse forest and not a tall one; most of the trees looked to be only twenty feet tall at most. The frost made the air like gold mist, and the sun hung like a burnished apricot low on the horizon in a blue sky.

Off the highway, cars and trucks were parked. We approached an enclosure of sturdy wooden posts and slats perhaps eight feet tall; this corral was the last in a series of corrals through which the reindeer were being funneled. There was enough room for about twenty people to stand inside, and an equal number of animals. About twenty to thirty reindeer at a time were released into this last corral, a brown-and-white blur of antlers and hooves. Some ran; others crowded together. Into this stew of animals waded men with rope looped over a shoulder and across the chest; sometimes they lassoed the reindeer, but in such close quarters it was often easier to simply grab the antlers, then the neck, and start dragging. Two or three people usually were required to hustle a single animal into a wooden corridor that led to the trucks and trailers.

This wasn't the autumn slaughter I'd seen decades ago in the Norwegian mountains, but a relatively simple separation process. Still the reindeer thundered around the pen. Their hooves are splayed to give them a good footing, and when they move, there's a clicking sound, tendon over bone. When they hear another reindeer's clicking sound going faster, they bound off with incredible speed. It's part of their survival system as prey animals. As one batch of reindeer was dispatched, another group was led into the fenced circle. Old bulls, cows, and yearlings often struggled after they were nabbed, but none escaped.

Anders brought me to Lennart. "How do you know your own reindeer in this group?" I asked him. From what I could see of him under his cap, he was a young, well-nourished man with an open, calm expression. "I mean, I know about the notches in the ear. I know, from books, that the pattern of the cut is the identity, but in all this commotion, how can you see the cut?"

"Practice." He spoke English, with an American accent. "And there are other ways to find your reindeer, from a distance. The way they run, or their size, or something about the antlers. It's like anything—you get a feel for it if you start young. The reindeer, they're all individuals."

Among the crowd of men I saw a few women, and some boys and girls. Children are often given their own reindeer. I watched a girl throw a lasso at a pair of antlers, saw the reindeer shy away. The mood was relaxed, remarkably, with all these animals bumping and bolting around, waving their sharp antlers and kicking when they were captured. Some men standing outside the enclosure even smoked pipes. But I felt wild and exhilarated around all that movement.

Eventually all the reindeer were accounted for, separated, and hustled into trailers. None of Lennart's herd had materialized, which meant, he said, that they were still up in the mountains, scraping away the snow with their hooves to get at the moss underneath. Or perhaps they were dead, killed by wolverines.

Anders and Lennart took me back to their base on Mount Dundret. The light was brilliant midday, the air sparkling and good to breathe. We piled into a Sami tent covered with snow to make a fire and have some lunch. Lennart did not plan to cook over the fire, but brought out a propane stove and a wok. He placed a slab of butter in it to melt, followed by chunks of reindeer. He set the coffeepot to boil and then started chopping up vegetables, which he threw into the wok with half a cup of soy sauce.

All this was very different from my day with the bachelors and Ailo two years ago, and Lennart wasn't wearing Sami dress (nor was Anders, but then, he wasn't Sami). Yet all the same, sitting on reindeer skins inside a chilly tent, warming my hands at the fire, was familiar and good; the smell of damp fur, the smell of hot coffee, even the smoke took me back to what I'd liked the very first time I set foot in a *lávvu*.

Lennart had grown up with reindeer, but while his older brother was taking over most of the herd, he'd opted to work with tourists. Pathfinder was founded in 1995, when he was in his late twenties. His first idea was to bring people here to the tents, make them food, and tell them about Sami culture. Although he still does that, he'd now joined with Anders to set up trekking expeditions over the tundra with reindeer as pack animals. The treks last over a week and take place in August and September, when the mosquitoes of the North have abated and the lichen and trees have begun to take on the bright colors of fall. Part of the mission of Pathfinder is educational. Those on the treks learn stories about past and present Sami history and culture, about natural history and herbs. "Our aim is partly to get people to slow down. We often stop and look at plants and see what there is to see. We don't always use the same paths. Our aim is to have little impact on the land."

One obstacle to trekking in the beginning was simple lack of knowledge about how to work with reindeer. The nomad life has been over for around fifty years, and in the intervening time, the animals have mainly been raised commercially for food, antlers, and hides. Llamas and camels and horses and donkeys are used as pack animals for tourists in other parts of the world, but since at least some segment of a population has continued working with these animals, there has been a tradition to fall back on. In the case of reindeer, that was not so, and it took Lennart talking with some Sami elders who recalled the reindeer caravans of their childhood, before the Second World War, to gain knowledge about how to tame reindeer and use them for trekking.

"The Sami," said Lennart, "used to be able to look at a reindeer and know what kind of working animal it could be. No one knows that now."

It's true that when animals are raised for slaughter, it matters little whether they are tame or not. Yet tame reindeer were important to the Sami for centuries. In the sixteenth century Olaus Magnus wrote that they, "with gentle compliance, faithfully serve the needs of man." That old relationship persists in the culture of the Sami, but not in practice. Tourism, in spite of its many drawbacks, is one of the few ways that tame reindeer have a place in Sami society.

After lunch we headed out to feed Lennart's reindeer. Here in the corral, I could get closer to reindeer than I'd been before, could take a good look at them. Reindeer are smaller than horses, bigger than goats. When attacked by bears or wolverines they're more likely to use their hooves than their antlers. They will rear up on their back legs and strike at their enemy head-on. Without their antlers, they look a bit like dogs, with rounded heads and soft muzzles. With antlers they are noble beasts, enchanted forest stags, glimpsed through the snow-laden candle spruce. Their antlers are partly used to establish hierarchy among them; in autumn the bulls battle in the rut. Their hides range from brown to gray to cream. A few are piebald and some entirely white. In Sami folklore the white male was magic. Their eyes are liquid-brown, bulging, wary, expressive. Frank Butler wrote, "the eye of the reindeer is very large and full, the outside black, and the animals always seem to be looking at you." They make a deep, satisfied roaring sound, lion-like, when they're happy or have eaten.

Anders and Lennart and I all stood there in the small forest, watching the reindeer munch on the brown pellets that Lennart had poured into the troughs. Up close I could indeed see how different the animals were from each other. A pale-brown yearling had slender antlers shaped like two question marks facing each other. A hefty cow seemed irritable as she shoved her muzzle into a trough and pushed a smaller animal away. Two old bulls stood side by side, digesting meditatively, apparently communing.

Thinking of the mystique of the animal, their resemblance to dogs and goats more than horses or cows, I asked Anders and Lennart if the reindeer reminded them of any other animal.

"A cat," said Anders surprisingly. "They're skittish in that way. Curious too. And never really domesticated, no matter how tame they appear."

In truth, the reindeer here did remind me of my cats, who keep a wary eye on me even after years of living side by side.

Lennart said, a little dreamily, "I never get tired of watching them. I could just stand here and watch them for a long time." To him, they were not like cats or any other animal; each reindeer was an individual. "It's not just the ear markings, it's everything about the reindeer. The Sami language has so many words for different kinds of reindeer, but it's also that you learn to recognize their expressions."

"Do you have names for them?"

"No names that they would recognize," he smiled. "They don't come to names. In the past the Sami used to bell them or some of them; they recognized the bells as belonging to different animals. Of course the wolves recognized the bells too."

The reindeer might not know their names, but when Lennart spoke to them in Sami—soft, throaty, coaxing—they came closer to listen.

I asked Lennart about dogsledding and whether his reindeer found it a problem. "It's not our tradition," he said, in the diplomatic way that was his hallmark.

Lillemor Baer had no such compunction to be tactful. "The Icehotel brings in dogsledding and snowmobiles. The noise of the snowmobiles bothers the reindeer, but the dogsleds are worse. Those dogs are scary to the reindeer. Reindeer hear the dogs and smell the dogs, and they won't cross the path where dogs have traveled. These tour groups use land without asking. They never discuss it with us. We can't use the land near the Icehotel for winter grazing anymore. It's useless to us now."

We'd met in the lobby of the Scandic Hotel. Outside, Kiruna had been transformed on this last day of the Snow Fest. Hundreds of people were gathering for the reindeer racing to begin in a couple of hours. The community center was packed with people trying to keep warm before the races began, but here in the Scandic all was relatively quiet.

Lillemor was small and stubborn and a bit fierce, in a likeable way. In her mid-forties, she had short, very straight red-brown hair, brown eyes, high cheekbones, skin roughened by an outdoor life. There was a deep confidence in her, of knowing who she was, without much outward display of it. I knew that one of the reasons she'd agreed to speak with me was because I'd identified myself as a journalist, and because she felt it was her duty to speak out about the situation with dogsledding. Yet she was also personable and sincere. She wanted me to understand; she didn't want to lecture.

She told me that the brochure was a new idea, that it had just been printed, with money from the Swedish government. They'd placed the brochures in all the hotels. "We've only done it because we're desperate," she said. "We want to try to speak directly to the tourists, to get them to understand what the problem is, and hopefully get them to take responsibility for how they use the 'cultural surroundings.' To see that it's not wilderness."

Lillemor herself had grown up in a reindeer-herding family and now owned her own herd. "We were four girls," she told me with a smile. "My father was very clever and my mother was supportive. I got involved with reindeer late—I was fourteen—but since then I've always had my own animals." Her grandparents on both sides were from Karesuando, a community northeast of Kiruna, on the border to Finland. Like many Karesuando Sami, they had been forced by the Swedish government to migrate southward with their herds in the early part of the twentieth century, when Finland closed the border. "No resistance was possible except that my grandparents did not give up their identity as

Karesuando Sami. They continued to speak North Sami and wear their traditional clothes. My parents also spoke North Sami, but after they married, they moved to Vilhemina, a South Sami–speaking area, where there was no one to talk to. That's why none of us girls speak Sami today.

"I just grew up speaking Swedish. Then I developed a sort of antagonism to people telling me I should speak Sami to be a Sami."

She smiled at the man who'd just joined us, Lars Jonas Allas, with whom she lived, and the reason why she'd moved to Jukkasjärvi in 1982. Lars Jonas, a thin, ropy man with glasses and an ironic glint, was one of the Talma Sami clan and a reindeer herder. "We work together," she told me. "But we don't mix our animals. My reindeer are my reindeer, that's that."

He nodded, and listened in as Lillemor went to the heart of the problem with the local tourist industry. "Why do they call it an industry, for one thing? If it were really an industry that was affecting our livelihood like this, we could be more effective in taking a stand. But there's no central authority. It's not like there's one person or company you can talk to. We have tried with the Icehotel; we have tried to organize in Jukkasjärvi. The local people, they don't like the dogsledding either—the dogs are dirty and noisy. People on walks worry about meeting dogs. The Icehotel doesn't have dogs of course, but they work with tour groups. They should pressure them. But the dogsledding tour operators pretend to be ignorant. *We don't see any reindeer around. We don't do anything to disturb them.* Meanwhile, the larger questions go unanswered."

What larger questions?

"Winter tourism. How big should it be? You get the sense everyone thinks, *No limit.* They want it to get as big as possible to make more money. How many people can be absorbed into a landscape?"

"What about the Sami Parliament?" I asked. "Can't the *Sameting* do anything?"

Lars Jonas coughed disgustedly. "The *Sameting* does *nothing*, can do nothing. It's useless to discuss the situation there."

"He is a member," Lillemor explained. "My cousin has been the president of the parliament. Lars Anders Baer. The Swedes don't listen to the Sami Parliament. No, we must try directly to explain to those who sign up for dogsledding how it affects us."

The three of us went outside, and I took a photograph of Lillemor before they vanished into the crowd. What could I do with this information? I did not want to be *against* the Icehotel and the people I knew there. It was a magical place for me. On the other hand, knowing dogsledding firsthand, I would not be sorry to see it banned from Lapland. I believed everything that Lillemor, with passion and good humor, had told me about the fact that dogs and reindeer didn't mix, but I had to be careful of my penchant for minority rights and David-and-Goliath causes.

One of the problems, I was beginning to understand, was who had the right to say what the landscape was used for and what it meant. Sweden had a long legal tradition of open access to the land, a concept called *Allemansrätt,* or "everyone's right." That meant, at its best, that little was completely private in the outdoors, whether the land was owned by an individual, a corporation, or the state. A camper could pitch a tent on a farmer's land, a fisherman could fish a stream, day-hikers could wander where they wanted in summer and skiers in winter. It was a social contract that had worked well when Sweden was less densely inhabited, before the advent of mass tourism. But now the Swedish sense of equality was coming up against a more fraught discussion of land use, into which tourists coming to see "untouched Lapland" would inevitably be drawn.

The cold was biting today, about −22°F, yet I guessed the crowd around the track in front of the community center to be about a thousand. Women in long sables and squirrel-tailed caps stood next to roly-poly snowsuited kids and parents with prams. Dogs in little jackets quivered and yipped; young girls in pastel parkas clustered together like fat tulips, giggling. From a stage in the center of the track, the MC, a radio personality, told jokes and tried to keep the crowd patient. Four Sami men, sensibly dressed in reindeer leggings, heavy fur caps with earflaps, heel-less reindeer boots, and embroidered wool capelets over their bright blue tunics, handled the reindeer and attached them to the sleighs. The sleighs were wooden, just like the one I'd ridden myself back during my first time in Jukkasjärvi.

Eight reindeer were tied up waiting to race, most of them looking anxious or feisty, or both. They fought when they got too close, swung their antlers about and charged, to the delight of the crowd, safely behind wooden barriers. Their harnesses were braided yellow, red, and blue, the national Sami colors. I could not help but look into their eyes, which did not see me, but were wild and restless. I had been looking forward to the reindeer races, but that was before my visit to Pathfinder and my time observing the herd and talking to Lennart and Anders about the characteristics of the beasts. Reindeer are not competitive, I knew now. This would not be like watching a horse race. I felt for a moment as if I had been transported to Jacobean England, to see bears being baited to the roaring approval of the crowd. Now we think of that as barbarous.

The racers were a varied lot, mostly young and male, but two young women also had volunteered themselves. The MC introduced them: one or two came from the South, that is, anywhere below the Arctic Circle, and one was from Australia, but most were local heroes from Kiruna and Gällivare who were cheered for past triumphs. They lay facedown on top of the sleighs, to which the reindeer had, very reluctantly, been harnessed. Their harnesses were attached to metal clips on wooden poles. They were off, two at a time.

The first of the dozen or so races was a bit staid, the drivers equally matched. The reindeer were fresh, the finish was close, the audience applauded dutifully and cheered for Kiruna. I walked around after three of these matches, to keep warm in the cold and to observe the crowd. I had grown tired, too, of the loud voice of the MC and his Swedish humor about following the rules, about the political implications of turning left or right. Viewed from a distance, the reindeer race seemed even stranger than close-up, for it was taking place in the middle of Kiruna's modern buildings, and every photograph I took, no matter what angle, had a '60s-style building in it. When I returned to the track, things were looser. In fact, a man was racing against a large Mickey Mouse mascot. At one point he had to leap from his own sled to that of the mascot's to keep the stuffed animal from toppling off.

Finally, some excitement: Two reindeer set off before the drivers were ready—they were standing on the sleds, not lying down. One driver fell off immediately and the other remained standing for a while, then ran alongside, then flopped back on just before the finish line. The crowd roared and applauded, banging their heavy gloves against each other.

Through it all, the Sami men kept working with the reindeer, unharnessing them from the sleds, tying the lathered animals, keeping them as calm as possible and away from each other and the crowds. Other than these men there seemed to be no great visible Sami presence at the Snow Fest. Down the hill a ways from the Scandic Hotel, a *lávvu* had been set up. You could go inside the warm tent, have some coffee, sit by the fire. Reindeer sleigh rides were also on offer, a single reindeer plodding around a track, hauling a sleigh packed with bundled-up, excited tots tucked under warm skins.

I knew that during Easter week in Kautokeino, in celebrations that drew thousands, the Sami raced reindeer themselves. But here, in Kiruna, in front of the Folkets Hus, not a single Sami competed for the prizes.

Down the hill, the sculptors were working frantically to finish their pieces before the judging at three PM. An English pair had created a very large, thin curved leaf. The Swedes tended to the abstract; one team carved a composition of a broken Corinthian column, a square cube, tilted up on one corner, a chess piece, likely a queen. I was rooting for the Polish duo and their monumental sculpture, *The Slaves,* which now had come fully into being, like something transported from a square in Warsaw.

The blue hour now began to creep upon us, for it was still late January and darkness came early even though the day had been sunny. A stage had been set up over by the supermarket and bank, and here the prizes for the sculptures were to be given out.

But first, a handful of local performers bravely took the stage: a bevy of cheerleading girls with pom-poms who flung off their jackets for a moment and let us see their midriffs (two wore long underwear), and then a chorus of women in full winter gear, who entertained us with a bossa nova in Swedish. The sculpture winners were announced, and Swedish teams took first and second place, which pleased the crowd. *The Slaves* won the popular vote though, which pleased us too. My feet had turned to ice, but I noticed a baby in a pram nearby smiling sweetly in her pink polar fleece. When you grow up in the North, this must feel absolutely normal.

Afterward, the crowds seemed to vanish quickly, and by six o'clock, the city was as deserted as an ordinary Sunday night in a small town in Sweden. I felt at loose ends, though, and in spite of the cold, walked around for a while. Not a trace of the reindeer remained in the center, and a few cars had already reclaimed the racetrack for parking.

I thought about wildness, about domestication, about my cats, which I suddenly missed inordinately. Lillemor had told me, "Once you tame a reindeer, it doesn't matter if it goes into the forest and you don't see it for months. When you find it again, it will return to being tame."

"How many reindeer do you have?" I'd asked her today, forgetting that I'd read you shouldn't ask reindeer herders how many animals they had. It was a bit rude, like asking someone how much money they had in the bank. I'd forgotten with Lennart, too.

Lennart had smiled and said, "a few," a traditional response. Lillemor had told me, "You can't really say you own reindeer. When the wind blows one way, you might have five hundred reindeer; when it blows the other way, you have none. Only the wind owns the reindeer."

13. WINTER MARKET

FOUR HUNDRED YEARS after Karl IX of Sweden decreed that permanent market sites should be established in the northern part of Sweden, I stood on a corner in the village of Jokkmokk, with several hundred spectators in fur coats, down parkas, and *gákti.* It was ten in the morning on a day cold enough to turn ears and toes to stone. Stomping our boots to keep warm, breathing out clouds of frost, we were there to listen to the welcoming speeches and to watch the reindeer *rajd,* a procession that officially opens the four-day-long Winter Market every February. The procession—a short string of reindeer led by a Sami elder, with young women walking behind, pulling children on the sledges—wound slowly along streets packed with booths; the *rajd* stopped frequently so visitors could take photographs and pet the reindeer. Even without the lead reindeer, a gentle pure-white animal with large, speaking eyes, the scene had a fairy-tale quality of just having sprung up overnight: a bustling medieval market superimposed over the grid of a modern Swedish town, along streets where only a few days ago cars had been parked.

Wooden booths lined the main streets of Jokkmokk, at least two hundred stands and all of them open to the winter chill, though they had protection on top and often on two sides. Some displayed homemade crafts: knives, cups, bags, and jewelry; some sold thick squirrel-fur caps and handmade wool jackets or knit mittens and socks; others offered calf- and reindeer-skin purses and wallets. Smoked reindeer was for sale, and frozen fish that hardly needed a freezer. Food stands abounded: hot coffee and *glög,* or punch; grilled sausages and shredded reindeer meat rolled up in flatbread, like a pita sandwich. At one corner of the market, a huge man, made even more enormous by his long bearskin coat and a fur toque thick as a sofa cushion, dispensed reindeer stew from a black kettle hanging over an open fire.

The Winter Market harkened back to long ago days when the Sami packed up their boat-sleds with the pelts of wild beasts caught in traps or hunted down—wolf, otter, bear, beaver, mink; with reindeer skins and hides; with antlers and bone; with haunches of meat, frozen through; with salmon dried whole, in the wind, or smoked to jerky-toughness; with white bundles of snow grouse, tied together at the feet; with oval birch boxes packed with cloud-berries gathered on warm days in late summer. They traveled the frozen riverways, from the mountains and forests to fjord inlets and river estuaries, to the market towns of Bossekop, Luleå, Umeå, Torneå, Jokkmokk. "They have also chosen specific places," wrote Olaus Magnus, "either in flat open fields or on frozen water, where they carry out such business every year and hold a kind of market, at which they offer for sale to the public wares which each individual has either made at home as a product of his own skill or acquired from some other place."

The Lapp Markets, as they were called, were times of celebration and inebriation as well as trade, of religious frenzy and judicial pronouncements. Afterward, the Sami drove their reindeer back along the frozen rivers, the sleds packed with iron kettles and silver spoons, with forged knives and metal traps, with wool cloth and embroidery yarns. Jokkmokk hosts the only remaining Lapp Market, though no one would call it that now. It still evokes a medieval fair of cacophony and color, the effect of times past heightened by the snow and the extreme cold.

The Icehotel under construction had reminded me of a cathedral in progress, with its workers wrapped in wool, trundling barrows and chipping at columns with chisels. Now as I walked between the booths at Jokkmokk, I saw an old woman bundled in wool scarves whose gnarled fingers poked out from ragged knit gloves cut off at the knuckles. I saw a man in the back of a booth lit by lanterns. He wore a leather jerkin over a thick sweater and had knife holsters hanging from his belt; on the wooden counter between us were laid out knives of all sizes. There were baskets stuffed with shapeless gray and blue socks and vendors who made change from soft reindeer-skin pouches. As darkness came on, candlelight and kerosene lamps flickered in the stalls. I heard the fat-crackle of roasting meat, smelled the acrid, comforting scent of damp leather drying.

I'd arrived in Jokkmokk from Kiruna a couple of days before the opening of the Winter Market, because the only way I'd been able to reserve a room was to agree to stay six nights. Beds were always at a premium during the fair, for the town has only two hotels, and the number of visitors runs at about thirty thousand. Jokkmokk's normal population is three thousand. Through the tourist office I'd gotten a list of several names and made some calls, and that was how I ended up at Irene's.

Irene Nordstrom was a widow in her late sixties who, unusually for a Swede, spoke little English. My room was in the basement of her ranch-style home. Uncomfortable, dark, and small, with an orange and brown color scheme, my bedroom had no door, only a curtain, and Irene, who generally used the room for storage, rarely thought twice about bursting in to chat. Irene charged me about eighty dollars a night and I felt lucky. Even given the exchange rate of the dollar, this was cheap compared to a hotel. Many people who came to Jokkmokk slept on the floors of friends' houses or on mattresses in one school or another. Upstairs in Irene's rose-petal and coffee-scented living room, ceramic figurines jostled for space on the windowsills with begonias and trailing ivy. Unassuming landscapes and dozens of framed photographs of her grown children and grandchildren covered the walls nearly up to the ceiling. One room was a workspace with a floor loom; Irene was a weaver and would be a vendor at the Winter Market, selling linen tablecloths, runners, and place mats.

She was plump and energetic and suspicious. She kept telling me that she could have rented out her whole house to visitors, but it was too much trouble to have a bunch of strangers wandering around among her private things. Yet she found my private things quite fascinating and seemed to take a shine to me too; every time I opened my mouth she was agog to hear an American speaking in a language she could understand. I'd grown used to the fact that Swedes found my Norwegian charming in a way Norwegians never seemed to.

I soon noticed that although Irene had lived for years here in Jokkmokk, the center of Swedish Sami culture and craft, she didn't seem to have a single piece of Sami handiwork in the chintz-upholstered, doily-dotted living room. She was an artisan, but in the Scandinavian mold; Sweden in particular is known for its glass, its printed textiles, its woven rugs and linens, its design of commercial, home, and industrial materials. Sami design and craftwork also have focused on form and function, the beauty of the utilitarian, but the traditional materials have been horn, bone, and wood, the size small and portable. In the Sami language, everything produced by hand was known as *duodji,* but *duodji* was not only a collective noun but also a concept: to be good with one's hands, not to be idle, to make what was needed, to make it beautifully.

Along with mass-produced souvenirs of antler key chains and dolls in Sami costume, I'd noticed true *duodji* on my first visit to Lapland. En route through the North, in Alta, Kautokeino, Karasjok, and Inari, I'd seen knives in highly decorated bone sheaths; cups hollowed out from birch boles, their handles inlaid with geometric patterns in antler and wood; finely wrought birch-root baskets; silky-soft leather coffee pouches embroidered with pewter thread; and elaborately carved bone spoons. These objects were the real thing: expensive, tagged with a certificate, locked behind glass. Once, these humble knives and baskets were part of everyday life in the tents and on the migrations. The self-sufficient Sami traveled light and used what was available: every part of the reindeer, every part of the birch and the willow. Their tools were minimal too: strap looms to weave ribbon bands, saws, knives and awls, needles threaded with reindeer tendon, chewed to make it supple. Any surplus from trade went into silver, which was easy to transport, and easy to hide. Sometimes the Sami gave silversmiths objects, particularly carved spoons and drinking cups, and asked for re-creations in silver. Silver gave status; it also had magic associations for the Sami.

Duodji "carries the culture, even when history oppresses," I'd read, and it was impossible to spend time in Sápmi without realizing the centrality of craft to identity. The museums were full of these objects, along with explanations of how they had been used during the nomad days, but a new generation had taken to creating and purchasing *duodji,* not because modern people could find a use for milking bowls and cheese molds, but because *duodji* could help define them as Sami and connect them with their ancestors.

How did one claim a Sami identity in the modern world? Lillemor Baer believed that speaking Sami wasn't necessary, but that keeping reindeer was. "Reindeer herders," she'd told me, "are the only true Sami. Because we are the only ones still living the Sami life." No matter that reindeer herding was no longer nomadic and instead was based on meat production; the reindeer owners had a protected place in Scandinavian society, and a clear identity as Sami.

"What about the ninety percent of Sami who don't own reindeer?" I'd asked. "And will never own reindeer?"

She'd shrugged—a little dismissively, I thought. "Then they must find another way to be Sami."

Since few adults over the age of twenty had had the possibility of studying their language in school and were unlikely to begin a language program now, that left Sami culture—making it and consuming it—as the primary way for most Sami to connect with their roots. If you couldn't have a reindeer in your flat in Göteborg, you could at least own a beautiful knife and a collection of Mari Boine CDs. You might not want to wear your full *gákti* to the office, but you could slip on a silver pin or ring with the Sami symbol of the sun.

At Jokkmokk Tenn, a metal workshop and showroom, I met Leif Öhlund, who learned his craft there and now works with five others making jewelry and small objects of pewter, silver, and gold. Like many Sami, Leif didn't grow up speaking the language, nor does he own reindeer. For him, like the majority of Sami, the creation and purchase of handsome objects using traditional methods and patterns confirms identity and helps connect them to their past. "When I was growing up," Leif told me over a cup of coffee, "you didn't always want to say you were Sami. That's different now."

Like Leif, some younger Sami had gravitated to the making of *duodji* and had come to Jokkmokk to study at the Sami Education Centre. The Centre was originally established in 1942 as the Sami Folk High School (similar to an American community college), but now focused on the Sami language and craft instruction in both Swedish and Sami. The crafts program had expanded over the years and attracted students from all over Scandinavia. This college, along with Ájtte, the Museum of Northern Environment and Sami Culture, and a few galleries here in Jokkmokk, were the places to see work by the masters of *duodji* such as Lars Pirak and Ellen Kitok Andersson. During the Winter Market, the rooms of the Sami Education Centre, upstairs and down, were filled with the work of students and Sami craftspeople who'd traveled from all over Sápmi to display and sell their wares. But the most artistic creations were to be found elsewhere in Jokkmokk, in galleries where a single knife and sheath might be artfully lit inside a glass box and the price was in the thousands of dollars. Collectors and museums would cough up the money readily; in the last few years the value of art handicraft had increased exponentially, with a premium offered for exquisite workmanship.

The practice of *duodji* had remained highly conservative for centuries; that was a large part of what allowed us now to see back into the past. Many modern artisans, or *duodjars,* diligently guarded the old ways: collecting roots by hand, winding pewter thread around reindeer tendon, refining the hand-production of baskets and knives to virtuoso elegance. Perhaps they even sewed secrets into the cloth, as had the Sami of times past, to keep the traditions alive and give the wearer power and insight. The more I learned about *duodji,* the more I could admire it, though my own fantasies of owning some really fine piece of Sami craftsmanship dwindled rapidly, given the price tags. Yet, in spite of my admiration, I began after several days to become a little put off by the very perfection of contemporary *duodji.* Each bowl, each knife sheath, each birch basket seemed more perfectly executed than the next. The variations were those of region and style, not of ability. I began to feel a harmonious but static quality to some of the *duodji;* personality shaped the making of craft, but originality and boldness were often missing. The old things—the cradles and bowls and spoons and boots I'd seen in museums—had had a soul to them. Much modern *duodji* wasn't meant to be used, but to be displayed. Once art and craft were one to the Sami; now art behind glass had taken precedence. The newly made artifacts had little of the quality the Japanese call *wabi sabi,* the beauty of the flawed, the mended, the imperfect.

I recalled Valkeapää's comment: "When people are so keen to make Samis into museum pieces—live in tents, herd reindeer—then something is wrong somewhere. When in addition to that they want Samis to reproduce old things which no longer have any practical function, it's not very stimulating to do anything. . . . The sign of a living culture is precisely flux and constant change."

It was the old things without practical function that Sami *duodjars* were making and selling to collectors for large prices, because perfection drove the market. The signs everywhere were of a thriving renaissance in Sami craft work. Yet when did conservation become stagnation? Nowadays there were Sami who'd attended art schools in the South or abroad, who were using Sami motifs in textile design (a well-known Ikea designer was a young Sami woman), or in their sculpture and painting. Two years ago in Inari, I'd watched a documentary, *God Is a Woman,* about the Karasjok-based artist Iver Jaks, who had been producing abstract sculpture, much of it with a mythological base, since the 1960s. The paintings of Marja Aletta Rantikk were expressionist howls of rage against the Laestadian faith. The Sami Art Group had approximately fifty members, working in graphics, painting, textiles, and sculpture. Some artists combined the practice of fine art with *duodji*. Perhaps the old distinction between craft and art didn't apply when much *duodji* was as high-priced and nonutilitarian as a painting or a sculpture.

Clearly some craftspeople in Jokkmokk chafed at the strictures of tradition, and this was most clear with fashion—perhaps not surprisingly, since the essence of fashion is change. Hanging on racks in schoolrooms that had been turned into boutiques were sleek dresses of thin reindeer skin, with V-necks and perhaps a ribbon of braid at the hem; short fur jackets, tight leather pants tanned green or gold, chic purses and hats, all with a bow to Sami tradition. One of the most popular events of the Winter Fair was the Fashion Show, which took place outdoors, in temperatures of −13°F. Young women appeared on an elevated catwalk platform among fir trees. While the rest of us stood with frozen feet, arms hugging our chests, hats pulled low, teeth chattering, the girls strolled out bare-armed and legged in leather dresses, or with coats unbuttoned as if it were a spring afternoon.

Within a day or two I realized the obvious: There were contradictions and hierarchies in the world of craftmanship, and the Winter Market wasn't the simple place it appeared in the brochures. For one thing, although Jokkmokk was the center of Sami *duodji,* others—Swedes mostly, but some Finns and foreigners as well—were here to display and sell their craftwork, which in Swedish is called *slöjd.* Like Irene with her linen tablecloths and runners, others came to Jokkmokk with knit caps and wool clothing, with carved toys and leather goods. Some also produced work similar to *duodji,* but generally less perfect, and less expensive.

Early on, before I realized that all the Sami-made *duodji* was inside, and all the *slöjd* was outside, I stopped at a wooden booth on the main street with a nice display of bowls for sale. These were whittled from the protuberances of birch trees and had horn designs on the handles with engraved lines darkened with ink. My attention was caught by a *náhppi,* or milking vessel. Once, when the Sami used every part of the animal, they'd also milked the tame reindeer and made cheese. Of all the once-functional items produced by the Sami, the milking bowl was most useless now. People still used cups and knives, still wore *gákti* and boots, still used harnesses and pouches, but in a world where animals were raised only for slaughter, almost nobody milked their reindeer any longer. This *náhppi,* shaped from a birch bole, had a lovely swirly grain and had been stained a light red. Its handle was inlaid with etched horn; it was a little crooked and uneven.

The bowl spoke to me and I asked the price, which at first seemed high, since I'd not yet understood what objects with the SAMI DUODJI label sold for. I put the *náhppi* down reluctantly, but kept talking with the woman, whose husband had created the work. They were from Vittangi, in the Torne River Valley. She said, with pride, that he'd been carving for fifty-two years.

I asked if he was Sami, for I assumed she wasn't. Somewhat defensively she explained, "No, but my husband knows many Sami, he has learned from them."

I smiled and moved on. I wanted something with the seal of approval, the true *duodji* label. But as the days went by I often thought of that milking bowl, for itself and because it raised larger issues of culture and appropriation. Did the old man who made the *náhppi* in the style of the Sami do it because he loved the shape and because he wished to honor his friends and neighbors in the Torne Valley, or because he thought he could sell objects that looked like *duodji* but were cheaper? Was he influenced by Sami culture—or was he appropriating it? These were not questions that concerned the Sami and Swedes alone: It was an issue that came up constantly in Australia with the Aborigines and in North America with the Indians and Inuit.

Still, from time to time, passing along the street on the way to a lecture at the museum or a concert, I looked in on what I thought of as my bowl, picked it up and held it. I spoke to the elderly man who'd made it. He said rather wistfully, "There were Sami in the family—long ago. We made things like this and that's how I learned." Once that might have been something to hide.

Eventually I bought the bowl. It had that unnamable quality of *wabi sabi* for me, because it wasn't perfect.

I wasn't the only tourist at the fair, or the only foreigner. Swedes who live nearby come regularly to the Winter Market, and scholars and artists participate in the lectures, film showings, and concerts that are also part of the celebration. But little is in a language other than Swedish and Sami, so there are limits to following some of the cultural events for most outsiders. I grappled, on and off, with what my role was, as a camera-toting, notebook-wielding American wanting to record and understand what I saw. In the Kiruna library, I'd pursued my interest in what others before me had written about Lapland.

It was astonishing to me how many writers had thought to write books about their travels and stays in Lapland. "I suspect that literature about the subject is up to a ton," wrote Ossian Elgström in the preface to *Lappalaiset*, published in 1919. He went on:

> The inhabitants of the place are particularly *over*-described. Untold volumes are published about them and their lives, their appearance and spiritual life, hair color and religion. Most of the writers, symbolically speaking, barely know how a Lapp looks, but books they write. They've traveled to Jukkasjärvi, or better Karesuando; they've witnessed Easter Sunday and seen the Lapps in the pews. Even better they've been to Abisko and gone on the motorboat to Pilomokiven's Lapp Camp. Others have taken their error to a deeper level; they have, as it's said, traveled with the Lapps, followed them on their trek over the mountains down to Norway and have under varying pretexts settled down among them and "lived their life" and with seriousness and diligence taught themselves the language so *that* has become a book. All swear truthfully that they don't know the Lapps, that they were foreigners and so on and so on, but between the lines you still read what remarkable men (women) they were, how secretly well they understood these Lapps they lived among, and how they with their trust and friendship and so on and so on, and how bad all the other books about the Lapps were and are. Amen.

I suspected Elgström might have been referring to Emilie Demant Hatt, whose 1913 book *With the Lapps in the High Mountains* described her trek over the mountains and her stay among the Sami of Jukkasjärvi and Karasuando. Indignant on her behalf (*she* had bothered to learn Sami—had *he?*), I had to wonder if that indignation was because I was now engaged in writing about Sápmi myself. As a traveler and a narrator of those travels, I wondered, *What is the right way to describe the people you observe, meet, and get to know?* I noted that Elgström, an artist and frequent visitor to these parts, didn't let his criticism of others stop him from writing his own books about the Sami, including *Hyperboreans: Travels and Investigations among the Jukkasjärvi Lapps 1919–1920*. He made detailed drawings, some reproduced in color, of the Sami, as well as humorous sketches of himself, his wife (called "the cook" in his writings), and locals like photographer Borg Mesch and Hjalmar Lundbohm.

The Kiruna library also had a complete collection of annual volumes of writing about the Swedish outdoors, published by the Swedish Touring Club (Svenska Turistföreningen, or STF, then and now Sweden's largest hiking association). Articles about Swedish Lapland grew in force from 1902 onward after passenger service to the North began. In 1903 STF chartered a train, the Lapland Express, to carry tourists up to Kiruna and then over the mountains to Narvik. These recreational tourists didn't particularly come to see the Sami; they arrived to hike and climb Sweden's stunning mountains and to see the Norwegian fjords. But naturally many of them came into contact with the Sami, as guides and as photography subjects, and of course there began to be descriptions of the colorful dress and manners of these people.

Far earlier than Elgström in 1919, some writers and travelers had worried about how to present the Sami. In the volume of STF writings from 1891, I found this advice given to prospective travelers:

> Remember that the Lapps are by no means any kind of wild animal, but pleasant and civilized people . . . You don't need to give the Lapps tobacco—ordinary treatment is better . . . At the least stay a month in company with the Lapps before you think of describing their national characteristics in your interesting travel memoir.

In *Lapponia* Johannes Schefferus had described the Laplanders thus:

> Besides their innate cowardice, they are strangely prone to suspicion and jealousy, being conscious of their own weakness . . . they are also revengeful. . . . The Laplanders besides are notorious

cheats. . . . They are also noted to be of a censorious and detract-
ing humor, so as to make it a chief ingredient of their familiar
converse, to reproach and despise others. . . . They are likewise
exceedingly covetous . . . yet they are very lazy withall. . . .
Their last good quality is their immoderate lust. . . . their pro-
miscuous and continual lying together in the same Hut, without any difference of age, sex, or condition, seems to occasion
this effect.

For centuries the critical words continued—and still went
on, albeit in whispers perhaps. Yet the younger generation of Sami
were often proud of their heritage and willing to move on. "It's
boring," as someone told me, "to always be focused on the wrongs
that have been done you. Everyone gets tired of that."

Times were changing. Lappology had become Sami Studies
and several universities in Northern Scandinavia now offered
programs of study with funds for research, publications, and conferences on minority culture, literature, and the politics of colonization in the Barents Region. Colleges in the United States and
Canada had also begun adding courses on the Sami to their traditional Scandinavian department offerings. The Sami, as the only
indigenous people of Europe, were suddenly hot. Additionally, a
number of descendents of Scandinavian immigrants found Sami
blood flowing in their veins—and this wasn't just wishful thinking.
The Sami, too, had emigrated to North America, hoping to shed
their pasts and begin again.

In the evening, late, Irene would pop down to my basement room
and stand in the doorway and wonder what I'd been doing. I described the fashion show, the conversations I had with people, the
lectures. My days were packed. I watched films, tried to follow lectures in Swedish. One afternoon I listened to Lennart Lundmark

speak on the "race-biology" movement in Sweden in the 1920s and
'30s, and how the Sami were affected by an ideology that reduced
them to non-Nordic and thus inferior. Lundmark is a Swedish historian who has written two very sympathetic books about how the
Sami had been exploited over the centuries.

I ran into Lennart Pittja, who runs Pathfinder in Gällivare. I
looked for Lillemor Baer, but the crowds were huge and we never
found each other. Down by Lake Talvas, where a local company
offered dogsledding trips, I saw Sven Engholm and his girlfriend
Bodil. He wore the blue jacket I recalled from the Finnmark
Plateau trip, and the horror of the experience returned vividly.
They were discussing dogs with the owners. I hid behind a large
man so they wouldn't see me.

Few of my adventures or observations really interested Irene.
The fair was a good place for her to sell her linens, but frankly,
she'd rather be on the Costa del Sol. She spent two months there
every winter now, and found the cold of February in Lapland hard
to bear. The Sami culture was of little fascination to her—and I
wondered why. I also wondered why I expected her to be more
involved. Why should she have Sami *duodji* scattered around her
house? I lived in the Pacific Northwest, which had strong traditions of art and artifact made by the Coast Salish, the Nuu-chah-
nulth, the Haida. I admired the carvings, masks, and prints from
these peoples, but did I have them displayed all over my living
room? No.

One day I came back to Irene's house to lie down for an hour.
I was going out again to hear a *joik* concert at the museum. She
loomed in the doorway, ostensibly on a mission to find more table
runners in a pile she kept on shelves in my room. "I don't understand *joiking*," she said, shaking her head. "What kind of music is
that? It's so monotonous. They're always *joiking* to their reindeer."

She laughed and I caught an echo in her voice of a much-repeated sentiment among Scandinavians in the North, at least of an older generation, to whom *joiking* was incomprehensible noise.

I'd caught a *joiking* and storytelling session earlier today among three men, craftsmen and reindeer herders from around Jokkmokk. One of them was Lars Pirak, a well-known artist who was here at the Winter Market as the Swedish equivalent of a Japanese Living Master. He was a humble man with a lively, worn face, and I was sorry that the language, especially the shifts from Sami to Swedish and back again, were so hard for me to grasp. The men told stories of their childhoods and relatives, and from time to time moved easily into *joik*. The room was jammed, many of us standing and straining to hear, yet the feel wasn't of a performance, but of a large family gathering to which we'd been invited. There was lots of laughter and a welcoming feel. Once *joiking* was as common as storytelling—some were better *joik*ers than others, but everyone did it, just like everyone wove or carved, as a part of everyday life.

Now *joiking* was like *duodji,* performed by the few for the many. Still this evening's *joik* concert at Ájtte, in spite of the stage and the ticket to see it, had an informal quality. Lars Anders Kuhnunen had *joiked* since he could talk, the program said. Lars Heika Blind was born in Karasuando where *joiking,* until twenty years ago, was considered the devil's voice speaking through people. Cecilia Persson, from south Sápmi, had been an actor. All three had quite different styles and voices, and none of them sounded at all like Wimme or Mari Boine. This was *joik* in performance, but it wasn't *joik* for entertainment. No amped-up instrumentals, guitar riffs, ambient techno overlays. One of the singers had nothing but her voice; the other two used drums as background percussion.

The Sami drum once played a large role in the spiritual life of the Sami. In the south of Sápmi nearly every household owned a drum and used it for purposes of divination. The drum skin was painted with symbols that reflected the lives of its owner, the sun in the center, and around the edges figures and symbols: goddess, reindeer, wolf, snow grouse, mountain, river, tent, skis, boat. To take a look at the future—would the snow come early or late, would the herd increase—the drum skin was warmed by the fire, and a brass ring or pointer of antler was placed on the skin. To the beat of a small hammer on the skin, the pointer moved over the illustrations. Wherever the pointer stopped the symbol could be interpreted, a little like a Ouiji board.

The drums show the physical world the Sami lived in and the spiritual world as well. In early times, there wasn't much difference. The Sami had a well-worked-out cosmology, and the drum was a gateway between worlds.

In the north of Sápmi, it was more likely to be the *noaidi,* or Shaman, who interpreted the drum in a dramatic ritual enacted before observers. While the Southern drums showed the sun symbol at the center, the Northern drums were divided into three layers; upper, middle, and lower worlds, each with attendant symbols. A skilled *noaidi* was able to move between realms; that was the source of his power. Often the Shaman was called in for healing purposes or to resolve a crisis in the community. Then he or she (though in recorded history the *noaidi* seem often to have been male) had to travel to the realm of the dead.

As in all ceremonies, the drumhead was warmed by the fire, and the *noaidi* beat the drum, calling on the helper animals inscribed on its surface to aid him in his journey. While he drummed, the Sami around him sang a special chant called the *luohti.* At a certain point the *noaidi* fell down as if he were dead, in a deep trance. It was then the job of a woman to continue to sing the *luohti,* which would keep the Shaman connected to the real world. The chant was like a thread that the *noaidi* could follow back after he'd finished his negotiations with the goddess of the underworld, Jábmeáhkka. If the negotiations were successful, the Shaman returned with her demands, which were most often animal sacrifices. In a recent film, *The Cuckoo,* which takes place around 1945 at the end of the war, there's a haunting scene of a woman trying to recall the old ways and using the *luohti* to sing a man's soul back to life.

The churchmen who missionized among the Sami saw the ceremonial drums as tools of the devil, and so did the Swedish state. Throughout the seventeenth and eighteenth centuries, hundreds and hundreds of drums were seized and burned, and those who refused to give over the drums often went to the gallows, as did anyone supposed to be a Shaman. If the Sami had struck at the Lutheran church and begun destroying Bibles and altars, there would have been outrage. But of course the Sami were widely supposed to be pagan and not quite human, their drums a symbol of Satan.

Not all the drums were destroyed. Ájtte Museum displays a handful of them in darkened cases. Their skins are cracked and split; some of them punctured and repaired. The illustrations are now faint on the brittle, parchment-like surface. Like many Sami objects, the drums are oval-shaped, the spruce or pine frames bent into two bow shapes then sewn or riveted together. Some said the wood had to come from the trunk of the World Tree. The reindeer skin was laid wet over the frame to dry and then affixed by thread made from reindeer sinews. At the back of the drum, from the frame or crosspiece, hung bear teeth and amulets or miniatures of boats and skis in silver, brass, or antler. The pictographs were painted on by the *noaidi,* blood-red ink from chewed alder bark.

On the way back to Irene's after the concert, when I was safely past the shuttered booths and party-goers, I couldn't help yipping like a coyote to the silver half moon as I walked down a side street. The cold went down my throat into my body; my soul careered out into the black heavens. So often in the past two years when I'd imagined returning to Lapland I'd seen myself back in the Palace of the Snow Queen, embraced by thick snow walls, looking out at the world through cracked blue windows of light. But the world was bigger than a fortress of ice where a child stood half-frozen and imprisoned, trying to work out the meaning of a single word. Whenever I reread Andersen's tale, I remembered again how much of the story was taken up with Gerda's brave adventures in "the wide world." I had left my own icy palace of grief and was traveling through the wide world now, outdoors in the cold night of the North and happy to be here.

I wanted to sing something about my sense of relief at having survived the full-on smash-up of my domestic dreams three years ago, about learning to live again, about having found a place on earth and a season that delighted me so much. "*Joiking* strengthens the heart and self-knowledge," I'd read in the concert program tonight. I wanted that self-knowledge, that strength of heart. I wanted to sing something, and so I did, low and then louder, a *joik* mixed with gospel and Joni Mitchell:

> The half moon
> In winter
> Lolo lulu lo lo lo

I could drink a case of you
And still be on my feet
Lula lo lo lu

I was lost and
Now I'm found
Lula lu lu . . . lo!

The next morning, the Winter Market was over. I left the far North again, for two last days in Stockholm and then, reluctantly, flew all the way back to my Seattle home, four thousand miles away.

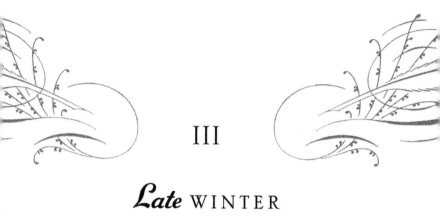

III

Late WINTER

14. UNTOUCHED LAPLAND

I OPENED THE WINDOW of my room at the Vinterpalatset, leaned out, breathed in. Snow cloaked the land, the birches were bare; but this April morning, spring wafted unmistakably in the chill air. The long white linen drapes fluttered in, over the bleached floorboards. I'd been awakened earlier than I liked by the sound of machinery, which turned out to be the mining company, LKAB, doing one of its test drills for iron ore in a small vacant lot behind the hotel.

According to IngMari Lundmark, the former mineworker and lottery winner, the ore under the Vinterpalatset was particularly good, 74 percent pure. That had sealed the doom of the hotel, as well as much of the town. The moving of Kiruna, rumored when I was here last year, was now a coming certainty. With the Chinese industrializing at a rapid rate, the price of iron ore had shot up, and LKAB, already the largest underground mine in the world, was laying plans to expand. First the railway tracks would have to be moved, then the major highway, the E10, that crossed the mountains to Norway. Then the workers' houses owned by LKAB; Hjalmar Lundbohm's historic home and the small park of birches that surrounded it; the Company Hotel, built for visiting Stockholm shareholders and members of the board, where the Swedish king stayed when visiting Kiruna; the listed City Hall with its clock tower; the vast Jugendstil wooden church in the shape of a Sami dwelling, voted Sweden's most beautiful building in 2002; the brick railway station and the old hotels nearby; the Vinterpalaset itself—all would have to be moved if they were to be preserved.

It seemed a shame that, just when I was growing fond of Kiruna, it was about to disappear—or at least remove itself to another part of the countryside.

In twenty years' time or less, this particular view, of white-skinned birches, of the terraced mountain, Kirunavaara, of a jumble of buildings across the white plain, would be gone. I pulled the window closed and the thin linen drapes fell quiet. Other views had disappeared over the years in Kiruna. In Borg Mesch's early photographs, Kirunavaara was whole and Sami herders still gathered on the lake with their reindeer and *pulkas*. This altered landscape wasn't one Emilie Demant Hatt had painted, or the one that Johan Turi had moved through on his skis. This view wasn't Lundbohm's when he arrived with the directive to manage the LKAB mine and create a settlement for the workers.

For me, still, this was the view I remembered, from my very first visit to Kiruna. It was the inner view that had changed. I'd known so little then about where I was, about the history of the place or the people who lived here. Now the days were lit from early morning to almost eight PM; my library card was still valid, and I could pick up the phone and call acquaintances. All the reading I'd done on Demant Hatt, Turi, and their circle brought me always right back here to Swedish Lapland.

I'd planned this late winter trip spontaneously and couldn't stay long. But I'd found myself missing the North over the winter, and come March I began to think about the Icehotel under the burn of the sun. As always it was the Palace of the Snow Queen that I dreamed of and the reality of Kiruna that intruded—now a welcome and happy intrusion, a reminder of how much this town had come to interest me.

Yesterday afternoon I'd strolled through Kiruna. The distance from the hotel up to the center seemed shorter; partly familiarity, perhaps, partly that the sidewalks and streets were almost bare of snow. In Railway Park, snow had been shoveled into hills; around the melting edges, the detritus of bottles and candy wrappers appeared. In the park, the sculptures from the competition at Kiruna's Snow Fest two months ago still stood, but they'd lost almost all definition. Here a swirl, there an indentation; mostly they were lumpy great blocks whose surfaces had melted and glazed as they'd shrunk. A balmy wind blew through town and, in particularly sunny patches, dry grass stretched up after a long cramped winter.

Stopping at the Folkets Hus, I'd noticed a display upstairs about Kiruna's upcoming move. Earlier that day the municipality had held a series of informational talks, soliciting opinions from the inhabitants of Kiruna; now, representatives of Swedish Railway System and the Highway System circled around the blown-up maps and plans, hoping to gather more comments. Even after I explained that I was just a visitor, they showed me around anyway. The citizens of Kiruna had gone home to dinner, so I would have to do.

Such a large-scale move was unprecedented in modern Swedish history, and various bureaucracies were concerned to present alternatives for the directions that the town could grow; the various schemas—"western alternative," "eastern alternative," and "central alternative"—were based on transportation first, and the fact that the LKAB mine also used the railway system. Once the all-important routes of trains and cars were figured out, human habitation could be planned around them. The planning process was very Swedish; the brochure I was given, "Kiruna— A Changing Town," was carefully laid out, with photographs of thoughtful-looking citizens of all ages, diagrams and tables of the decision-making process, simplified maps with arrows and lines. The mine was illustrated by a large gray oval around which the various possibilities for the railway and E10 circled, sometimes through, sometimes around, the ochre-shaded outlying areas of Kiruna and the small brown lump that indicated its center.

The brochure described Kiruna as:

* *a town built on a mountain in an arctic region*
* *snow-rich a large part of the year*
* *a town with strong resources: mining, reindeer herding, space research, environment, tourism.*

And asked some questions:

* *What's good about today's Kiruna?*
* *What would make Kiruna a beautiful town?*
* *How can Kiruna become a leader in the field of environment?*
* *What should a visitor experience in Kiruna?*

Optimistic city planners saw a great opportunity for Kiruna to reinvent itself. After all, they reminded us, Kiruna had a long history as a planned environment, at least at its inception in 1900. It was Sweden's first "climate-adapted" town; the houses were built on the hillside, where the air was slightly warmer, and the streets were shaped to minimize the winds, with abrupt turns and small squares. During the '60s many of the wooden houses were torn down, and apartment blocks went up instead, along with the community center and the large parking area in front of it: an eyesore the 364 days of the year when it wasn't being used as a track for racing reindeer. But the memory remained of Kiruna as Lundbohm's socialist experiment, where workers had had decent living quarters, a communal bathhouse, and schools for their children.

Now there was a chance to remake the town, with money from the government and LKAB. Kiruna could become not only architecturally attractive, but efficient, energy-conscious, a city of the future. As usual, there were naysayers and kibitzers. People whose homes and businesses were located above the subsidence zone were less than thrilled. People who stood to lose their views over the lake and valley were not happy. People who distrusted LKAB and the Swedish state muttered grimly that the mine was a monster, gobbling land. "What if we go to all the trouble to move the town, and then we have to move it again in a hundred years?" Historic preservationists warned that simply moving buildings from one spot to the next was complicated. "To move that church—you know, that church was voted the most beautiful building in Sweden in 2002—is a major undertaking. It took the city a year to figure out how to paint it, and then to do it. How do they think they're going to move it? And where?"

IngMari Lundmark, one of Kiruna's amateur historians, said, "Yes, you can move Hjalmar's house, of course you can move the house somewhere. But what about the birch woods around it? What about its close view of the mountain and the mine? That's what gives the house significance."

The Sami were, as so often, caught in the middle. If the town moved southeast, in the direction of the airport, it would encroach upon the district of the Laevas Sami; if it moved northwest, it would impact the Gabna Sami. The migration path of the reindeer from their winter pastures to the spring calving area in the mountains was already complicated and tenuous, carved out and negotiated across roads and railway lines, past the airport, around the mountain of Kirunavaara and the mine. What would happen if the mine took up twice as much land, and the town moved one way or the other?

After looking out the hotel window at the view for a long time, I slipped on my warm coat, left off the hat, and walked in the morning sunshine over to the Samegård, once the guest hostel for Sami living in Kiruna, and still a small hotel. It also housed the museum and some offices. In one of them, a young Sami named Hans Inga took the time to print out some maps for me of three neighboring Sami districts, or *samebys,* around Kiruna and Jukkasjärvi: Gabna, Laevas, and Talma, with black lines that showed how the reindeer herds migrated through this area.

Hans Inga was a member of the Laevas *sameby* and adept at utilizing a software program that had been developed for the Sami reindeer herders in 1998. Along with satellite photographs to show the best feeding grounds, GPS, and cell phones, the software was one of the many ways the adaptable Sami had used technology to help make modern reindeer husbandry efficient.

Yet the maps also showed the complex questions facing the Sami who lived in the districts around Kiruna. The *samebys* of Laevas and Gabna were long and narrow, their narrowest portion precisely where the town and mine proposed to expand. I'd known, theoretically, about the partition of Swedish Sápmi into reindeer districts; I'd seen their long, skinny shapes on maps often enough. But only in Hans Inga's office, and afterward, when I went off with the map printouts in my hand, could I see how Kiruna and the mine lay like twin spiders in the middle of this region, webbed in streets, encircled by industry.

This was not a new problem; the initial damage to the reindeer's winter grazing area and migration route had been done before—more than a hundred years ago—when Lundbohm surveyed Kirunavaara and became the managing director, when, with the best intentions, he tried to create a Utopian city for mine workers. The demand for iron ore had gone up and down, now it was increasing again. It drove Sweden's trade balance and was the reason for the king's visits to this apparently out-of-the-way place. In addition to the mine, Kiruna now had industry and a burgeoning space research program that included a campus in Kiruna and a rocket launch area called Esrange in Jukkasjärvi. Then there was tourism. Once it had been confined to the sunnier months, when Kiruna was a gateway to the mountains and brought skiers and hikers. Now tourism was, thanks to the Icehotel, a yearlong industry, with its own expansion plans, most of them in the area adjacent to Laevas and Gabna, in the Talma *sameby*.

Where were the Sami and their reindeer in the proposed move? The brochure about "Kiruna—A Changing Town" mentioned reindeer herding in passing—just one more element among many to be considered in the inevitable, indisputable reality of LKAB's need to expand—but there were no photographs in the brochure's tasteful spread of Sami herders or reindeer. The brochure's colorful maps, unlike Hans Inga's, showed none of the migration routes up into the mountains. In the competition for land and water, the Sami were likely to be losers again, as they had often been in their long history in Scandinavia. In Norway, especially on the Finnmark Plateau, the issue of Sami rights had gained traction in the last twenty years. But the Sami population was larger in Norway, from forty thousand to fifty thousand, in a country made wealthy by offshore oil and with an overall population of just four and a half million. In Sweden, there were only twenty thousand Sami, perhaps twenty-five hundred involved in reindeer husbandry, in a country of nine million Swedes, with an economy that depended on iron ore and hydroelectric power.

The Sami of Scandinavia's inland forests and tundra had always organized their society in *siidas*. Originally these were village units and kinship groups. Each *siida* controlled an area for its own use, and these areas had clear boundaries. The *siida* migrated within the boundaries of the area from spring to fall; in the winter its members gathered as a community in their winter villages. Before large-scale reindeer herding came to be, the inland Sami had a more diverse economy; they fished and hunted as well as grazed some reindeer. Their ownership of the forests, mountains, rivers, and tundra was based on "immemorial usage."

But what that meant had varied throughout the centuries; and sometimes it meant very little.

The first political divisions of Lapland began with the merchants who traded with the Sami from the fourteenth through sixteenth centuries; they broke the vast tracts of the North into so-called Lappmarks. Within these trade-specific Lappmarks, however, the Sami still formed themselves into *siidas*, still gathered in the winter and migrated in the summer and fall. In 1543 the Swedish King Gustav Vasa affirmed in a letter that the Sami could enjoy certain rights on their side of the Lapland border, but his son, Karl IX, replaced the *siida* system with church parishes. The state intended both to convert the Sami to Lutheranism and to incorporate them more fully into the Swedish tax system. Karl IX proclaimed the Norwegian coast and Finnmark to be part of Sweden; Denmark (which ruled Norway) and Russia also laid claim to them, which is why the Sami in the region were forced to pay taxes to all three countries. Eventually, of course, the coast and almost all of Finnmark went to Norway, and those Sami came under the rule of Denmark.

Meanwhile, in seventeenth-century Sweden, the state was busily encouraging agricultural settlement in Lapland. The Lappmark Proclamation of 1673 gave farmers the right to settle in the North without consulting the Sami about land and usage rights. In 1751 the border between Sweden and Norway was finally pinned down in a legal document. The Strömstad Border Treaty has a thirty-paragraph appendix known as the Lapp Codicil, what the Sami sometimes call the Sami Magna Carta. It states that the reindeer from Swedish Sápmi continue to have the right to cross the border into Norway. It also makes provision for Sami neutrality in case of war between Norway and Sweden. The Lapp Codicil has been in dispute almost since its signing, with Norway often having prohibited the migration on the grounds that it destroyed farm pastures in the valleys.

Over the next century the Swedish government issued a flurry of often contradictory letters and proclamations, sometimes claiming the right to all "vacant" land in its Northern provinces, sometimes recognizing the long-standing right of the Sami to use "vast mountain expanses such that only the Lapps and their reindeer can earn a livelihood there." Sometimes the government sought to protect the Sami, sometimes to disregard them, but always the state claimed its right over the choices of the Sami and its right to set the terms and conditions of Sami use of the land. The Reindeer Grazing Act of 1886 laid down the boundaries of the fifty-one *samebys* where the Sami might practice reindeer husbandry.

The *siidas* thus became *samebys* in Sweden, and the large areas that the Sami had used were geographically tightened and legislated. Most of the reindeer districts are long and thin in shape and trend slightly from south to north, from the winter grazing grounds at lower elevations to the calving areas and summer pastures in the high mountains. And the term "immemorial usage"? That was as subject to stretching and trimming as it ever was, especially when the State's economy was involved. After all, it was never as if the Sami actually *owned* any land in the North. The care with which the Sami had treated their environment worked against them. As Rauna Kuhmunen, a contemporary Sami scholar, has noted, "the fact that the Saami reindeer herding culture has left relatively few physical traces in the landscape has become a disadvantage for the Saami who need evidence in the form of cultural traces of our existence on our land."

Yesterday, while in the Folkets Hus, I'd picked up a handful of brochures outside the tourist office. I noticed that the Talma Sami's handout—addressed to guests visiting Jukkasjärvi—with its background on reindeer and dogs, its quiet plea for visitors to be respectful of the reindeer, was no longer to be found. Instead there were many more flyers offering dogsledding treks, many more attractively designed, full-color brochures touting the beauty of the North and of Untouched Lapland, Europe's Last Remaining Wilderness.

By now I was weary of this constant harping on Lapland as the last remaining wilderness in Europe. Certainly, compared to heavily urbanized regions of southern Europe, northern Scandinavia, with its boreal forests and tundra, was relatively empty. But everywhere people were fighting over the land. The Finns were cutting their forests, the Norwegians were prospecting for minerals on the Finnmark Plateau. The Sami were constantly in court to protect what reindeer habitat they still had left. Well-intentioned people who lived here battled too, over how much land should be used recreationally, for boating, hiking, and hunting, and how much should simply be set aside for animal and plant habitat. There was much in northern Sweden that could be considered wilderness—a string of national parks in the mountains, Sarek, Padjelanta, Stora Sjöfallet, and Muddus National Parks, all of which were now included in the UNESCO World Heritage Site, Laponia. Yet the Swedish national parks had highways and some facilities; they were popular backpacking and climbing destinations.

More important, all of the parks fell within one of the seven *samebys* of the region. Laponia, in fact, was a World Heritage Site not only because of its natural beauty, biological interest, and wildlife, but *because* it was a "cultural landscape," that is a landscape where the Sami and their Stone Age ancestors had lived for approximately nine thousand years. All over this area archaeologists had found the remains of dwelling sites, graves, fire pits, as well as tools, some dating back to the arrival of the first hunters in the North after the glaciers began to recede.

Lapland, particularly the slice of Lapland that surrounded Kiruna, was only a "wilderness" in the parallel reality of promotional language. It was hardly a wilderness for any tourist who walked around Kiruna, took the mining tour, or even went up the stairs of the community center to see the displays about the moving of the town. It was a wilderness constructed for tourists who lived farther south in cities, tourists who could be whisked from the Kiruna airport directly to the Icehotel for three days under the *impression* that they were at the end of the known world. Untouched Lapland played on the longing of many of us from cities for the pristine, the undefiled. We didn't know, perhaps did not want to know, about the vanishing reindeer pastures, the clear-cutting, the hydroelectric stations, dams, and mines.

The complaint of some in Kiruna that the tourists never came into town and that the Icehotel tried to keep them out in Jukkasjärvi eating at the restaurant and shopping in the gift store was valid. To come into town, to see the offices and apartment buildings, the parking lots, and then to see a huge mine in operation right nearby would break the spell that the visitors were in virgin territory, in a Northern fairy tale. I, too, as soon as I'd arrived in Kiruna several years ago, had only wanted to get away from it.

Rebecca Solnit talks about the issues of wilderness and indigenous people in her book *Savage Dreams,* half of which is devoted to Yosemite. In 1864 Abraham Lincoln set aside the Yosemite Valley as a park to be overseen by the new state of California. Like the Shoshone, who were ousted from Yellowstone, the native Ahwahneechee of Yosemite were pushed out by the first whites; and a mind-bogglingly short time after their eviction came writers like John Muir and photographers like Carleton Watkins and Ansel Adams to conceptualize for the rest of us what Nature should look like, to erase in ecstatic prose and to crop out via the camera lens all evidence of settlement and cultivation. "Millions of people a year," writes Solnit, "crowd together here to see virgin wilderness, a natural phenomenon they recognize thanks to cultural intermediaries."

The same method could be seen in how Lapland was presented to the rest of the world, as empty and pristine, as a painting of snowy tundra and frosted trees, to be looked at and admired. The United States Wilderness Act of 1964 defines wilderness as "a place where man is a visitor," that is, a viewer who comes, photographs, and leaves. In this view nature is a thing apart from us and we can thus imagine it as untouched, and worship it as undefiled in a world where so much else has been exploited and destroyed. It's hard for the Eurocentric imagination to see a landscape as both inhabited and undefiled; it must not be inhabited if it is beautiful. The recurring words "Untouched Lapland" in the tourist literature spoke to that dream of landscape as pure, and the images used to illustrate that purity were heavily censored and controlled. The only history that was admitted was sanitized: a man in a blue and red *gákti,* often seen from a distance or from the back, leading reindeer across a snowy terrain.

This manner of visualizing the North was no new thing; yet my British travelers, Butler, Gourlie, and Chapman, however rhapsodic their prose about landscape, had never presumed to present Lapland as empty. Empty of foreign visitors, yes, but not empty of people altogether. Their travel descriptions invariably mentioned the Sami households and communities of northern Scandinavia. Condescending as the British might be about the locals, at least they saw them in the landscape. The new versions of the landscape presented to tourists emphasized wilderness, and even the tourism organized by the Sami fell into that mode.

One of the brochures I found in the racks of the Folkets Hus especially irritated me when I first opened it up. Against a stunning two-page spread of well-wrapped-up tourists, each in his or her own wooden sledge pulled by a reindeer, the reindeer harnessed together in a line, all of them traveling on what looked to be the frozen, snow-covered Torne River, the text in English and Swedish read:

> It could be today, yesterday, or a thousand years ago, because the landscape of Sápmi is practically unchanged in all that time. The

brilliant midwinter light which takes you through the same splendid forests, tundra and magnificent mountain ranges is the same as it ever was.

Our forefathers and we, the present day Sami, live and have lived close to nature for thousands of years.

I paged bad-humoredly through the irresistible images of the brochure: reindeer herds, lakes and forests, the Icehotel, the old-fashioned buildings at Jukkasjärvi. Not a single picture of the mine, the industrial area of Kiruna, the airport, the highway, even the town. Not a single picture of a Sami wearing ordinary clothes, driving a car, talking on a cell phone.

At least there were no dogs, I thought. At least this company, Sápmi Journeys, seemed to be Sami-owned. At least it was respectful and non-exploitative; it didn't treat the Sami simply as local color. As I calmed down, I looked more carefully at the familiar images of the brochure and realized that this was the outfit down the road from the Icehotel; this was where I had had my own encounter with reindeer racing, my meal in the tent with the bachelors and Ailo.

I decided that when I went to Jukkasjärvi in the next couple of days, I would see if I could speak with the people who ran Sápmi Journeys.

I found Nils Thorbjörn Nutti, a compact, athletic man of about forty, dressed in jeans and a zippered ski shirt, sitting in front of his computer in his office upstairs from a souvenir shop in the small historic area of Jukkasjärvi. He offered me a cup of coffee and we sat down to talk in between his two tourist groups of the day. It was getting near the end of the season, but tourists were still coming to the Icehotel, still signing up for an adventure with Sápmi Journeys.

Nils grew up in a reindeer-herding family in the Saarivuoma district, which borders that of the Talma. He lives in Svappavaara, down the E10, about twenty miles from Jukkasjärvi. He'd originally worked with Yngve Bergqvist, the CEO of the Icehotel, getting tourists over to Svappavaara, but Yngve eventually suggested an arrangement by which Nils set up shop down the road from the Icehotel. This was after Yngve and the local Talma Sami, in whose district the Icehotel is located, had a falling-out.

Yngve had a personal friendship with Nils as well as a satisfying business relationship. Sápmi Journeys was featured in Icehotel brochures and their Web sites were linked. For most tourists on package tours, it made sense that the tent down the road was their first contact with the Sami. In the eyes of the local Talma Sami, Nils was "imported." To them, this was a crucial distinction. To tourists, who could hardly grasp where they were, much less that all this wintry barrenness had a history, it meant nothing. All Sami were the same, weren't they?

"I consider myself a kind of cultural ambassador," Nils told me. "We are the first and usually the only contact a tourist from abroad will have with the Sami."

Nils was not the first Sami to go into the tourist business, but until the last ten years, it had been relatively rare. Up in the high mountains to the west, at a place called Nikkaluokta, the Sarri family had been working with tourists since around 1910. They were one of five Sami families from northern Norway who settled near the intersection of three valleys at what is now the gateway to Sweden's highest peak, Kebnekaise. Already reindeer herding was seen as insufficient as a means of supporting a family, and the Sarri family soon became involved with the burgeoning Swedish hiking movement. Until 1971, when a road up to Nikkaluokta from Kiruna was finished, most of their energy went into transporting tourists up into the mountains. Now they own a thriving tourist center at the end of the road that includes a conference center, cabins, a restaurant, and shop. The Sarri family still practice some reindeer husbandry, but they are members neither of the Laevas or Gabna districts. Their tourist complex, visited by twenty-five thousand each year, sits in between the two *samebys* and the spring and autumn migration paths of their reindeer herds.

For years, the Sarris were considered sell-outs by other Sami; now, with a younger generation finding it next to impossible to make a decent living from reindeer, cultural tourism has taken root, and the Sarris are now seen as smart, savvy businesspeople who have recently taken to providing cultural information about the Sami as well as overnight accommodations and meals. According to recent statistics, there are now about forty Sami-owned tourist enterprises in Swedish Sápmi. A dissertation by Robert Pettersson notes that they're not excessively commercial and that most are conducted in connection with the reindeer-herding life. Many of the enterprises are owned by women, who use the income to supplement what the family earns from reindeer. Most of the enterprises are modest. You could visit or stay in a tent, hear *joiking,* eat Sami food, practice your lasso-throwing and sled-driving. You could purchase Sami handicrafts, eat some reindeer with home-made bread, hear a little of the old ways, if you were so inclined. Pettersson quoted one of his interviewees:

> It's a thin line. We're here to sell them our everyday lives, but these lives are the same as other people's lives. So there has to be a touristification. Entrepreneurs must decide for themselves where to draw the line, but they must create a saleable and interesting product.

Some of the more ambitious of the young Sami tourist entrepreneurs offered treks with reindeer, such as Pathfinder, run by

Lennart Pittja, whom I'd met last year outside Gällivare. Like Nils, Lennart was serious about finding a way to make money from visitors to Sápmi in an ethical way. Both Pathfinder and Sápmi Journeys are members of an organization called Nature's Best, which only gives their seal of approval to environmentally responsible tourism. The Sami tourist organizations promote tourism based on culture and activities with reindeer; they do not run dogs or organize snowmobiling expeditions. They see their role as partly educational, and not only in regard to foreign tourists, but also to Swedes. For, still, in the twenty-first century, the Sami figure very little in Swedish history classes. There had been, in fact, something of a backlash against them since the late 1980s, when they began to achieve greater visibility and a small measure of power.

Wasn't it better that Sami represented themselves to tourists rather than having their culture used and distorted? Wasn't it better that they themselves were able to profit from the selling of their culture? Because tourist operators everywhere in the far North had seen that the Sami were a draw. "I employ twelve people at the height of the winter season, six people year-round," Nils told me. "I educate the young people who work for me about their culture and history, give them a chance to share that with tourists, as well as to think about their own heritage. What other kind of work could the Sami do that would combine with reindeer herding?"

He told me frankly that he sat in two chairs. He wanted to see tourism regulated—particularly some fast-growing areas like snowmobiling in the forest and dogsledding—yet at the same time he wished to see it expand. He wanted the culture of the Sami better known, yet he wanted to keep it "exotical."

I didn't need to point out the contradictions to Nils. He was a smart and caring man who knew far more than I ever would about the complexities of living as a member of a minority indigenous group in a larger society that both wanted to use you and assimilate you, depending on the fashion of the time. Yet, I walked away from our conversation troubled, not by him—I'd liked him very much—but by something I could hardly put into words.

I looked at the two tents on the other side of the Jukkasjärvi church and the corral in the distance, where a quick movement through the trees told me there were reindeer. I remembered my ride around the track—it had been fun, of course—and the meal that Ailo prepared for us on that bitter cold day around the fire. I recalled the taste of the coffee and the fried reindeer, and the stories that he told us. They'd been wasted on the bachelors, perhaps, but in me the spark had gradually caught fire.

I hadn't, as it turned out, been satisfied with one afternoon of Sami culture. I had instead learned more and more, on my own and through people I met, like Jorma Lehtola and Lillemor Baer. I'd allowed my interest in Johan Turi and Emilie Demant Hatt to ripen. I'd come to the North years ago as an escape from my life at the time, through a yearning to see something completely different: darkness and ice. I'd found myself in a tent with five British bachelors and Ailo, and, without knowing it, my life had begun to change.

Who was to say that couldn't happen with others who came here to Jukkasjärvi, others who, without the chance to see something of Sami culture, would merely stay overnight in the Icehotel, take a dogsledding trip, and return to London or Tokyo? Nils and the guides who worked with him wouldn't encourage either romantic or harmful stereotypes of the Sami, the ones that many Swedes had grown up with. They'd make sure the visitor went away with a sense of the long history of the Sami and their connection with this land. They'd give the urban dweller some taste of a culture that went back thousands of years, no small thing to offer those of us who are rootless without being nomadic.

What troubled me then? Perhaps that this form of Sami tourism, sitting in tents, was only a representation of the past. It was, at its most innocent, as Pettersson's informant admitted, "touristification." At its worst it perpetrated a myth that the Sami still lived in their *lávvus,* still wore *gákti* every day, and still traveled by reindeer. Admittedly I'd gone much further in my explorations of Sami culture than most would, but what had helped were festivals, museums, and conferences organized by contemporary Sami out of the experience of having a foot in both worlds. At the film festival in Inari, I'd begun to understand the Sami as important actors on the world stage when it came to indigenous rights. I'd admired their commitment to the past and their adaptability as a people who did not see themselves apart from the world, but made common cause with Amazonian Indians, Guatemalan Indians, Alaskan Inuit. Their interests were often broader and more sophisticated than their apparent isolation in the far North would lead one to expect. The Norwegian Sami Ole Henrik Magga, for instance, was the chairman of the UN Permanent Forum for Indigenous Issues who'd grown up in a reindeer-herding family in Kautokeino and, after studying biology and mathematics at the university, did a doctorate in Sami linguistics and became a professor.

Was a brief tourist visit to a tent, a ride on a reindeer sledge, a step to understanding Sami history, Sami resilience, Sami political goals? Or was it a hindrance; did it keep the Sami firmly in the distant past, no threat to anyone? And what about this notion of wilderness? That the Icehotel and the Kiruna-based tourist businesses promoted Untouched Lapland was not surprising, but that the Sápmi Journeys brochure extolled a landscape that "was practically unchanged" for a thousand years seemed to be against history, against the modern Sami political struggle, against the evidence of one's own eyes.

I walked away from the tents and the corral, through wet, soft snow around the little red church to the small cemetery, to the large granite stone that marks the spot where Johan Turi was buried in 1936. I suspected that few tourists ever walked through the churchyard and that fewer would know who Turi was if they were to come across this granite marker. Yet at his funeral, the red wooden church behind me had been filled with mourners.

I thought about the Sami way of inhabiting Sápmi, which was not to see Nature as something else, something outside oneself, but as a living consciousness. That had been Turi's way; he had, in fact, been incapable perhaps of seeing landscape differently than as home to animals, including the human animal. One of my favorite passages in *Muitalas sámiid birra* described the Sami custom of greeting their summer camp thus:

> *Hail to you, hail to you, Mother and living place!* And then they give something, and so they beg the Haldes [spirits] to take care of their herds, so that the reindeer do not die, and the calves grow big.

> The Lapps call the earth, or their living places *duovddagat* (literally "ground that is lived on," in contrast to the wild tracts). They say, when it is a beautiful *duovddagat,* or a good reindeer *duovddagat,* that it is such a lovely *duovddagat* that it smiles.

> And when you are good, and all things go well, then you think that the whole living-place rejoices, and when things are sad and you sorrow, then you think that the whole living-place weeps, and all the stones and trees and everything in the whole world, and it does not gladden you any longer, and nothing that was nice before is nice any longer, and the days are so long that they never seem to end. And when it is a bad place for reindeer, then it is a bad living-place.

The landscape, I tried to remember as I walked away from Turi's stone in the direction of the frozen Torne River, is not *out there*. We are part of it, we use it, we love it—or should love it— not because it is beautiful, but because it is our living-place.

15. "AS LONG AS WE HAVE WATERS"

A MILE AND WORLDS AWAY from the Icehotel, I was spending the day with Lillemor Baer, the reindeer herder I'd met last year. I sat in the kitchen of her rambler-style house in Jukkasjärvi, while she made lunch. She placed several whole salmon trout in a pan and scooped up about a cup of soft butter and dumped it on top, then stuck it in the oven. Then she put another giant knob of butter in a cast-iron frying pan and melted it on top of the stove, before throwing in chunks of smoked reindeer meat. "No vegetables," she commented. It was an Atkins Dieter's dream.

Earlier we'd done some driving around in the district. I'd asked her to show me the Talma *sameby* winter grazing lands. I'd expressed some hope that we might see her reindeer. No, she said, they were already up in the mountains, most of them, but perhaps we'd find an old reindeer she'd been looking for. She had some dried moss in the back of her station wagon that she'd feed him if we found him. He was about seven years old, she told me, *old,* and she'd nursed him when he'd been sick once, which made him tame.

She'd picked me up in the parking lot of the Icehotel. She looked the same as I remembered her: small and active, with short, straight reddish-brown hair and brown eyes above high cheekbones in a rounded, slightly weathered face. As we drove through Jukkasjärvi's few streets into the forest, we passed a tourist group of snowmobilers. The light was strong, but it wasn't sunny; in fact, snow would begin to fall in a few more hours. Lillemor stopped her Volvo from time to time to show me something. "See, that's where reindeer have been grazing, you can tell. Underneath the trees, where the snow is gone, those bare patches. This is the kind of landscape that the reindeer like in winter, under the Scots pine, where the moss grows."

She stopped the car again to point across the forest to a mountain in the west. "That's where the reindeer are," she said. "Kattuvuoma. Up by Torneträsk. They left early this year, they weren't happy with the winter grazing areas."

"Do reindeer just leave?" I asked, "Do you try to stop them, or slow them down?"

"If the reindeer simply want to move, we can stop them. If they *really* want to move, we can't."

Reindeer are sensitive creatures. When they're disturbed, they migrate, when they don't have enough food, they migrate, when there are too many dogs or snowmobiles or noise, they just go. The Talma *sameby* has, collectively, about six thousand reindeer, owned by about a hundred people, though in unequal numbers. Lillemor's reindeer are her own, earmarked with her cut. She brought her herd with her when she came to Jukkasjärvi to live with Lars Jonas Allas in 1982. She doesn't work with the herd herself during the migrations, however, but leaves the management of getting the reindeer from one place to another to one of the Allas brothers, Börje.

We turned into a drive and parked near a house that belonged to yet another Allas brother, Per Olaf. The Allas family is well known to those at the Icehotel and in Kiruna, few of whom would refer to them by name, but instead as, more cryptically, "that family you have mentioned." The Allases had been outspoken for a long time on the subject of tourism, and dogsledding, and their rights in general. They were not shy about using the law when they could. This branded them as troublemakers.

Per Olaf came out to greet us as we sat in the car and told Lillemor that her old reindeer hadn't been seen for a week, that he'd probably left for the mountains. While they talked, I looked around. On top of a shed roof was a tangle of antlers and a reindeer head with antlers attached. The cold had kept it from decomposing, and it still seemed to stare over the yard calmly regarding us. There were two reindeer skins being stretched, in traditional fashion, over an oval of branches. Several snowmobiles in various states of readiness were parked in the yard.

When we set off again, Lillemor told me about the reindeer and said, "This will probably be his last winter." She said that Per Olaf's mother was already up at Kattuvuoma, and that the rest of them would follow soon.

Lillemor's year goes like this:

From November to sometime in April she and Lars Jonas and Per Olaf's family, who make up a grouping in the Talma *sameby,* live in their houses in Jukkasjärvi, near the winter grazing grounds. April through July is spent up in Kattuvuoma, where they also have homes, on the northeastern side of Torneträsk, the huge mountain lake that was the source of the Torne River. Kattuvuoma, on a relief map of the mountains, is a tiny speck in the middle of nowhere. The major highway, the E10—which comes up through northern Sweden to Kiruna and then turns west through the mountains before dropping sharply down to the Norwegian city of Narvik on the Ofotfjord—skirts the southern side of Torneträsk. In the past, Kattuvuoma could be reached only by boat, and that's still how Lillemor and the rest of the family get there in summer.

Near Kattuvuoma is where the calving takes place in May. In July and August the herd moves across the border to Norway, to feed on the rich grass in the valleys, and Lillemor and the others go with the animals and live in tents. The young calves are earmarked during this time; the owners spot them together with their more recognizable mothers. Then they return, the Sami and the reindeer, to Kattuvuoma, sometime in late August and September. In early October comes the roundup and sorting of the reindeer back into ownership groups, and then the reindeer migrate back to their winter grazing lands around Jukkasjärvi. Slaughtering time is in December.

In recent years, slaughtering, as I'd heard from many people, had not brought in much income. Reindeer meat was being imported from Russia, at much cheaper prices. Since the breakup of the Soviet Union, the Skolt Sami of Russia's Kola Peninsula had been permitted to market their reindeer for profit; there were others in Russia who raised reindeer for slaughter as well. In Russia, unlike Norway and Sweden, the exclusive rights of Sami to participate in reindeer herding wasn't defended.

"We tend our reindeer, we take care of them, but we aren't making money from them," said Lillemor. "It's a big problem."

Russian meat production that cut into Sami sales is one problem; another is the lingering effect of Chernobyl. In April of 1986, winds blew radiation north to central Scandinavia. In south Sápmi, the radioactive particles came down with the rain and contaminated the lichen, which is one of the mainstays of the reindeer's diet. Some thirty thousand head of reindeer were destroyed that fall when it was found that the meat contained dangerous levels of cesium. The industry had recovered slowly from that natural catastrophe. Slaughtering often now took place in early fall before the reindeer began to paw the snow for the lichen underneath.

The Norwegian and Swedish states intervened constantly in the business of reindeer herding, and had done so for two hundred years, deciding where the reindeer could graze, how many herds could be accommodated in an area, and who was allowed to carry on the herding tradition. The states saw value in keeping the Sami and their reindeer viable; the question was how the industry should be managed. Environmentally, the reindeer—at least too many reindeer—were sometimes held to be destructive to habitat. By forcing the Sami to become more "efficient," that is, to focus on reindeer as animals for slaughter only and to build up herds of few males and many females, the states had contributed to the mechanization of herding. The Sami now relied on snowmobiles and helicopters to herd the reindeer. There wasn't time to simply follow the animals back and forth on the migration paths. The Sami now had houses, many people also had other jobs, and then there were the children—they needed to be in school. The reindeer were often trucked to and from their grazing grounds, and helicopters flew above, dropping bales of hay for them to feed on in remote areas.

Then there was the issue of predators. In times past, the bear, the wolf, the lynx, and the wolverine had been the bane of the Sami. A wolverine could move into a herd and destroy half a dozen animals, more than it could eat. A pack of wolves could decimate a small herd. Turi had been a wolf hunter at a time when the Sami relied upon such men to protect the herds, but all Sami had grown up fearing the power of predators. Yet, by the end of the twentieth century, with wolves almost extinct in Norwegian-Swedish mountains and wilderness areas, a different policy had come to prevail. The Swedish state, for instance, had made it a new priority to protect the wolf and to monitor its revival. Reindeer herders were reimbursed for each animal that a wolf had killed. Reimbursed, that is, if a Sami could find the dead reindeer and prove a wolf had killed it.

The Sami, who had to bear the burden of being romanticized as ecological saints, as a people who had lived in harmony with nature and whose wise use of land had preserved much of northern Scandinavia, were also paradoxically cast as environmental villains, who had "too many" reindeer for the fragile tundra and mountains and who would shoot a wolf as soon as look at it.

Lillemor and I had come by this time to the end of the road. In front of us was a large closed security gate, with cameras and a manned booth. It looked like something out of a James Bond film. This was the entrance to Esrange, a space research facility run by the Swedish Space Corporation, a company owned since 1972 by the government. Kiruna and its environs had early had a connection with auroral and upper atmosphere research. The Kiruna Geophysical Observatory, established in 1957, had become the Institute for Space Physics (IRF). I'd never visited its campus below the mountain of Kirunavaara, but the bus from Kiruna to Jukkasjärvi went by it and dropped off and picked up space engineering students and researchers. IRF focused on phenomena in Earth's upper atmosphere, the ionosphere, and planetary magnetospheres—layers and layers above us in the sky that most of us, usually concerned with a radius of a few feet around our person, rarely think about. They routinely measured for radiation of the human-error sort as well as for solar radiation. Lately, of course, they had contributed measurements of the thinning ozone layer.

Esrange was Sweden's small version of Cape Canaveral, with facilities to launch rockets, unmanned spacecraft, and weather balloons. Esrange was initially built in 1966 by ESRO, the European Space Research Organization, which included Belgium, Denmark, France, the Netherlands, Italy, Switzerland, Spain, the U.K., Sweden, and Germany. The aim was to establish a coordinated program for peaceful space research. Cooperation among the European countries lasted a relatively short time. By 1972, the Swedish government was running the site as the only civilian space center in Europe. Swedish researchers have developed services that can be used commercially, such as maritime surveillance systems and remote sensing or satellite pictures. There's now a Space Division and a Remote Sensing Division.

Esrange also makes its facilities available to researchers from elsewhere in the world who wish to launch their own rockets and balloons. The site includes a central complex with offices and conference rooms, a restaurant (the Space Inn), several hotels, a radar station, a satellite receiving station and a GPS reference station, garages for cars, buildings for payload preparation for the balloons and rockets, chemical laboratories, ground observation stations, and rocket and balloon launching pads.

Esrange had been on my radar screen, so to speak, for quite a while. Attracted by the brochure in the Folkets Hus that showed a lovely green sweep of Northern Lights, I had almost made a tourist office–sponsored visit out here last year but had run out of time. I knew that Kiruna was one of the Aurora Borealis monitoring stations, along with Tromsø and Sodankylä, Finland, for the wonderfully named European Incoherent Scatter Facility, or EISCAT. I continued to feel gypped that I so rarely saw the "magnificent sight of the Northern Lights in the polar sky," as the brochure put it. Perhaps enhancing my experience of this dazzling spectacle with knowledge about what I was seeing, to paraphrase its text, would help with actually seeing the Aurora. I'd also understood that Kiruna was marketing "scientific tourism" to Northern visitors, and that Esrange was part of the push to attract more tourists to these parts.

The one thing I hadn't grasped from the material I'd read about Esrange was its location: nearly eight square miles in the middle of the winter grazing grounds of the Talma *sameby* reindeer herds.

The story of Lapland is the story of colonization, exploration, and expropriation; and that hasn't ended even though contemporary Sami now have parliaments, cross-country cooperation, and links with the Human Rights Commission at the U.N. All over Sápmi the Sami are struggling with state and private interests over how traditional grazing lands are being taken and used for other purposes than providing reindeer with the habitat they need. In Finland, the Inari Sami have seen their forests reduced to stumps by a state-owned wood products company. They've fought back by taking their issue to the U.N. and contacting NGOs to help them make the story visible. In return they've been harassed by forestry workers and the local Finnish population. In Norway, an international mining company has secured rights to gold and platinum discovered on the Finnmark Plateau, not far from Karasjok. Ninety-six percent of the plateau now used for grazing reindeer is claimed by the Norwegian state, which has granted the mining rights to Tertiary Minerals, based in England. The Sami Parliament in Karasjok disputes the authority of the Norwegian government to give away such natural resources and not to involve the Sami in decisions that could mean both destruction and profit. Battles also loom over oil and gas exploration in the far North; the Sami have already begun to organize to protect the landscape from the effects of the environmental damage that will certainly result from mining and oil and gas projects.

Most though not all Sami districts in Sweden have something in their grazing areas to contend with—a town, a ski resort, hiking, and fishing lakes. In the district farthest south in Sápmi, the Idre *sameby* was contesting plans to invest more than a billion Swedish kronor into the ski resorts that already exist in the mountains. The point of view of the ski resorts is that Sweden needs to build more lifts and develop more slopes, allow for more vacation housing and the infrastructure to support it. They plan to develop the land, they say, in a way that will be environmentally friendly in addition to creating three hundred new full-time jobs in the tourist industry. Against them are pitted the thirteen reindeer owners of the *sameby,* who have pointed out from the beginning of the project that the ski resort developments would cut off the reindeer migration path between the winter grazing grounds below and the upland summer pastures. Already the emphasis on increasing tourism in the area has created more snowmobile courses in winter. As for the summer pastures, recently a golf course was built squarely in the middle of them.

The Leavas *sameby* had Kiruna's airport, part of the town of Kiruna, and, up in their mountain area, skiing in the winter and hiking in the summer. The Gabna Sami had the LKAB mine and Kiruna, as well as the famous tourist spots of Abisko and Riksgrensen in the mountains. "We have the Icehotel in the south of our district and Esrange in the north," said Lillemor as we drove back down the road, back toward Jukkasjärvi. "We have no idea how much land the state eventually will decide to appropriate for Esrange. We have very little say in the matter."

I had heard at the Icehotel about plans for getting more of that hotel's guests out to the space facility. "They're launching huge balloons—*huge*—that will float over to Canada and gather information about the ozone layer." There was talk of shooting people up in space, just so they could feel how it was to be weightless. Now I was seeing Esrange from a wholly different perspective, that of a reindeer frightened by loudspeakers and kept out by fences.

Lars Jonas joined us for lunch, along with a godson in his twenties. Per had trained to be a pilot, but had decided to become a reindeer herder instead and was learning something of the trade from Lars Jonas and Lillemor. The men had been out in the snow dismantling the engine of one of the snowmobiles and came in, washed up, and tucked into the fish and the reindeer, served with home-baked flat bread. Lars Jonas had a way of speaking Swedish that seemed inflected by Sami, so much so that I couldn't understand him well and was sorry to miss what I could tell was a good sense of humor. The joke at lunch was how Per had learned piloting at the state's expense, but couldn't learn reindeer herding that way. It's unusual for anyone who isn't born into a herding family and inherits reindeer to become a herder. Seven or eight hundred head is the minimum, Lillemor had told me, and really you need more because of bad years, and there always are bad years.

There are Sami, of course, who own fewer reindeer, and they pay others to work with them. A number of Sami need to work other jobs. Often, it's the women in the family who work outside the home while their partners and sons manage the herd. Some women who own reindeer are reluctant to marry, since the rules of the *sameby* specify that only the "head of the household" can become a full voting member of the community. Since in Sweden it's common that couples don't formally marry anyway, this is not always a problem; an unmarried woman can vote. Still, Sami women reindeer herders are few and chafe at the outdated barriers to married women gaining full membership in the *sameby*. Lillemor is active in the *sameby* and works with reindeer, but she still takes on outside jobs from time to time. One of them is to work with archeologists at Sami sites from the past. They clear away the brush and trees where there were once old corrals and slaughter pits, and in some cases reconstruct the corrals.

The two men ate hugely, and then we had coffee. Lillemor had gone outside and brought in one of the chunks of reindeer meat that was air-drying in a line of chunks from hooks along the porch. The meat was cured in the same way that Spain's *jamon Serrano* was, in the cold winter wind, and had the same glassine look when sliced into thin strips.

Lillemor advised me to put the strips in my black coffee. "Studies have shown," she told me with a smile, "that the stimulus you get from coffee with reindeer meat, especially pieces with fat, is much greater. People can go a long time without eating a meal if they drink lots of coffee with reindeer like this."

The reindeer gave the coffee a salty tang, not unpleasant.

"We are thinking of starting a reindeer food business here in Jukkasjärvi that would bring more value to the animal's meat." She thought that visitors to the Icehotel would possibly buy dried and cured reindeer in packages. I chose this moment to ask her about tourism. Did she think that was an occupation that combined with herding?

She looked thoughtful. "We tried to do tourism," she said. "When the Icehotel first came, we arranged some tours, talked with people. But then more and more people were coming to the hotel, it was going in the way of mass tourism. . . . The problems started with the dogsledding. . . ." She stopped, as if she didn't want to get into that right now, and then sighed.

"Last year, I used to go out on the main road of Jukkasjärvi with the brochures about dogsledding. I would stop individuals and tell them about the Talma Sami, the Sami who lived in this area. I would try to educate them, one by one. They were often very nice people. They listened. But it's tiring. And you don't know if it really changes anything overall. This winter"—she paused—"I haven't really felt like it."

I told her that I didn't see as many of the brochures around as last year.

"The Scandic Hotel won't let us put them in the lobby. We asked to meet with them. They wouldn't."

Then I told her a little about my conversation with Nils Thorbjörn Nutti, and how I had learned something from my odd afternoon with the bachelors, Ailo, and the reindeer on that very first visit.

She sighed again. "The problem is: to sit in a tent, to guide people around on reindeer, it doesn't say anything about how we live now. It's historical. When you talk about Sami life that way, you become exotic, you become what the tourists want. How do you work with tourists and not become what the tourists want to hear and see? If I were to work with tourists, I would tell them about our rights. Our rights to land and water. That's what I would focus on. Not sitting in a tent like in the history books. Or having reindeer in a corral down here in the summer. The reindeer have their noses pointing toward the mountains. That's where they want to be."

Lillemor, I knew, was very conscious of Sami rights. She had a small office in this house, and there she'd shown me notebooks labeled by years, beginning sometime in the 1600s, that showed the taxes that individual Sami had paid to the Swedish state, in the form of fur pelts, dried fish, and reindeer meat and skins. Yet while the Nordic states gave away land to Norwegian, Finnish, and Swedish settlers for animal husbandry and farming, and their taxes proved ownership, the Sami's taxes were never considered proof of anything.

Sami scholars have begun to challenge the general belief that the Sami were "vagabond Lapps" who did not own land. They point to the *siida* system of the Sami, in which individual groups migrated within carefully defined boundaries. Families held the land in common and claimed exclusive rights to use their specified areas for fishing and reindeer herding. Outsiders were only welcome on the land if they came for trade or in marriage negotiations. Each *siida* had an assembly that managed resources and controlled the admittance of new members. Every member of the *siida* had voting rights. When the settlers from outside the *siidas* began to come into traditional Sami areas to farm, initially the two groups lived side by side. They intermarried and the settlers purchased land from the Sami. It was in the 1700s that the states began to seize traditional Sami land without compensation or acknowledgment, and to claim that the Sami had never owned it in the first place.

For many modern-day Sami, the majority in fact—long disenfranchised of their reindeer herding and fishing rights—the taxes paid, the agreements reached, the border issues meant little or nothing. Their emergent identity as Sami was based on culture and language. But for the 10 percent of the Sami who own reindeer, reindeer husbandry is what makes one Sami, and laws, taxes, and history are still crucial in maintaining Sami rights. To Lillemor, the Lapp Codicil wasn't ancient history, something for the history books. It was part of a treaty between Norway and Sweden that should still be honored. She and other Sami often met with lawyers in Stockholm to pursue their case, and she seemed to think that it would soon conclude with the right of the Talma *sameby* to cross into Norway more freely than they could now. For Norway was now in the forefront of Sami rights, attempting to enshrine in law what had been foggy for so long.

When I was a high school student we had a social studies teacher who opened our eyes to the reality of the American government's mistreatment of the Indians. But even he never suggested that the Indians could overturn history. He spoke only sorrowfully of all the treaties broken, as if treaties, signed and sealed, could just be forgotten. Many Sami reindeer herders, Lillemor among them, declared that agreements could not just be put aside. They were still valid.

Snow had begun to fall outside, thick, fat flakes, but still Lars Jonas and Per worked on the snowmobiles. Lillemor and I drank more coffee, and she showed me photographs of her parents and her sisters. All the sisters owned reindeer, and all of them, she insisted, smiling, were as determined on justice as she was. One sister was active in forestry and traveled often to Canada to work with indigenous groups there.

On her walls were paintings by Sami artists. I thought I recognized a painting by Lars Pirak. In a corner glass display case she had half a dozen beautifully carved knives and other Sami *duodji*. While Lillemor answered the phone, I looked through bookshelves and took out a Swedish-Sami edition of *Giela giela* (*Ensare the Language*), a poetry book by Paulus Utsi, the teacher of *duodji* in Jokkmokk and witness to the deforestation and damming of the North.

As long as we have waters where the fish can swim
As long as we have woods where the reindeer can graze
As long as we have woods where the wild animals can hide
We are safe on this earth.

When our homes are gone and our land is destroyed
—then where are we to be?

I also pulled out her copy of Emilie Demant Hatt's *With the Lapps in the High Mountains.* It was up at Torneträsk that Demant Hatt and Turi had lived together in the fall of 1908, working on his book *Muitalus sámiid birra.* Demant Hatt had traveled in those mountains to the places that the Talma Sami called home in the spring and fall, including Kattuvuoma. A year or so ago, passing through Stockholm, I'd taken a look at Demant Hatt's Lapland paintings, which were stored in the basement of the Nordiska Museum. She had bequeathed them to the big Swedish museum in part because of her friendship with the Swedish anthropologist Ernst Manker, who had done much to record and collect the culture of the Sami in the first half of the twentieth century and who'd helped establish the museum.

With the help of one of the curators, I'd photographed the canvases, most painted during the '30s and '40s. Reindeer caravans crossed ice bridges in the polar blue light; tents glowing like triangular orange lanterns dotted the snowy tundra. Figures in blue and red warmed their hands around a yellow fire under a starry sky streaked with the Aurora. I could almost breathe the cold in the air, know the numbness in my feet and hands as I looked at the canvases.

I'd given Lillemor an enlarged photograph of one of the paintings, of women in a boat, crossing Törnetrask. I said I wished Demant Hatt's Lapland paintings could be on view somewhere.

"The local government asked for comments about the 'new Kiruna,'" I said. "I thought of writing on the comment sheet, *Build an art museum. Bring Emilie Demant Hatt's paintings of the landscape and the Sami here.*"

Lillemor had earlier told me about the plan to build a new parliament for the Sami, a building of their own, not just a renovated schoolhouse. The prime minister had set aside a large chunk of money. The Swedish Sami Parliament would rival Norway's in Karasjok. It would be part of the new Kiruna.

"They've had some meetings to get our input," said Lillemor, "asked us what we wanted. Everybody, all the Sami, at the meeting had the same idea. 'We want it to be welcoming,' we said. 'For everybody. We want it to be like—a kitchen.' A kitchen where you didn't have to ask, where you could just come in, make yourself a cup of coffee, sit down and stay.

"It's not like that now. They meet you in the reception of the parliament building and ask you what you want, do you have an appointment? I mentioned that at the meeting, and one of the women who works at the parliament, *not* a Sami woman, seemed surprised. She said, 'But you can come anytime. Come to me, and I'll show you around.' To *me,* she said that. Show me around the Sami Parliament building."

"Did you ever think of running for parliament?" I asked her. I knew that Lars Jonas was a member, and that, in spite of sighing over its ineffectiveness, he considered it important to belong.

"Ha," she said. "No, I like to stay on the outside. So I can criticize."

Lillemor gave me a ride back to Kiruna. On the way she wanted to stop by the Yamaha snowmobile dealership and take a look at a secondhand snowmobile to buy for the godson. She said "Yamaha" a couple of times before I got it. I thought it was a Swedish word, *jámaha,* that I didn't know. My language skills were definitely fading after many hours of trying to listen in Swedish, speak in Norwegian, and take notes in English.

While she talked to the manager at the dealership, I roamed around the bright new machines, with their sleek lines and candy colors. Personally I didn't particularly like snowmobiles; they were noisy and polluting. I agreed with Nils Thorbjörn Nutti that, unregulated, they were probably a bigger threat to the environment than dogsledding. But snowmobiles were part of Sami life, no way around it, and if you were looking for Sami, you'd find more here than in a tent by the Icehotel. If tourists only knew it, the Yamaha dealership *was* the Sami experience. But how could this be made available to outsiders? It wasn't exotic, it wasn't colorful, it was just life. In her decisive way, Lillemor was already walking out the building. "He says the snowmobile is no good, no point even looking at it."

The snow fell heavily now. It no longer seemed like spring, but a return to winter. We drove the last mile or so into Kiruna. I'd moved to the Kebne Hotel, which was always packed with mining engineers. I had the same view, to the west, over the plain to the mountain.

"Why don't you come to Kattuvuoma in October, for the roundup?" asked Lillemor. "You want to see reindeer. Then you'll see reindeer."

At that moment I wanted nothing else but to see thousands of reindeer thundering around in the high mountains. I'd like to sleep in a tent and drink salty coffee and learn the Sami language. My life in Seattle seemed so far away; my usual preoccupations had vanished. I understood how the young Emilie Demant from

Copenhagen had decided to join a nomad family for a year, and kept finding ways to return to the far North. In later life, when travel was almost impossible because of the German occupation of Denmark, when her heart began to fail her, she painted dozens of canvases of Lapland from memory and said that more than anything she wished she could go back. How did she contract Lapland Sickness? How did a child born in California catch Arctic Fever? From reading "The Snow Queen"? Or did I catch it when I first arrived in Kiruna in the blue hour and stepped off the train into a cold blast of snowflakes?

"Don't forget about October," Lillemor said, as I got out of the car, and the snow swirled around me in soft thick circles. "October 10–11 is our roundup. See you there?"

It was a less a question than an invitation, and as her blue Volvo disappeared down the street, I thought how much I'd like to take her up on it someday.

16. THE ARCHITECTURE OF MELTING ICE

ARNE BERGH STABBED a long stick into the roof of a suite at the Icehotel and poked vigorously until he hit something solid.

"No danger yet."

Every day at this time of year Arne or Åke Larsson took a walk or two through the building and did what they called "security checks." This mostly consisted of jamming sticks up into the ceiling until they found the hard shell of ice. If they found no hard shell, if the stick kept going, they blocked off the room, no discussion. If enough rooms had soft ceilings, they closed the hotel for the season. Today it was April 6, and the hotel was booked through the 20th, two more weeks. To close earlier would be to take a financial loss. But the weather, after a cold, sunny spell in mid-March, had turned warmer. The snowstorm of the day before yesterday hadn't stuck. This morning the sun shone, and the nights weren't cold enough to re-chill the snow. The road down to the church at Jukkasjärvi was bare and black, and the parking lot was slush, with drifts of dirty snow piled up around it. Planks of wood had been placed over some of the particularly mushy-wet sections of the path leading from the reception building to the Icehotel. Birds sang in the unleafed birches and spruces. Spring was in the air.

And still the Icehotel stood, as magical to me as when I'd first seen it being constructed: a series of large white bumps next to the Torne River, still with its big double doors of reindeer skin and antler handles, still with its ice-block blue windows. Inside, it was colder than outside, the usual 23°F, while the temperature outside was 34°F. I'd been walking around the grounds of the hotel with no hat or gloves and with my coat open, and I strolled into the hotel in the same way. But soon I had to fish out the mittens and then the soft hat, and zip up.

Inside, there was a sound of quiet dripping and a smell of damp reindeer skin. The ice sculptures glistened, and if you ran your hand over them, your hand glided instead of sticking fast to the ice. On the floor of one room, thirty little sculptures that had once been meant to suggest penguins were now more reminiscent of large teardrops.

"The process of melting goes like this," said Arne. "The sun's rays cause a molecular change in the snow. The roof thins. Water runs down through the walls. There's water on the floor, then the ceiling opens up. There's no avalanche, no general collapse. The columns in the hallways, the ice sculptures, and ice furniture will stand as the snow melts around them. Every day it will look different."

We were standing in the central hallway as he explained this. The central hall was formed of Gothic arches, supported by columns of ice. This year the columns were square and heavy, not cylindrical. Several ice sculptures emerged perpendicularly from the inner walls of the hall. If you looked closely at them, you could see they'd begun to buckle from the sheer weight of the snow pressing down.

Over the last four months, from around December 1 to April 1, the snow that built the Icehotel had compressed from gravity's downward pull, but also through the fluctuations of temperature that happened at the beginning and end of every season, which caused the building to alternately warm up and ice up. This made the roof very tough ("I could drive my snowmobile on top of the hotel," said Arne, "even now"), but it had also caused the height of the hotel to drop substantially, by at least two feet. New-fallen snow exerts a pressure of 441 pounds per 35 cubic feet, while casted snice, that mixture of snow and ice, had a pressure of 992 pounds per 35 cubic feet. The pressure of ice itself is one ton per 35 cubic feet. Right now, at the end of the season, the pressure of the hotel's walls was at 1,323 pounds per 35 cubic feet.

In effect, the building, which had started life more as a Snow Motel, really had become an Icehotel. This compression naturally had had an effect on the rooms, all of which had become smaller, with lower ceilings. "Some rooms have aged gracefully," Arne said, as we ambled around the corridors, "some, not so much. I try to get the designers to think into the future, to think not just of how it will look when they finish, but how it will look in some months."

One artist-designed suite that I thought had aged particularly well was titled "Cave." Its entrance was tricky to negotiate; first you had to walk up a few steps into a sort of anteroom, then down about twice as many steps into a bedchamber that had been dug into the snow beneath. Stalagmites, carved to protrude up from the ground, had now fused with the ceiling to become stalactites. The crumbled surface of the interior, with icicles dripping, had probably become more cave-like than when it was fresh and new last December. In contrast, another room with a bed-canopy of ice blocks was now unusable. Chill water droplets rained down upon the bed, whose reindeer skins were covered in plastic sheeting.

The two rock and roll Swedes, Båvman and Almeiros, had designed a suite they called Fillmore North, with a carved curtain swag over a stage. Mats Indseth had done a witty room with giant mammoth bones and the body of an archeologist half buried nearby. One very special room on two levels had a section like a child's dream of an urban landscape, with a compact, New York–style city carved in ice. Another ice-de-resistance room, the da Vinci Suite, featured a life-size carving of *The Last Supper,* as well as Leonardo's drawing of a man with his arms and legs akimbo, etched on ice and pressed between two clear slabs.

Some rooms had their beds covered in plastic, but for the most part the reindeer skins were dry. The catenary arch, used in forming the suites and sleeping rooms, ensured that as the hotel melted, the water ran down the sides, and the walls retained their shape even as they compressed. Gravity's pressure was most apparent in the hallways. These arches had originally been the shape of a children's drawing of a house, with a modified peaked roof and straight sides. But the house-shape had become more like an Arabian tent in a wind: The roof seemed to swoop in a downward curve, and the walls bulged out into the corridor. Arne said he wished now that they had designed all the forms of the hotel using the same catenary arch of the sleeping rooms; there would have been less maintenance. "But it's a work in progress," he added. "We've learned by doing."

The hotel's architects had been able now, after fifteen years, to take measures in advance when building. The walls of the southern-facing corridors were six and a half feet thick. Outside, along the impressive wall of ice bricks at the end of the central hall, they'd placed another outer wall of even bigger ice blocks, for double insulation. Inside, the ice bricks had developed lovely lines of hoarfrost, like fluffy icing, between their rectangles.

"I'm the one who's most interested in the melting," said Arne. "I walk around with my camera after the hotel closes, taking photographs every day or two, looking at the new sculpture that's created, at the shapes that emerge, at the way the walls and sculptures begin to be reflected in the water forming into small ponds on the ground. Openings appear, the light penetrates the ceilings. It's unbelievably beautiful, almost mystical."

As the 75,350-square-foot hotel turned soft and slushy, electricians and other workers would rush to remove miles of cables, LED lighting, and lamps before the thirty thousand tons of ice and snow began to slip, unaided, down the banks into the Torne River. The river would eventually absorb the hotel, but about a month ago, it had also provided some of the building blocks for the future. In late February or March, as the sun grew higher and stronger, snow blowers spewed out snice to cover the river's surface and keep the ice frozen. Then tractors with special saws moved in, cutting four or five thousand rectangular blocks, each weighing about a ton, and transported them to the refrigeration warehouse. There the ice would be stored for the following building season; the blocks would turn into windows and columns, as well as the ice bars and ice glasses that Jukkas AB sold around the world. It was Arne and Åke who'd invented the glass made of ice. One day they were having a whiskey in a plastic cup in the Ice Bar; the next, they were boring holes in small chunks of ice to hold liquor. By the following day, the bartender was begging for more glasses. The two created a machine that could cut and bore as many glasses as needed. Jukkas AB now makes 2.5 million ice glasses a year.

As always, I marveled at the enormous project that was the Icehotel, marveled too at Arne's unfailing enthusiasm for ice architecture and ice sculpture, an enthusiasm so intense that it extended even to melting ice, transforming itself day by day into smaller and smaller shapes.

"Raindrops Keep Falling on My Head" was playing as I walked into the restaurant across the street, where I was to finally meet the man behind the Icehotel, the man who'd done so much to put northern Sweden on the international itinerary: Yngve Bergqvist. I'd heard a lot about him, and in truth I'd been expecting a sort of Swedish Donald Trump with dimples—cunning, acquisitive, bullying perhaps. He was quoted in one article as saying, "I don't think I spend a lot of time wondering what people will think or if I have stepped on anyone's toes." I was unprepared for a tall man in black with a handsome, quiet face and gentle voice who came up to me at the buffet. "Mrs. Sjoholm?" he asked tentatively. "Do you mind if I join you for lunch?" In every photograph I'd seen of him he'd been wearing a large fur-trimmed hat, so I didn't recognize him at first. His balding head gave him a tonsured look, and his eyes were dark and soulful. He did have dimples though, long ones that slanted through his cheeks—a boy as well as a monk.

Even people who thought him a bit arrogant and overreaching in his business ambitions tended to like him personally. He was a mover and a shaker on the local scene; people said that was because he didn't come from the North. He didn't have that fatalistic attitude of the born Kiruna-ite, who either stayed and worked at the mine, or left for the warmer south. Yngve had wanted to make more of Jukkasjärvi, the Torne River, and northern Sweden. He'd begun with summertime activities and ended up as the new Uncrowned King of Lapland, as Hjalmar Lundbolm, the mining director, had once been called. Yngve's "product," however, wasn't as concrete as iron ore. It was, as befitted our virtual times, something more amorphous—an experience shaped and sold. He had taken what to many people was a drawback of traveling in the North—wintertime darkness and cold—and marketed it as a luxurious, exotic commodity.

"The more I thought about it, the more certain I became that winter must be something that could be sold," Yngve had told an interviewer in a book about the origins of the Icehotel. What he told me, with disarming quiet pride, over our lunch of salmon and potatoes, was that Jukkasjärvi had gone from being a *kalle holle,* slang for "cold hole," to a "cold center."

"Cold has been redefined," he said. He'd been one of the first in Sweden to grasp how to redefine it and not just to display ice sculptures for people to look at, but to create a larger experience, one that would involve touch, smell, hearing, taste, an enveloping sensual experience of cold.

Yngve had looked at the Torne River and realized that, unlike Harbin and Sapporo, which had large snow festivals but where all the ice was artificially frozen, here in Jukkasjärvi they had a natural resource, if they could only figure out how to use it.

The success of the Icehotel seems remarkably swift in retrospect, but at each stage there were decisions, uncertainties, questions. The idea of a hotel, of a snow building providing lodging didn't come right away. The first two years were devoted to showing paintings in a snow structure. The next step wasn't necessarily obvious, but Yngve seems always to have been able to take a next step. Once the basic structure of the hotel was established—the rooms, the chapel, the ice bar—he realized that without a better marketing plan, the ice hotel would remain a little-known local phenomenon.

Yngve needed a business partner if the Icehotel was to grow, and he found it in Absolut Vodka, Sweden's premier spirit company, which already had a sophisticated advertising campaign and an instantly recognizable image around the world.

According to legend, initially Yngve couldn't even get his phone calls returned by Absolut. So he took matters into his own hands. He asked a photographer friend to snap pictures of vodka drinks sitting on the ice bar; these photographs they then distributed to the European media and waited to see what would happen. The media, predictably, went wild, and Yngve soon found himself taking a call from an Absolut executive. A partnership was born. The Icehotel would call its drinking lounge the Absolut Ice Bar and only serve Absolut Vodka. They would, every year, use elements of the famous vodka bottle shape in the design of the Ice Bar—the entrance, the chandelier, the back-of-the-bar wall—so that every photograph taken, by individuals or the press, every film clip shot in the bar would in effect be an advertisement for Absolut.

Absolut has proclaimed itself well pleased with the arrangement. The company makes sure that ice from the Torne River is distributed throughout the world, in the shape of ice bars, sculptures, and glasses, in connection with their advertising campaigns. Absolut emphasizes that Jukkasjärvi's ice shares many of the same qualities—"values"—as its vodka distilling process. As an advertising executive at Absolut put it in an article I read:

> A block of ice is a combination of three elements: nature, technology and transparency. Ice embodies simple forms and common sense. Ice is a natural product. It reflects openness. It is ecological. The purity and transparency incorporate the values that are shared by all the major political parties in Sweden.

Purity, in fact, was the mantra of the Icehotel and its growing line of "ice products." Two expensive coffee-table books about the Icehotel were for sale in the gift shop, both rapturous meditations on purity, impermanence, transparency, and the power of marketing. Ice from the North, that is, pure ice, unsullied by sewage, by toxic waste from factories, by a myriad of human and inhuman byproducts, was promoted as something special, a valuable resource. In a world where the glaciers were melting and clean water was becoming an out-of-reach basic need for many peoples, the Torne was marketed as endlessly available, clean and pure—naturally frozen into convenient blocks from which glasses to hold liquid, vodka preferably, were created.

But wait—how could the Torne be that pure? It's true that it was one of the last undammed rivers in Sweden and that it stretched for 435 miles, flowing from Torneträsk to the Gulf of Bothnia, but it was still a river that ran along human habitation, it was still a river that was used by reindeer, snowmobilers, and dog-sledders in winter, by swimmers and boaters in summer. IngMari Lundmark had told me once, in a conversation about local dog-sledding, that one of their neighbors out in Jukkasjärvi, where her daughter Anneli had a weekend home, owned a kennel on the banks of the river. "And he takes very bad care of his dogs and lets their dirt and things build up. Then in the spring, at the end of the season, he takes a hose and sluices it all down into the river."

"If he does, he shouldn't," said Yngve, hearing this. "He's not a man we work with. Of course we test the river water regularly. By February and March, when we take the ice from the top layer, any impurities have settled to the bottom, which is what makes the ice so clear." My question rattled him a little though, and he knocked his glass over. The water spilled onto the tablecloth, and we both moved to mop it with our napkins.

I didn't doubt the ice was probably fine for drinking—the freezing cold would kill off the bacteria of course. What was more disturbing to me was the attachment the Icehotel industry had to the river's clarity as a commodity, when in fact the frozen river was so much more than a harvestable ice field. The Torne was a living, moving substance, and, even in the winter, the river was a pathway for skiers, snowmobiles, dogsleds, and even cars—someone had once driven me from one side of the river to the other, just for the heck of it. The Icehotel needed the river for many reasons now, and its marketing department needed its purity.

Like most businesses in the capitalist world, the Icehotel has to expand in order to keep solvent, yet there is no plan to keep increasing the size of the hotel or even build another hotel in Sweden. In 2001 the Ice Hotel Quebec-Canada or l'Hôtel de Glace opened about thirty miles west of Quebec City. The plans for this hotel were franchised directly from the Swedish Icehotel and it looks quite similar, though it has just thirty-five rooms as opposed to sixty and is only open from early January to April. Being nearer to major metropolitan centers, the Canadian Ice Hotel also draws thousands of visitors who don't stay the night but simply pay to look around or to attend a wedding or business meeting. Like the Swedish Icehotel, the one in Quebec follows the model of offering an ice chapel and ice bar, with reception spaces and winter activities. These two ice hotels keep in close contact and try to maintain their mystique, even as a variety of other snow and ice lodgings have opened, with greater or lesser success, in other parts of the world, from Alaska to Romania. The technology is not that complicated, especially with snow-blowing machines, and the public's interest in structures of snow is not yet satiated.

Besides putting their name in all caps with a registered trademark, the Swedish Icehotel now markets itself as "the original Icehotel," and looks for ways to brand itself more firmly in the global market. To that end the Torne River has become a crucial part of its identity. It's not just a river in Sweden, it's firmly merged with the Icehotel's image, and with Absolut Vodka's as well. The Icehotel and Absolut have joined together to export Absolut Ice Bars and glasses to distant places. The first one opened in Stockholm at the Nordic Sea Hotel. Like the bar in Lapland, it's kept at a temperature of 23°F, and drinkers don silver thermal ponchos with fur-trimmed hoods when they enter to drink high-priced vodka from ice glasses.

Another bar was opening soon in Milan "with new white and shining ice . . . arriving directly from Torne River in Swedish Lapland," according to a press release. The first design would include a reproduction in ice of da Vinci's *Last Supper,* to be transported by truck and installed in the space, which would also be kept to a winter chill temperature. Ice Bars were planned (and now have opened) in London, Tokyo, and Copenhagen, all constructed with ice from the Torne. Every six months, Arne Bergh and a small team from Jukkasjärvi would travel to one of the Ice Bars and install new sculptures and décor from river ice that had been shipped by container ship and truck from Lapland.

"The plan is to bring ice to people who would not, for many reasons, think to actually come north. That way we are not so dependent on tour operators," Yngve said, flashing his dimples. "The Ice Bars will help with our general economy by providing a more consistent financial flow. And they will act as advertisements for the Icehotel and Absolut. Of course."

One of the things so disarming about Yngve was his frankness. Another was his insistence on sharing the credit for the Icehotel's achievements whenever possible, such as praising the young American architect Mark Szulgits from Arizona for his contributions to the design of the hotel and the exported ice bars. Like Arne, Yngve had the air of being delighted with the possibilities of ice and snow. I remembered Rolf Degerlund's story of Yngve coming up to him after he expressed the public wish to direct at a theater in ice. The next winter, the Ice Globe theater was up and running.

"Since we aren't expanding the actual hotel," Yngve said, "we are trying to create other products, here and abroad, that complement the hotel. No more than two each year, so that we don't overextend ourselves. This year we have allied with a man running 'Elk Safaris'—going out to look for elk in the winter landscape. There are the ice bars, of course. And we hope to do more with Esrange—scientific tourism. Perhaps with people going up in balloons . . . who knows?"

Along with the Ice Globe productions, which had included theater, opera, a *joik* concert, and even a magical act, Yngve had encouraged dogsledding and Sápmi Journeys. He spoke warmly of his friend Nils Thorbjörn Nutti and told me of a skiing trip the two men and their wives had recently taken, but when I mentioned Lillemor Baer and her campaign against the dogsledding, he looked impatient. "There are people you can work with. And people you can't. And some Sami . . . the family you've mentioned . . . are not people who find it easy to compromise. The dogsledding company we are connected with here at the Icehotel does not go on reindeer-grazing land. We don't have control over what other operators do."

I thought of what Lillemor might say to that—why was it the Sami were always the ones expected to compromise? Hadn't they done enough of that already? But someone came over to speak with Yngve, and he soon found he was needed elsewhere.*

---

* In February 2007, Swedish Television (SVT) ran an evening news story on Lillemor Baer and the Talma Sami and their fight to inform the guests at the Icehotel about the problems to reindeer grazing caused by dogs around the Torne River. According to SVT, there are now twenty dogsledding companies and some two thousand dogs in the Kiruna area. (The Kiruna tourist office says the correct figure is half this.) Lillemor told me on the phone that she had been contacted by Peter Salmonsson of the Kiruna tourist office. Together he and Yngve Bergqvist hoped to find a solution to the problem by working with the Talma *sameby* to control and/or license the dogsledders.

❄

Just before we shook hands and parted, I remembered to ask about a curious item I'd read in Swedish in a local magazine, something about 3-D glasses that would be given to tourists who came to Jukkasjärvi in the summer, glasses that would somehow create the winter world of the Icehotel.

"We're working on that now with an interactive company based in Umeå. They will be headpieces fitted with glasses that will construct a virtual reality of the Icehotel using digital pictures taken from different angles—360 degrees. You can stand in the place where the Icehotel usually is and actually 'see' it. You can be warm, it can be summer, yet you can walk through the ice suites, see the ice sculptures.

"They're thinking of applying the same technology at Esrange and even Kiruna," he added. "With Kiruna, they would create how it looks now, how it looked in the past, how it could look in the future."

Since almost everything that Yngve turned his mind to seemed to happen, I didn't doubt that within a short time, these interactive headsets would soon be available. Of course he had not done it alone—he had done none of this alone—yet it was clear to me that without Yngve, the Icehotel would never have been more than a very cool idea. Almost single-handedly Yngve had managed to get a vast number of people to rethink winter and to transform Jukkasjärvi from a cold hole into a world-class tourist destination. The Icehotel had turned traditional tourism topsy-turvy in northern Sweden. "It used to be that summer tourism was 75 percent of the business; winter only 25 percent, if that. Today it's completely the opposite." He added, "Now we have to think of ideas to draw people here in summer."

Those who followed stories in foreign media noted that 40 percent of all articles about Swedish tourism were now about the Icehotel, many of them appearing in the British press and on television, and most so beautifully illustrated and presented that fully a third of foreign guests to the Icehotel are now British. In a world of global warming that leaves formerly snowy countries green and brown all winter, Lapland could be made to represent not only Santa Claus and fairy tales, but also something healthy. I'd read some of the media stories about the Icehotel, and one of the things that most intrigued me was the very success of the hotel in getting writers to adopt the terminology of the hotel's PR machine, which was, in its quiet Swedish way, as relentlessly on-message as the current administration in my country. The same words were used over and over: pure, clean, remote, untouched. A place where you could drink the river still.

After leaving Yngve I wandered around again in the hotel and its environs for a while. Although there were still plenty of people about, casual visitors as well as hotel guests, on this Wednesday in early April there was a slow, end-of-the-season feel to everything. Guests and workers walked about bare-headed, without hunching against the cold and gasping when they came inside the reception. The glitter and sparkle of winter was over; no photographers set up tripods, no cameramen filmed commercials.

The Ice Chapel had been designed this year by Tjåsa Gusfors, the flaxen-braided puppeteer I'd met during the construction of the Icehotel on my first trip. She'd not only returned the following year, but every year, and had become a true ice artist and architect. One of her projects in 2004 had been an outdoor drive-in in Kautakeino, with a huge screen of snow, for the annual Sami Film Festival there. Not only was there an amphitheater of reindeer-skin-covered seating for the audience, but there was a section for those who arrived by snowmobile and were happy to sit on their bikes during the films.

The Ice Chapel was closed because it was dripping too much inside. The last performance at the Ice Globe Theatre had been a week or so before. Now, a chunk of the theater wall had crashed down and was a pile of snow. In the Absolut Ice Bar the bartender was chatting with a couple all dressed up in the Icehotel's standard attractive snowsuit. The pair was drinking something cold and pink from square ice glasses.

I found a kick sled outside the bar and went down to the frozen river and began walking and sometimes sledding along. A light snow covered the ice. The Sami might have called it *áinnádat,* a surface (with new-fallen snow) upon which fresh tracks are easily seen. Or they might have called this stretch *jodáhat,* good going. The Sami words to describe snow are interactive, which make sense if your livelihood depends on being able to read tracks and to access travel conditions for you when on skis and for your reindeer. Purity is not a category in the Sami language. Fresh snow is simply newly fallen snow without tracks.

I kicked and walked farther and farther down the river. In a couple of days I'd be back in Seattle, where we were having a warmer spring than usual. The tulips were up before I left last week; some trees were already flowering. I turned several times and looked at the Icehotel, at the hotel re-created every year from the most basic material: water. If I wore a headset with digitalized pictures from past re-creations, what would I see? A woman wandering around a building site, clinging to her notepad and camera and courage. A woman who'd come North to ease heartbreak and to explore darkness and cold, a woman at the beginning of not only one winter's adventure, but several.

When Gerda found Kai in the frozen center of the Palace of the Snow Queen, he was almost dead with cold. But her tears washed away the splinter in his eye, and after that he could see. The two of them made their way back down from the icy North to the South again, visiting some of Gerda's old friends: the Finn woman, the Lapp woman, and the little robber girl. Gerda and Kai walked through spring, and by the time they came to their old home, the roses were blooming. They noticed that they had somehow grown up, and now they forgot "all about the cold, empty splendor of the Snow Queen's palace as if it had been a bad dream."

And the story ends, "There they sat, two grown-ups, and yet they were children, children at heart—and it was summer. Warm, blissful summer."

Perhaps Kai and Gerda weren't two friends but two sides of the same soul. Gerda's resourcefulness and loyal love were what healed Kai's stubborn icy heart and washed the splinter from his eye.

Soon this frozen river would break up and begin to flow. In another two months, the scene would be unrecognizable. The long days of the midnight sun would bring about a transformation as trees leafed out, bugs hatched, and water poured south through northern Sweden. The Sami had almost as many words for water as they had for snow: *áhparas,* a very deep place in the river; *oalli,* the main channel of a river; *goatnil,* still water, near the bank or by a stone in the river; *savu,* a smoothly flowing stretch of water in a big river.

I'd traveled often in Scandinavia in the late spring and summer and knew the beauty of the blue fjords and the flowering apple trees, of the deep lakes surrounded by firs smelling of sweet sap, of the rivers that rushed down through, from high, snowy mountains. Hans Christian Andersen loved heat and sunshine, and for him and probably most readers, a return to the South and summer, "warm, blissful summer," was an emotionally rich, satisfying ending to Kai's long hibernation and Gerda's brave journey to find him and love him back to himself.

I'd never completely accepted that ending, even as a young girl. Was it because Gerda and Kai were now grown up? However much we dream of adulthood's power as children, no child really likes the prospect of life narrowing to what grown-ups think of as satisfying. The end of "The Snow Queen" marked the end of Gerda's adventures in the wide world. What was left for her but to marry Kai and settle down in Stockholm?

Yet in reading the story again recently I'd seen that Andersen had left open another ending, another possibility, in the rebellious figure of the little robber girl "with a shimmering red cap on her head and pistols in front," who'd appeared in Gerda and Kai's path on their southward trek home.

> It was the little robber girl who had grown tired of staying home and was now on her way north, though later, if it didn't please her, she might head for other parts. She recognized Gerda at once, Gerda recognized her, and they both rejoiced.

I had a feeling that if Gerda ever tired of life with Kai, of sunshine and roses, she'd go looking for her friend with the red cap and the pistols. Meanwhile, I was with the little robber girl in spirit, headed North.

I was out of sight of the Icehotel now, far away on the snow-covered still-frozen river, sliding along on my simple kick sled, no desire to turn back yet, into the wide world, rejoicing.

ACKNOWLEDGMENTS

I THANK Ragnhild Nilstun for originally inviting me north and for providing an unforgettable Christmas in Norway, as well as for commenting on the manuscript in progress. Laila Stien also offered much-needed warm hospitality in Alta and set me on a new path when she told me about Johan Turi and Emilie Demant Hatt. Her cross-cultural knowledge was essential in my first months in the far North. In Norway I'd also like to thank Harald Gaski, John Gustavesen, and Øystein Aaspas. I'm especially grateful to Lars Børge Mykevold of Árran, the Lule Sami Center in Tysfjord, for reading the manuscript and offering valuable insight into contemporary Sami life.

In Sweden, I'd like to thank everyone connected with the Icehotel, who answered countless questions about construction and operation. Arne Bergh was especially generous with his time and knowledge. Helena Sjöholm smoothed my way with cheerful kindness. The information office at LKAB helped me to see what was under that mountain in the distance. Nils Thorbjörn Nutti in Jukkasjärvi and Lennart Pittja in Gällivare added greatly to my understanding of tourist ventures undertaken by the Sami themselves. The tourist office in Kiruna has always been an excellent resource and I particularly thank Yvonne Niva for helping with one of my trips. Tore Nilsson and others at the Kiruna Library offered assistance and a library card. Mats Spett, Anneli Lundmark, and Lisa Jones contributed to my understanding of many aspects of life in Swedish Lapland. Without Barbro Behm and IngMari Lundmark, I would never have seen the variety and richness of life in Kiruna or understood the strong ties that bind people to this part of the world. I appreciate Lillemor Baer's courage, clarity, and sense of humor, and thank her for everything.

In Finland, great thanks go to Jorma Lehtola, my essential guide to Sami film, music, and popular culture, and the staff of SIIDA, particularly Sari Valkonen. Long may their innovative film festival continue.

Thanks to June Thomas for asking me where I'd like to go for *Slate* and not being put off when I answered subarctic Scandinavia; and to Robert Fogarty of the *Antioch Review* for his interest in all those essays about snowflakes and reindeer. Special thanks to Anne Fadiman for encouraging me to write about reading Hans Christian Andersen in Lapland for *American Scholar*. And to Robert Lescher for being a wonderful agent—thank you.

Some of this book was written at the Barents Literary Center in Sweden, the Villa Kivi in Finland, and the MacDowell Colony. For the space and time to work, I am exceedingly grateful.

My friend Jan Wright, whose life was sadly shortened, was a reader and midwife to many of the early chapters. I also thank Michele Whitehead, Marisa Solis, Trish Hoard, Roxanna Aliaga, and Jack Shoemaker of Shoemaker & Hoard.

Betsy Howell braved the dark, the cold, and the rental dogs. I thank her for helping me get through a long winter and supporting me in every possible way.

SUGGESTED READING

Andersen, Hans Christian. *The Complete Fairy Tales and Stories,* trans. (from Danish) Erik Christian Haugaard. New York: Anchor Books, 1983. A new translation by Tiina Nunnally of many of Andersen's best-known fairy tales is also available. New York: Viking, 2004.

Beach, Hugh. *A Year in Lapland: Guest of the Reindeer Herders.* Seattle and London: University of Washington Press, 1993, 2001.

Butler, Frank Hedges. *Through Lapland with Skis and Reindeer.* London: T. Fisher Unwin, Ltd., 1917.

Chapman, Olive Murray. *Across Lapland with Sledge and Reindeer.* London: The Bodley Head, 1932.

Dahlström, Åsa Nilsson. *Negotiating Wilderness in a Cultural Landscape: Predators and Saami Reindeer Herding in the Laponian World Heritage Area.* Uppsala, Sweden: ACTA Universitatis Upsaliensis, 2003.

Gaski, Harald, ed. *In the Shadow of the Midnight Sun: Contemporary Sami Prose and Poetry.* Karasjok, Norway: Davvi Girji, 1996.

Gaski, Harald, ed. *Sami Culture in a New Era: The Norwegian Sami Experience.* Karasjok, Norway: Davvi Girji, 1997.

Gourlie, Norah. *A Winter with Finnish Lapps.* London and Glasgow: Blackie and Son, Ltd, 1939.

Helander, Elina and Kaarina Kailo, eds. *No Beginning, No End: The Sami Speak Up.* Alberta: Canadian Circumpolar Institute, 1998.

Kulonen, Ulla-Maija, Irja Seurujärvi-Kari, and Risto Pulkkinen, eds. *The Saami: A Cultural Encyclopaedia.* Vammala, Finland: SKS, 2005.

Lehtola, Veli-Pekka. *The Sámi People: Traditions in Transition,* trans. Linna Weber Müller-Wille. Fairbanks: University of Alaska Press, 2004.

Magnus, Olaus. *A Description of the Northern Peoples,* 3 vols., ed. P.G. Foote. London: The Hakluyt Society, 1996.

Manker, Ernst. *People of Eight Seasons.* New York: Crescent Books, 1972.

Paine, Robert. *Herds of the Tundra: A Portrait of Saami Reindeer Pastoralism.* Washington and London: Smithsonian Institution Press, 1994.

Schefferus, Johannes. *The History of Lapland,* trans. Acton Cremer, 1664. Stockholm: Rediviva Publishing House, 1971.

Turi, Johan. *Turi's Book of Lappland,* trans. (from Danish) E. Gee Nash, trans. (from Sami to Danish) and ed. Emilie Demant Hatt. New York and London: Harper & Brothers, 1931.

Valkeapää, Nils-Aslak. *Greetings from Lapland,* trans. (from Sami) Beverly Wahl. London: Zed Press, 1986.

ABOUT THE AUTHOR

BARBARA SJOHOLM is the author of *Incognito Street: How Travel Made Me a Writer*. Before changing her name in 2001, she published a number of works of fiction, mystery, and nonfiction as Barbara Wilson. *Gaudi Afternoon,* a comic mystery, received a British Crime Writers Award for best thriller set in Europe and was made into a film starring Judy Davis. Her memoir *Blue Windows: A Christian Science Childhood* was nominated for a PEN USA award in Creative Nonfiction as was *The Pirate Queen: In Search of Grace O'Malley and Other Legendary Women of the Sea*. Her essays have appeared in the *New York Times, Slate, Smithsonian, Antioch Review,* and *American Scholar,* among other publications. She has also translated several books from Norwegian and is currently at work on a translation from Danish of *With the Lapps in the High Mountains* by Emilie Demant Hatt. She lives in Port Townsend, Washington.

To contact her and follow links to Sami organizations and other related websites, please see www.barbarasjoholm.com.